27/10/2005

To Kassendra

Pain of Heart

Lord's Daughter

Patricia Ivan

THE CHOSEN ONE

Channelled with
PATRIZIA TRANI

BALBOA
PRESS
A DIVISION OF HAY HOUSE

Balboa Press books may be ordered through booksellers or by contacting:

Balboa Press
A Division of Hay House
1663 Liberty Drive
Bloomington, IN 47403
www.balboapress.com
1-(877) 407-4847

ISBN: 978-1-4525-0961-7 (sc)
ISBN: 978-1-4525-0963-1 (hc)
ISBN: 978-1-4525-0962-4 (e)

Library of Congress Control Number: 2013905505

Because of the dynamic nature of the Internet, any web addresses or links contained in this book may have changed since publication and may no longer be valid. The views expressed in this work are solely those of the author and do not necessarily reflect the views of the publisher, and the publisher hereby disclaims any responsibility for them.

The author of this book does not dispense medical advice or prescribe the use of any technique as a form of treatment for physical, emotional, or medical problems without the advice of a physician, either directly or indirectly. The intent of the author is only to offer information of a general nature to help you in your quest for emotional and spiritual well-being. In the event you use any of the information in this book for yourself, which is your constitutional right, the author and the publisher assume no responsibility for your actions.

Printed in the United States of America

Balboa Press rev. date: 05/28/2013

I dedicate this book to my loving soul parents, Jesus and Mary Magdalene, who I thank for their ongoing healing and support.

Patrizia Trani
2012

Jesus

My most beloved ones, you are all the embodiment of the greatest love, because we share your experience of life, of healing, of understanding, and of our continuing ascension and renewal of existence from soul.

I come to you to share this blessed gift through the words, healing, and miracles that this living and enlightened tool can provide, and I hope that you will allow yourself to receive and enjoy the unfolding blessings you will experience. I thank my daughter and her apostles, healers, and scribes for their dedication and faith in this uplifting process and clarification of our renewing earth. It is one unified, alongside heaven. May their souls reach to yours through our unending love.

Jesus Christ

Mary

My dear children, we arrive together to greet the dawn of earth's ascension, where all humans now will become the light of their soul. No more shall enlightenment be false and held by few who claim it with misuse of power and abuse of nature.

With you we are one force of soul united to bring you back to your most heavenly state of perfect health, perfect love, and perfect support so that you can, through this healing tool and journey, use your creations fluidly and enjoy your existence radiantly. My daughter and her team give you this guide and tool to enable you to easily and joyfully throw off conditional existence in exchange for eternal clarity of life. I thank my loving daughter for this immense opportunity to create, to open humanity to their infinite unity and divine choice, and to be all that their souls have chosen to be.

Mary Magdalene

Contents

Acknowledgements

First of all, I would like to thank Simone de Visscher for bringing forth the words in this book. Her channel, her creativity, and her vision, as well as the endless hours she dedicated to compiling and editing this book, are immeasurable. She sees channelling as a gift, an offering of Love. *As She Is,* I thank you.

To Clare Murray, for your dedication and time as a very gifted channel and medium. You have continued to deliver the most insightful messages from Spirit, enabling many healings to be identified and truth in unconscious to be revealed, accepted, and healed. A gift unto the earth. I thank you.

To all of my clients, you have continued to inspire me as we have grown together throughout this extraordinary year of 2012. It has been a tremendous journey of learning and awareness and release of anything which no longer serves. And we have, with courage, with authenticity, with grace. I thank you.

A special thank you to Gabby Barrasso, my business mentor and my gracious friend, who has inspired, supported, and motivated me towards pursuing and achieving my goals without limitation. She imparts gifts of passion in creativity, which illuminate the power we all hold. I am extremely grateful, so thank you, Gabby.

Last, but certainly not least, I would like to thank our loving and patient families and friends, additional staff, and helpers who have all contributed in their very special way in the creation and production of this book.

Introduction

The Chosen One

The Chosen One, as channelled by Patrizia Trani and Simone de Visscher during 2012.

This extraordinary book offers channelled writings and conversations with God, blessed loving guidance from Jesus Christ, and words of inspiration and strength from Mary Magdalene. We share experiences that are personally relevant to you all, broadening your awareness and understanding that we are part of a collective consciousness that is expanding and evolving faster than ever before.

The 2012 global shifts have rocked the human experience. They have marked the end of primitive and self-limiting thought forms and called into being the true power you hold. Energetically, an irrepressible urge has surfaced to push your creative force towards an authentic and dynamic process and to live in full awareness of your potential, creating it now. This urge unveils your world from the inside out and calls for you to release unhealthy energies, genetic encodements, and negative belief systems, allowing a renewed co-creative perspective and a total unification of body, mind, and spirit. Want to be happy, in love, successful, healthy, and wise? Does that sound like a fairytale? That it isn't! We reveal the end of what has been an illusionary suppression of the most powerful beings on earth.

The Chosen One includes channelled writings that reveal sacred teachings, guidance, and love, touching the hearts and souls of all who read her pages. Real-life events that encompass every area of human experience, are delivered to reveal, guide, and heal. It is unlimited, it is enthralling, and it is personal. There are no misconceptions and no ego, just simple guidelines and revelations beyond your cognitive thinking. This is an opportunity, offering you back your life as you were meant to live and love it.

These words begin to shift energy just by your holding the book, and by reading it, a union of body, mind, and spirit is inevitable. Miracles follow. It is simply so. It is as complex and as simple as you allow yourself to understand and integrate it. But it is nevertheless your connection to your highest being, your God self and powerful creator of the real, authentic you.

S de Visscher, 2012

About Our Healer Channel

Patrizia Trani

We welcome the ascension of the planet and conduit channel of God. The Mother and Father will assist the planet and the entire Universe in this time of great shifts.

God's healers, masters, and angels assist many living lights whose quest is to bring heaven and earth into alignment. Patrizia is fondly known as this: a living light of God's profound healing love.

Working with her soul parents Jesus and Mary Magdalene, she harnesses the infinite awareness, the rapid cleansing and removal of disease, dysfunction, and ailment, which is usually locked in genetic and past-life (false) body records, as well as within the physical, chakric, and etheric layers.

Patrizia retrieves the essential soul being in every healing she does in order to align it within both physical and God bodies as one united force.

Over the continuum of time and through her awakenings throughout her life, she has refined her learned healing skills with the masters, saints, and angels, guiding and unfolding greater levels of healing, resulting in miraculous change and transformation for all who have come to her. Her genetic lineage on her mother's side challenged her to rise to greatness through adversity and the expected roles that she has had to balance as a wife, mother, and healer of God. Patrizia has reached a pinnacle point in her passion and focus to continue her work in her life, so that she can embrace the entire world with her God gifted healings. This is the drive of her soul towards the ascension, awareness, wellness, and infinite creation of health, harmony, and enlightenment for all mankind.

May the journey and answers found through this life's work begin your personal journey to Soul Integrated Ascension.

God the Mother
God the Father

Amen

How to Use *The Chosen One* as a Healing Tool

Much like many of the books that have existed for the centuries, this book is for the healing and enlightenment of mankind. It represents a rare opportunity to allow its readers to receive both understanding and answers to the many issues they may be experiencing. It is an oracle and will gently and directly reveal, through its short-story format, how to deal with all matters, blocks, or difficulties. Open this book at any page with the intent to find the answer to an issue, and it will be simply presented to you.

Many people in this day and age refer to both traditional and non-traditional tools for guidance. But this book will help you to begin your personal self-awareness journey. It will reveal what you need to unblock by recognizing, then healing, what is miscreating in your life.

Once you begin to work with this book, it will advance your self-trust with what is and what is not in alignment with your life and soul path in the quest to become unified harmoniously.

This book works with you like your very own guardian angel, because the answers to your heart's needs for your life path are all here. It is just waitin to unfold, to enrich, to support, and to uplift your existence into its truest, most vibrant expression.

Open this oracle and open to self-understanding and to soul alignment.

You are the Chosen Ones.

With all my love,

God

The Chosen One

Understanding the Messages and Healing for You

Congratulations on obtaining a copy of *The Chosen One*.

In it, you will find eight chapters individually titled by subject matter, and then a series of short stories within each category or subject. Each story was channelled using a method called *automatic writing*, during which a conversation began of clairaudient, clairvoyant, and clairsentient nature. The impressions, images, words, and emotions were transferred onto paper at exactly the same moment that an energy healing was being performed. The specific subject and its healing then produced the messages and, more importantly, the wisdom required to evolve within the matter in question and ultimately to creatively move forward in your life.

The words, the wisdom, and the experiences contained within this book carry a frequency of light, which is inherent to its Source. It is a subtle but powerful vibration of love that will help you to eliminate what you no longer wish to create in your life. It does not matter from where you came, or whether you are male, female, young, or old, rich or poor, these elements are merely the exterior dynamics of a much higher, richer, wiser being who is really you.

When we consider and accept that human life is based around a series of common experiences, we realize that our "differences" are few and our true inner desires are even fewer. We all long for love, security, inner peace, joy, connectedness; yet sometimes, these fundamental desires seem unreachable. Why? In truth, this is the natural state of your being in its purest sense. It is your earthly incarnation and its experiences that map a mixed bag of pleasure and apparent pain. So we investigate, from an evolvement perspective, why we choose our genetic, karmic, and human family and the soul group we incarnate with. Not only do we choose to experience, but we intend to acknowledge, learn, rebalance, and release so that we can cease to function from negative patterning and false belief systems. Once an aspect or soul lesson has been understood and cycled through, we no longer need to revisit it in anyway, and one can progress.

All life and life experience is a miraculous unfolding adventure, with you in a starring role of your very own box office movie! But in this film, you have the power to change the script at any moment, as you are the director as well. As the plot thickens and you observe the unfolding scenes, you continue to create and express, respond and relate. It is a very healthy perspective to adopt a bird's-eye view as you step out and watch yourself and your life unfold, giving you a clear message of what needs to be addressed and healed. People no longer view themselves or their existence as coincidental or part of a series of random events. You are the most valuable energy being you could ever love and cherish. And remember: along the way, you are never alone. You are always being guided, nurtured, protected, and loved by the benevolent and angelic beings assigned to you for your life's purpose throughout your life's duration.

Trust his team of love will ensure your safe and timely arrival at your destination, just as you chose to experience it.

Use this powerful text as an oracle, a gift from your angelic team to assist you with clearing and/or healing aspects that are presenting for you at this very moment. Sit quietly, take a deep breath, and centre yourself. Open the book at any random page and trust that the story in front of you carries the message and healing vibration especially for you. And while the characters and the scene in the story may describe a different time and place, trust that the energy brought forth within the pages is connecting to you as your mirror for your awareness and healing.

And so it will be done.

Perfection is the magnetized force of the Law of Attraction, which plays an integral role in your life as you choose it.

You are and always will be,

The Chosen One.

Message from Jesus Christ
30/3/13

Out of the waters of existence, I launched out onto the land, and yes, it took great strength! To remain at the bottom of the ocean, within the depths of my soul, would allow me seclusion and silence, but this is a passage in time, an experience I must rise from, to continue my passage forward.

And so I deliver this message in easy, clear language for all to understand.

Your experience of your physical lives on earth is a series of relationships, emotions, intentions, actions, desires, and passions. It does not matter from whence you came; every human has the same fundamental needs and wishes for his or her life. Every human wants to feel God alive within and clearly hear her guidance. And we are within you. Throughout the challenges you encounter and the blocks that you ponder, you are never alone. Rather than it being some sort of misunderstood punishment (which is one of the greatest lies ever told), it is merely a reminder of what you may have been ignoring. Passion drives the human spirit forward. If something intercepts your passion or your good intentions, acknowledge and listen. This is what we guide you to do. Listen. Listen to your heart. What is your heart saying about your existence? Are you happy and fulfilled in every area of your life? If you cannot truthfully answer yes, then you are seeking here.

Ultimately, the human experience is one of creating, learning, clearing, acknowledging, and, most importantly, growing. The people writing this book understand human challenges of every kind. They are humans, after all.(humorously). They have encountered and experienced all levels of fear, such as disease, depression, jealously, external interference, dysfunctional relationships, poverty, and discouragement, just to name a few. Those symptoms and effects were the result of what connected to them, on some level.

Each human understands that they have a very different experience in human form than that of Spirit. But as loving, evolving, and expansive souls, you wish to allow these experiences to create an opportunity to heal and grow. That is the goal not only for oneself, but for all of humanity. What happens when the entire human race shifts, learns, and grows from her life experiences? The planet ascends, and you will reach the state of nirvana.

Cycling through of the history of humankind, there have been some very significant evolutionary shifts over the last two thousand years. It has certainly evolved in so many ways; however, it is time to reveal to you, the people, that your very existence, is for each other. Your love and compassion for yourselves and one another is to reach your goal. Your desire and passion for unity with one another and God is aimed to create and experience planetary and human ascension. There is no division in this. You have all decided that whilst your individual agendas are certainly part of your growth process, your collective ascension and unifying love force you have within keep you engaged in the desire to keep returning (reincarnating) and releasing inauthentic beliefs and practices.

The goal is to eliminate all negativity from your existence, to experience your life as a love-inspired creation. Eliminate fear, violence, greed, hunger, and jealousy. Every negative human condition you still create, experience, and accept is no longer required to understand yourselves.

The Chosen One relays this message. It is about the painful, growth-seeking, and humbling experience of being human, yet trusting that which the heart yearns for will become. There is no human challenge, no physical, emotional, or psychological pain, which will hold you back.

You will become your highest vision of yourself.

I lead by example and reveal *The Chosen One*.

With much love in transcending your existence,

Jesus

Message from Mary Magdalene
30/3/2012

Hello, my child. Yes, I was student who then became teacher, teacher of the wisdom to bring forth to humanity from Jesus Christ.

His direct connection to God was a continuous channel of grace, and as he filtered the information and delivered it to the people, I too listened.

Over the years, I was a testimony to some ill-fated events and painful human experiences. Certainly my own life could have been viewed as one of sacrifice; however, quite to the contrary, I saw it as a great gift. All life is.

It is an opportunity to join in oneness with the Creator and all that is. And oneness is your natural state of bliss.

My existence as Mary Magdalene was a multifaceted experience, as was Jesus's life and our intention together, and it was designed to leave an imprint on humanity. The one or ten questions you are driven to find the answers to? Well, they spark the delicious curiosity of the human mind, enquiring for your life meaning, even though your soul already knows it all so well.

Without these questions, you cannot bridge the gap and understand the less than random sequence of life events you experience. You seek so that ye shall find, and it will never be any other way.

I represent and deliver the element of feminine empowerment in all of her miraculous, nurturing, and creative forms. Historically, when the great goddesses and priestesses of our earth were replaced by ego, power, and fear-led empires, the shifting of that darkness had to cycle back around to balance. It had to be much greater than before if people were going to learn, grow, and evolve to their highest potential. Life simply could no longer exist in those former realities, unless we chose to heal and rehabilitate our experience with soul.

I was to lead a procession of many loving, passionate, creative women in history, who would be denied their power and their greatness, and most often challenged or tortured to their death. I would remain behind a curtain of a male-dominated, church-led hierarchy who would mislead and openly lie to the masses. I would remain with my head held high as I was called many cruel names, knowing my heart bore no injury, as I am of pure God light and service to humanity. Perhaps not for this moment, but unto the ages, many years forward, as my sisters did bear the injury of the forefathers and mothers, the degradation, the misuse of their bodies, and the denial of essence of the life-giving power within them, we release and pray, as this is accepted no more.

All women who have experienced fear; dominance; physical, emotional, or mental abuse; unworthiness; and devaluing of your whole being: you, my holy sister, walked in my name for humanity's sake. The sins of the forefathers and mothers who allowed such acts have cycled many times on the planet, as all life cycles must balance with karma and personal and planetary evolution. In celebration of great days ahead, we prepare by releasing the binds of the past and balance the scales once again.

The unity of female and male energies on earth is essential for our growth and co-creation. Without this, our existence and process of healing individually and collectively is compromised. The union of the Twin Flame and Soul Mate is one of the sacred rites of your existence. We are led by a great desire to unify and join in love, and it will always be so.

Your current personal challenge may be that you are not living the life you wish to create, your current physical health is not as you desire, or perhaps you are not happy with yourself and you practice no self-love. If your relationship with your partner (or yourself) is not creative, growth-filled, nurturing, and nourishing for you both, what you seek to understand is the greater knowledge and practice of love in balance, which allows the expression of tenderness and support for you both and for yourself. This will reflect on and influence experiences in your relationships, personal empowerment, self-worth, self-love, mothering, birthing, decision-making, and teaching.

Through my energy, lovingly present to you now, and the living example of my daughter incarnate, the feminine human experience is delivered and shared, relaying the parts of your existence that require you to powerfully acknowledge your choice, to change your life today.

The feminine is finally cycling from the darkest of ages through to the love and light of the God Mother's creative, honouring, and nurturing embrace on earth. We see ourselves in each one of these experiences as we experience them together in *The Chosen One*.

With much love and celebration,

Mary Magdalene

May 2012

Chapter 1

Christ Consciousness

What Is Christ Consciousness?   25/6/2012

Listen with your heart, bless'ed ones, to what I am about to tell you.

You are light. You embody flesh to experience yourself as human. Your essence, your soul, is a vibration of love that emanates light.

Christ consciousness is the food of God light. It is light "plugged in." As you reside with your physical body, your frequency changes to accommodate and feed internal organs, blood production and nourishment, hormonal secretions, digestion, and energy production. Christ consciousness is a vibration that has a specific set of subfrequencies to match its host.

Your energy healing allows Christ consciousness to be filtered through your vessel and spirit, to feed all dynamics of a healthy and harmonious existence. Whether that be for your emotional, physical, mental, or genetic healing, the body's translation will filter the healing to the required area and level.

Eventually, when one reaches a state of surrender (of human/bodily/societal/ego leadership of self), the consciousness of Christ, in its pure love and wisdom, will be the only frequency one needs to live in bliss. This is the state of nirvana that you all strive towards, often with complete unawareness.

Christ consciousness allows you a symbol or essence of God vibration that was once embodied in my physical (and now in my non-physical) body for you to follow as an example. When you reference that level of consciousness, you are embarking upon a clarity of love so pure no disease can be present in its light. It is from whence you came, from where you sprung, from the Source of creation. Just like a seedling sprouting in the warm spring air, upon your descent your frequency had to filter into a body and remain attached during your incarnation. Your Christ essence, your God vibration, connects you condensed form on earth in your physical life with your physical body.

When you pass from this earth and return to your true magnetic source, you will reunite with the essence of you in heaven, and you will have accomplished much. I would not send you on a journey without food, without water, without the very basic requirements to survive, my loved ones, and so my love will always be there to reach upward for.

We are the same. Our essence is made of the stars, the cosmos, your blood, our blood; our hearts beat to the same rhythm.

Christ consciousness is the fuel, the love, the healing, the knowledge, the joy, the grace; surrender in your last breath.

We are always united.

With love upon the earth unending, it will always be.

Jesus

Jesus's Egyptian Temple and Training with the Priestess 22/9/2011

Jesus meets the temple priestess with a warm smile and "Welcome, Isaiah. We have been looking forward to seeing you. Please sit. We will begin ."

Jesus sat with the priestess at the temple garden and shared his knowledge. He could speak freely and without reservation with her. The purpose of their connection was to reveal to Jesus his ancestry. He already intuitively knew of his purpose, his gifts, and cosmic truths. He simply wanted to know the beginning. Physical embodiment of the bloodline began in ancient Egypt and Judea: feminine Egypt, masculine Judea.

The priestess began to speak with Jesus about such things as meditation practises, crystal healing, water healing, levitation, and transcending the body to heal all levels of life and consciousness.

Jesus had a very evolved chakra system, particularly his crown, third eye, throat, and heart. He listened to the teachings and absorbed the encoded symbols into his crown to initiate further light infusion of his physical body. This connected his energy stream to God in a very powerful way. The energy stream to God's universe was to be tapped into and accessible to him. Jesus believed undoubtedly in his abilities and the truth of his being. The meditations were at different locations— sometimes held in a temple, or in the garden, or at the nearest mountaintop. Jesus would have clear and concise messages about all he was about to embrace and all he was to encounter. He practised diligently. The temple priestess conducted the esoteric teachings over months and allowed and guided Jesus to follow his inner knowing. He would fast for long periods and only drink water. The water purified a thousandfold to give him healing hydration within his body.

"Still the mind and external thoughts." He became a master and could sit in meditation for hours and hours. To move beyond the confines of the body was the ultimate test. He bilocated to the Apostles on a few occasions, and they were somewhat surprised and frightened at first, thinking something had happened to him! But it was in fact an energy body bilocation, all done whilst his physical body was sitting within the temple grounds in meditation and prayer. Jesus and Mary did this often to one another during lengthy periods of time apart. Breath work was also a fundamental part of the training: being able to sustain the body on very little volume of oxygen. The breath becomes shallow and very slow when bilocating or healing distantly. Embalming with ritualistic oils of frankincense and myrrh added to the opening, and all physical sensations could be completely surpassed. This proved to be a necessary skill when he was later hung on the cross to be crucified.

Your beautiful queen, your wife Mary, has direct lineage here, and she too is "encoded" and well trained in these practices.

"I know she is far exceeding my skill level, and I am blessed to have her greatness, her beauty, courage, and knowledge in my life."

Jesus lived and trained at the temple for three months before returning home to Mary Magdalene and their child.

Note: Jesus had been there before; his mother, Mary, had sent him there to train with the priestesses at age thirteen.

Amen

"Amour, mademoiselle. That is you. You are love, the great mother of all humanity." We are the fiery feminine and consciousness that embodies the light of God, and we are to continue the story. She escaped in the night by boat with two children and a baby in her womb.

The great Mary Magdalene was hidden within the safe confines of the mountainous area in and around Languedoc. The Cathars were loyal to her. She embraced a people and a region who were god/goddess/earth worshippers. Rituals and practices involving the sun, the moon, the seasons, and solstices were part of the divine design of human existence, and people of this locale were well practised and connected.

Mary Magdalene was smuggled into France via Italy and took refuge with these like-minded people. Immediately she felt at home with them. Rumours began to circulate about her identity and recent past. She had already survived a near arrest and death penalty. She was aware of Jesus's survival after crucifixion, and she was strongly focused on her family, living with and within her. It was an awe-inspiring time for these people. As the locals approached and gained more confidence, she would impart knowledge and the teachings of her husband's visions and his transcendence: their purpose was to reveal the coming of a new world that encompasses only love and no war, where children will incarnate to reveal only more of their true god selves.

Every woman and child wanted to meet and touch her. Many children asked to brush her hair. The men knew they were in the presence of a great teacher. Those who were unsure soon realised that this warm woman was a great writer, teacher, and healer. As a woman, she feared nothing, and her voice sparked attention to all who were near. She began to preach divine truth, the words of God, as it channelled through her and through previous teachings she had received alongside Jesus. Before long, she had a following and scheduled teachings and prayer sessions.

It was important to keep Mary's whereabouts secret, as Rome was a threat. Mary was able to travel to various towns and later meet with Jesus at various intervals as they went on pilgrimages across France and into Egypt. She had the support of the local community, who looked after the children if the journey was to be perilous or weather conditions were unfavourable. As Mary settled into her new life in the South of France, she continued to write, heal, and perform "workshops," as we call them today.

News of a miraculous prophetess and healer swept the countryside, and Mary's following became strong.

Apostle Simon accompanied Mary on travelling pilgrimages to ensure her safety, along with the five or six others in the entourage, depending on whether the children were accompanying them.

The wealth and the generosity of the people and the region supplied an abundance of food, water, shelter, clothing, and love to their much-loved new queen and her children.

Christ My Father 22/9/2011

The Christ, my Father, was a Nazarene born of the royal house of David to reveal his healings and teachings to the Holy Land and beyond. Ultimately, his knowledge of pure Source was to reveal and teach that God resides in us all and that our entire existence over many centuries and thousands of lifetimes is intrinsically linked and will eventually embrace an evolvement and a sustainability of a future and a wondrous transcendence of life on earth. Without this evolvement, we simply cease to exist. Our planet and mother universe are dramatically shifting. Earth's energy grids no longer support our previous life and the expulsion of energy in the former way. We are ascending, and this process has been coming into reality over thousands of years. The ascension master, teacher, healer, and great master Jesus, the Christ, professes the time draws near. "During my incarnation, a large majority saw me as a heretic! A lunatic!"

But my words, my presence, and my power would emanate from my heart, as depicted in many artistic forms. This would link me directly to God, ensuring that at first a few, then many, then a great mass, understood and felt the presence of a Lord through a God of love, not manipulation or masochism. The seed was laid, which was most important as a taste, to ensure that each and every human born thereafter was encoded with the reality of love as truth. This truth being that love is the only true desire of us all. Guilt or regret has no viable use today, as you have moved significantly past the former entrapments and karmic lessons to provide progression. We can now do this with a fully engaged heart, with the desire to love as your reason and just cause.

With joy, we acknowledge that two thousand years later, we live within a society that allows more freedom to express and live out this truth. It is a necessary introduction to the next process for human existence. Again, without encompassing this newly integrated pattern and embracing it with compassion and love for self and one another, the healing and changes to old beliefs cannot occur. My family, my lineage, and our beloved God. We are at the forefront of such enormous change, but thankfully, at this time, without the monumental physical wars against truth. The areas of warring, power and manipulation, starvation, etc., on the planet will diminish. It will be very quick when this occurs, as it will be an act of universal correction. I guide you so much and reveal as you enquire. I will show you the steps you need to take. The re-emergence and revelation of the bloodline and her soul-purpose followers will be not without reaction, but it will be nothing you cannot handle. Jerusalem provides you with further clarity and verification of your lineage and past. The Holy City traced my footsteps to Egypt, where I followed my ancestors and learned of ancient teachings of esoteric medicine, healings and doctrine. Within the physical plane and spiritual level, this anchored me to my former/present/future existence, which was wonderful at the time. We all must understand our past to know our future. However, there are many people still engaged in their highly speculative thought forms who are disconnected from their hearts truth. Earth life was a heavy and unconvincing process in that time, and even thousands of years later, there are still those who have not elevated their consciousness. This is mainly due to the fear they harbour of a pending freedom and responsibility they have never experienced in body. If their current personalities and ego selves do not allow the release of these fears, their energy bodies and physical bodies will not be able to maintain or sustain healthily in the expansion of this current frequency. It simply cannot be so.

Languedoc, in the southern region of France, has your genetics encoded strongly. Here you will learn more about your Mother, your people, and where your bloodline extended. As it was, the beauty and magic of the secrets were to be protected and revealed to the earth when she was ready to learn, so many years into the future. Many, many, courageous and beautiful souls stood in devotion and dedication to hide, protect, and even move, when necessary, the treasures of our existence. The divine truth of this immaculate life. We would assign and include many people to see the survival of the Holy Grail when the time comes that the next level of consciousness emerges and earth is ready to accept her role and her reason. We are the new revelations of the old. There is a higher consciousness that is ready to be born, and you will be the Chosen Ones to deliver it.

Research, retrace, and reveal with a new perspective. Your life, here and now, is so very exciting. When some express fear, you will fear not, as this is their residue, and there is no threat. You are strong and vital as you have always been.

More, much more, will be revealed, all in time.

With joy in my heart.

Joy is infinite.

Image of earth with blue light around.

Amen.

Mary Magdalene:

You carry my blood; do not fear. I am with you throughout your entire journey, from start to finish and, of course, beyond. My beautiful angel child, it is nowhere near over yet. And with every well wish and the acknowledgement of a "fear to clear" dynamic, it is all very relevant. Feel the breeze on our lips and sense carefully, knowingly. The landscape looks solid, large, and unchanged, and yet the difference will be always what you feel. The atmosphere may appear different even with familiar surroundings. The breeze is blowing softly, and the sun is warming your skin. Your sensitivity serves you well, as it did me, and with your heart engaged, you will witness the evidence and fruition of your prayers. Do not harness any discouragement, for it truly is not yours. Be a light unto the darkness and with that, inspire others to be that also. If we join or connect to a lower aspect, we only feel low ourselves, and it is not you, my darling.

Your book—it is good, very good. You are well aware that the information now being realised and taught carries with it wisdom and tools for humanity. These will be understood in clear, easy language, as well as feel good to the soul. You will prosper, and it will bring great recognition and higher learning. Unlike myself (in my physical incarnation), the fears that relay as threats are not dangerous to you. You live in the perfect time to bring forth the wisdom, the love, the perfection of this life you were born into. For all who live in your physical lives right now, stop and be grateful, as you are so very blessed.

During your life with me, I often worried for your safety, as we lived in physically turbulent times. We were sometimes unchaperoned, but you, my brave heart, you were unafraid, displaying the courage and determination of ten men and many more.

And now, my star, this is perfection, as is all of God's universe. It is with clarity and love that the wisdom and, ultimately, the healing of humanity is accepted to allow your god selves to nurture and guide each one of you. Be it that they wake and entrust, for all the angels are singing, *Hallelujah! Hallelujah!* Today's language serves to communicate the time of awakening more precisely. There are now words and terminologies used to explain so many emotions, thoughts, and visions that were unavailable to me in that time.

Your deliverance of the texts can be simplified with these new words, and lengthy explanations will be needed only for some subject matter, or for people who are yet to clear many programs, including over-articulation/heart disconnection/intuitive blocks that are firmly in place.

You are embarking on an incredible journey. All of your asking for help has not gone unheard. I/We hear you. Believe it. Some things are part of your higher learning, and some things are in place because you believe them to be an obstruction. Disengage in what displeases you, and much of the aspects will be gone. You have the power to shift mountains of thought and its energies.

The first book, *The Healers Journey*, is about you; it is about us. In fact, it's about all of humanity in relationship with one another. It is your gift to your brothers and sisters of the earth and for her healing. You have created and brought forth (and will continue through many texts) great knowledge, banded and united together with past and present beings. They are people who have loved and served alongside you before. They live this as their truth. Acknowledge, love, and care for each other.

The Healers Journey imparts a history, a history of your being and where it all began. And like looking at your photo album of baby pictures, pre-school, primary school, and then high school, the people who share a karmic and/or soul-aligned history with you will present on your path and therefore in this book, as they share a journey with you on more than a physical level.

On a personal level for you, *The Healers Journey* has already been superseded by your current experiences at this time. You are already many books ahead energetically, physically, and emotionally.

It's like a popular movie that gets released at the cinemas. The actors and producers have long completed the film by the time it's released, and then suddenly, twelve months later, the media wants to talk about it like it is a current creation. But the writers, actors, and producers have already moved to the next project. So in creative flow and prosperity, their achievements, rewards, and interviews are in current time.

And so it is the same. Do not stop and wait for anything. Continue as you are aligning all future flow.

You are protected and guided always.

Three hundred copies of the book is sufficient for the Centre.

Infinite love. Feel the wind on your lips.

Soaring towards the light.

That is all.

Mary Magdalene:
The Great Goddess   13/10/2011

Jesus and Mary Magdalene, we thank you for your presence. Mary Magdalene, with your radiant smile, you are showing that you are pleased with what we now understand and acknowledge during the time in which you lived. The male-dominated church hierarchy portrays manipulation and female persecution that lasted centuries after your incarnation. When the people lived in the harmony with Mother Earth and the ways of the Great God/Goddess, all of life had a cycle of joy and a life spark that was honoured and nurtured and was made manifest for continuing life and creation to birth and grow, to age and transform. This evolving cycle is honoured and naturally known by women as a feminine philosophy overall.

She is the Feminine aspect manifest, it is that purest power, and it is her natural state. Mary Magdalene and her own mother were healers/teachers who were forced to conduct their work underground or face persecution. The official and respected presence of women as Priestesses and healers/health practitioners had long been removed from the Temples. These were now led, run, administered, and serviced by priests and men only. The world was at war, and the existence of the average person was treacherous, particularly near the cities. People were told what and how to believe, what to think, and what to pay, and the consequences were imprisonment or death. Life was extremely two dimensional, violent, and provocative.

The emergence of Jesus during this time was of course purposefully significant.

The role of women in Jerusalem at this time and consistently around the world was that of possession, initially by her father and later her husband. This made well for a good future, to be a humble wife and mother, in service only.

No woman made a spectacle or was regarded as powerful. The role of a priestesses and goddess was considered blasphemous, and for witches and demons. The temple holy men were determined to burn that out of existence.

So most women, if they were healers or were performing energy work (which in truth was their natural state of living anyway), or if they were using natural remedies or goddess wisdom, etc., would keep this very quiet. Only inner circles, close to their families, would know.

Mary Magdalene was from a prominent family lineage. She was wealthy and educated. She had the opportunity to learn to read and write. She was articulate, beautiful, and socially and worldly educated. Her mother was of a royal lineage. Jesus and Mary Magdalene were not betrothed to begin with. She was promised to another, but she refused to marry him, even though that was unheard of in those days. As she practised and nurtured her own innate abilities as a healer and intuitive, she was very aware of the twin flame union destined to her in a man who mirrored her passion and abilities. She even read it in tealeaves and knew it to be true. Mary Magdalene lived by the philosophies and healing of the Great Goddess/God as representation of the ultimate union of male and female energies as equal creators, to bring forth the ultimate creation in flesh, the physical form of joy and love on earth.

The goddess clans or groups secretly existed, and Mary was of teacher status. Her personality was not one to be quietened, and therefore she was always reminded by those who loved and were concerned for her to be cautious of the words she spoke so openly and publicly. Man has no compassion or leniency for what he perceives is a threat to his ego.

"Fools!" she'd exclaim, "Where will this lead our race, our people, humanity, the children and their future? We must express our messages of love and their real reasons to live; otherwise, I see no use in the embodiment of the flesh only to experience savagery!"

The temples and their leaders were infuriated with Mary's presence around Jesus or anywhere, as she had made quite a significant impact on those around her. A woman who was unattended by her husband or not chaperoned must be a harlot or a loose woman. But Mary was not married and not betrothed. She was educated and was known to be connected to the philosophies and teachings of the Goddess. Those who felt threatened by her felt terribly uncomfortable in her presence.

The threat was illuminated through savage rumours of prostitution and of her being a whore. Her beliefs and strong associations with fertility rights, healing, and women's circles cemented this further and as such, she and other women were being hunted, persecuted, and eliminated, and were labelled less than wholesome society members by temple and political leaders.

But none of this deterred her.

She was a queen and representative of all women, as she illuminated and reminded them of a firm and undeniable truth: that the natural power within the womb is a holy and nourishing vessel of light, bringing forth life in a physical embodiment through babies, allowing each and every goddess in all women to shine forth.

With love and gratitude,
We conclude for now.

17

Mary Magdalene ,

Be sure it is so that there is no other greater challenge nor blessing than life itself. My work as a Healer began early. I remember as a young girl placing my hands on the livestock birthing to assist in her in a holy action of bringing forth a new life. It would be so magnificent, so exciting to watch her work the energy, the pain she'd use as her force, sustaining a presence and vitality so pure and very beautiful.

Much later as I developed relationships around family groups and trading partners, as well as the orphanage and prayer groups, I came to know other women who were practising spiritually or whom I believed worked within a Mother Earth consciousness and belief system. There were many surfacing and forming beliefs. The temples were full of men who led their prayer work with judgement and inequality! Ridiculous, to claim they worked in alignment with God. My appearance sometimes startled people, as I loved colour. My wavy auburn hair fell down my back, and I presented as being self-assured and powerful in the way of the Great Goddess I revered. My energy vibration and channelled knowledge, dream journals and prayer sessions would speak of universal truths, great challenging processes to experience for humanity. I was to play such a large role in mankind's ascension process, and if I'd known beforehand how hard it would be, would I do it again? Absolutely yes, with every last breath.

Sienna was a woman I knew from the orphanage. She always made an effort to speak to me about God and the path, and I would enjoy her enthusiasm about her more structured belief. I offered some examples of God's less invasive, more compassionate and loving expressions. She gazed upon me, sometimes appearing so engrossed in my words, and then suddenly I'd be aware I'd been channelling divine truth. I would love it, connecting in those moments.

In the Temple of Isis, among many others, I had always worked in this way. I would acknowledge God and my angel of mercy and protection to be flowing in and around every spark of my existence and the process would begin. My God self, my all wise one, the healer, the teacher, the prophet, and the sage. There is no separation, nor is there any denying, we are all the same and part of the one.

I had to deliver a multifaceted message, and I had to experience love and loss, overcome by grief and severe danger. I would be labelled and hunted, diminished and trodden upon, to push through it all and reveal my inner strength of God. My belief in who I am and what I had to reveal came from within my denied existence. Denied only to those who refuse to see that all of creation and the continuance of the human race is balanced upon the recognition, grace, love, and gratitude of the God and Goddess in union and in co-creation.

Sienna looked at me wide-eyed. "My Lord, you must write that down, Mary! They are God's words channelled directly through you. The clergy would want to hear this. The temple could not deny they are words of such height, no woman could create them." What transpired from this conversation was a script that was written and delivered to the temple. The clergyman shook and choked! He gasped and held his chest, yelling "Blasphemy! From a witch!"

The protection and tax paid by my family ensured a better position for me (not to be arrested), but my honour and name would be slain just the same. This is the originating fact behind being called whore. I was also not married and would freely walk unchaperoned, which was not taken lightly, and so my integrity, my name, my honour, was quickly trampled on. I was a double threat, as I am woman.

This betrayal, and any other judgemental and low-vibrational frequency of mindless, ego-driven power consciousness, is no longer. Humanity has evolved to a level to accept and integrate the God self, the Goddess self, your earth angel purpose and divine reign over your planet. The time is here, and my daughter now leads you forward. Embrace and dance the freedom you hold to express the truth freely.

From the light and love of God.

They came with many, on horseback, with shields and weapons, with armour and protection, to arrest me. How ironic that, first of all, they felt my presence was powerful enough to overcome them. And secondly, they shook within as they threatened me as a criminal and heretic. An obscene interruption of their abusive lives, they heard their own voices within warning their very souls that what they were about to do would impact on them forever.

I surrendered to their will. I didn't fight, nor did I scream. I offered peaceful co-operation. It was not necessary to push, punch, or verbally abuse me. Could I have struck them all with the hand of God and made a dramatic escape? Perhaps, but that was not the ultimate plan and was not the course for humanity.

What threatened them so intensely was truth, love, innocence, equality, and true power, none of which they practised, although many preached. I remained focused on calm and retreated into my inner world, calling to my God. In an instant, we communicated, and her love language of hope and recognition of illusion was within me, even in the face of great physical pain.

The unfolding of events, the individual, as well as the collective impact on every person involved, created such a huge opportunity to heal, and if not, then not.

It is a choice aligned to your desired evolvement. They, you, all people have choice. Your action in response to an attack will be your position in future events. Do not retaliate, as it always, always_beckons further abuse. Rather, retreat, pray to your God and your Creator, rest in her arms, and heal all ill intent. If they are not of you, walk away, but don't forget to bless them on their journey. This is when the disconnection of their fury takes place. They no longer affect you or your life. It is truly a large drum capable of making a lot of noise, but it has nothing inside to threaten with. Retract as I did from the noise and the drama and retreat into prayer. The sound of the horses, the rattling of chains, the pulling, the verbal abuse, and the grand show disappeared far into the distance as I meditated and prayed.

Noise, anger, and theatrics are illusions of an underlying fear of true power.

You are God connected and hence harness true power.

Call upon me, and within a moment, I'll be by your side.

With love, Jesus

This child who lay in my womb, this child of light, is calling upon me, her mother, telling me that her arrival is not far away. I've paid attention to each passing moon, and yes, I hear the voice of my beloved as well. He assures me he'll be with me as soon as physically possible, but at this time, he cannot. I have four close confidantes with me, three men who travel, apostles by name and protectors till death. In no way physical harm can come to me; my guardians of earth, they surround me by day and some at night. My soul-sister, my friend and my companion, Esther—without her, my feminine outpourings may be solitary. I thank god for her every day, for her selflessness, her dedication, and her courage. I love her much, and she will assist me, as doula, to bring forth my child.

I grow weary as the weight of my child tires me. Fortunately, the cold allows me (us) to wear extra layers and cloaks to hide my bulging belly. I do not want anyone to see me. I want to acknowledge my need to protect and conceal.

My mind and my heart has been telling me for some time that I must reach France and take refuge with the faithful, the men and women who have built fortresses to protect themselves. Peter and Phillip have been calculating time and distance, but I have slowed in recent weeks. Esther keeps me focused.

We enter the village at night, and some lights are on in a few houses. We approach an inn to hope to obtain a room for the night, but the hostel owner approaches and speaks: "You are the Expected One. We have received word of your arrival. We have arranged for your safe refuge and a place for your baby to be born. For a queen, we see no beauty for you in my humble inn; the place you will reside is just over the hill. See the great stars twinkling in your honour? We await confirmation you have arrived safely. Two horsemen will guide you and our entourage."

I arrive at the beautiful house within a short ride.

Esther and I settle into our room, and she prepares warm water to bathe. We are greeted but allowed to rest, as the journey has been quite long and hard.

At three in the morning, I awake with strong pain; I know my baby is coming. Esther jumps up to my side. She calls to Peter to alert the nurses to be aware the time is near. A large tub of warm water is permitted in the room with soft fabrics.

Throughout the three hours of labour I experienced startling visions. Between contractions and during, I'd see future, prophetic events my child and I would share.

She's a sacred being, a child of divine importance, a gift to humanity—a God Child indeed.

The sweat poured from my belly as Esther stoked the fire more, more fire. She threw the resins and aromas into the fire, helping the birth process. I was at one with the mother of all creation . . . I was *mother*, in control of my experience of integrating soul with body of both daughter and myself. Just before her arrival, I had an out-of-body experience. I saw myself giving birth, labouring, breathing, and suddenly I travelled in an instant to Jesus.

I appeared beside him and smiled lovingly. "We have a daughter, my love. She awaits you."

We were in a beautiful garden, and it was daylight.

I returned to my body. One final push, and she was here.

Such peace, an angel in my arms. I cried unto my God, thanking him. (Esther cried with joy, kissing my head.)

There began our journey.

Encodement of Christ Consciousness

Now I want you to take a big inhale through your nose and fill your lungs entirely to their full capacity. Then exhale out through the mouth, fully exhaling. And again, in through the nose, fully inhaling to fill the lungs, and out once again through the mouth. One more time in, and out.

With your eyes closed, I want you to "see" the access point between you and God. I call this "the void." The colour you would see within your vision is blue/black, almost like a beautiful piece of lush, thick velvet. It has a vibration that creates a small wave of movement. The sensation you feel when viewing this is absolute *peace.*

In the centre of the blue/black void, far in the distance, is a small star. It appears like the only small diamond glistening against the velvet. Now focus on this and, at the same time, acknowledge the space within your heart centre that has the matching diamond point or star.

Just sit with this for a moment, seeing and acknowledging the glistening diamond against the velvet void whilst seeing and acknowledging the matching point within your heart.

Suddenly you will see and feel an extraordinary alignment. The two diamond points will begin to acknowledge each other and magnetize into alignment, to be within the same energy stream or channel. In an instant, once all is perfectly aligned, the two points connect. The diamond-white light explodes from the void and from your heart at the same time. The infusion of

26

love, of minds, and of soul wisdom is that which consciously reconnects the universal umbilical cord of Divine Mother, of God, our creative force and eternal nurturer. We return to the womb of creation and of our existence to understand, truly, from where we came.

Your memory, the knowing of your purpose, of your soul's desire to explore your human existence, will be completely realised at that moment and your belonging to an infinite love complete.

Suddenly you are aware of four white pillars that surround you and provide your Temple. It is ethereal and made of light, and it is that which houses your being during your incarnation on earth.

It is God's house within you.

Rainbow colours of energy begin to encircle the temple. Faster, faster, faster, until the background of black velvet and light expand and disappear, and the temple turns into a bright-blue sky and earth is viewed at a ground level.

Your infusion and your connection to the divine is akashicly, ethereally, karmically, spiritually, consciously, genetically, and physically complete.

We give thanks. Amen.

Chapter 2

Past Life Healings

Humankind is created in the image and likeness of the creative source. In fact, we are that creative source. We are made of God energy; this is who we are. We are God, self-experiential in every moment, pulsating to the frequency of light, which is urged to move and create fullness and expansion, and expressing itself in every moment of physical life.

We live eternally in that our essence flows in a continuous movement of physical incarnations and creative source energy. Throughout this continuous process, we are supported and guided by specific and non-specific beings. We refer to guardian angels or guides as some of these beings; others are just supportive sources energy gently embracing you and guiding you to your evolvement on path. "Past" lives, as we refer to them, indicate your soul's energy hosting with a physical body and life for a designated period. It indicates an "in-life" and an "out-of-life" experience. However, the truth be known, it is a shift in experience within a physical perspective and a transition into ethereal form which continues the life you are. The physical body, whilst miraculous and infused with God light (your soul), has a time span and cellular production and degeneration in its design. This allows your experiences to be evolving within a span of time and in relationship with human/earth relativity and time span. As a hundred years pass in earth time, an average 1.2 life spans are experienced and a continued "community consciousness" shifts, which expands to societal and nations re-evaluating and reassessing their needs, motives, and service to each other and the planet.

Over a number of life spans, a soul will explore his expansion and loving wisdom on many levels. From a perspective of the individual, it also ultimately creates a perspective of co-creative experience as we affect and seek growth together. Consciousness is raised, and whole nations clear old patterns, beliefs, and ideals that no longer serve the earth's ascension process.

It is all happening simultaneously, in all time directions and across all realities.

A soul who has lived and experienced five hundred births and deaths of physical reality, as well as simultaneous non-physical realities, will be linked to those energies of existence through a fine blue-silver cord. It has an order of wisdom and evolvement. It is perfect and entirely non-judgemental. It is simply the journey of soul, which allows a reference point of acknowledging particular repetitive behaviours or beliefs that require healing and releasing. We do not know where we are going unless we observe whence we came.

In allowing one to acknowledge and release patterns or beliefs of the past, we are obtaining the ultimate freedom we were created to enjoy. Endure the beauty of God's design in every moment as you create the ultimate version of your ultimate self. She sits at the right-hand side of the Father and to the left of her Mother and as the Holy Trinity, a celebration of love is expressed. And so it is for all.

We all have multi-levelled soul pursuits in that our individual perspectives seek to grow and evolve to the oneness we innately know and desire to experience, *and* we concurrently push the wheel of existence of all humanity (as well as non-physical planes) to collectively evolve together.

Past lives are your personal travel diary, your transcending and interpersonal time-machine, allowing the human experience to cooperate with genetic, karmic, and soul purpose. It also works in relationship with biological and environmental dynamics to further enhance and create the experience. It is opportunistic and perfect. It is God's wheel of life. It is perfection and ongoing. The connections and lives are infinite.

Amen.

It is what it is. And yes, there was a past life where this man lived a royal life. This particular life fed his soul, and I will tell you why.

Zaraf Elijah Khan was Arab royalty, specifically from the Old Persian Empire. Zaraf loved gold—the higher in carats, the better, 24k and 32k. It was so pure, it would bend in a warm hand. Zaraf was son of a Persian king, and there was no shortage of the finest of wares, items, food, dancers, and wine. War and combat were the largest problems, but they became a fact of life. "It is what it is," his father would say.

Zaraf was like any other child and was interested in the way things worked in the world. "Father, why is it so? Father, why are there poor people? Father, why does gold glisten so? Father?" He had many questions, day and night. There was no one else to keep him company or occupied. Zaraf would wait for the camel-driven carts that would bring in the gold, jewels, and wares from faraway lands. They were mostly gifts (or political currency) for his father and the fear of his power. Zaraf's father was a very powerful man. As the cartons and crates arrived, Zaraf was so excited! He just couldn't wait to see the jewels, the vases, and particularly the gold! He felt something extraordinary happen when he touched the gold.

Zaraf stood in front of a large crate. Workers of the king were all around, ensuring safe passage of the gifts. They allowed Zaraf a loo" and to play. Zaraf opened a box and uncovered a sealed, tightly packed wooden box with Egyptian inscriptions on it. *Wow!* he thought. He wedged a crowbar in to open it. The streams of light and gold were blinding. No one else could see.

He became frightened, but the rush of excitement took over. What a magical mystery he was revealing, but no one else could see what he saw. He opened the box once again, but this time he looked past the light streams as he gently lifted the ark from the wooden box. "The Ark of the Covenant," he said with amazement and disbelief. Could anyone else see this? Obviously not! Only Zaraf was meant to see it. The blinding gold was warming and beautiful to him. Zaraf knew he'd come across something powerful and mystical.

This extremely ornate piece was made of pure gold and was scripted with hieroglyphics. It held the mysteries and secrets to be revealed to the one who would receive it. The ark looked a little like a boat, and its course was to sail across many seas across many lifetimes, ensuring the balance of emotional health to all of humanity.

"Why me?" Zaraf enquired.

"Why not?" was the reply.

He laughed to himself. "I like that; a humorous God!" Zaraf noticed the incredible detail inscribed on this sacred piece. He began to overview his life. Yes, his father was wealthy, powerful, and lacked nothing, but what did he really have? Upon the dawn of his father's death, no amount of power, food, or money would stop the army of angels who would come forth to collect him. His father's army of ten thousand Persians had no power over these angels.

"This is the Truth. I know it to be so. I have a great secret to reveal, but how? The Egyptians have passed the gift, and it has fallen into my hands. I will be put up on a podium; I will be questioned like Heraclius. I have not the education to withstand the philosophers, the leaders, the critics. My fear overwhelms me. I hold the ark, and I suddenly experience the healing of my ill-feeling stomach. This is too great for me to hold. I cannot. I do not have the status, the power, the courage, the knowledge, to see the covenant be given to the people, adequately, safely. I shall return it to sea!"

Zaraf quietly snuck out the following night, carting the very heavy ark in a wheelbarrow. He had pondered whether to bury it, but that didn't feel right at all. "The Ark can be set free to the ocean and allow the gods to direct it to a worthy one. Now, that's a good solution." And so that's what he did.

Zaraf set the ark out to sea and watched it drift away. He felt a deep sadness, but he mostly experienced a sick feeling in the stomach as he watched it drift from sight. He told himself, "It will be given to a person, as directed by God, who knows what to do."

Golden treasures continued to be gifted to the kingdom, and Zaraf searched every crate for that special item which would enlighten him and allow him to feel God in his midst, but he never received such magnificence again. Gold made him feel safe, loved, secure, and protected, and he later deeply regretted releasing the ark.

He later had a dream of a beautiful angel who appeared to him, telling him the ark would be returned when he was ready.

He waited and waited. It never physically returned, but he often saw it in his dreams.

Blocks: Crown, Heart, Solar plexus.

Healing has taken place.

"I will kill anyone who gets in my way! Whether that be blood, brother, friend, or foe. I am the next in line to receive my rewards. I have fought and led a five-thousand-strong army. I have killed and sent many men to their death. I will be recognised as a hero, and I will not allow some buxom young pigs to stand in my way. I don't care what family or bloodline you're from."

Adhim was a fighter, a soldier of high rank, who fought many wars and led many victories against the Persians, Babylonians, and Greeks. His recognition from the Great Pharaoh earned him much pride, not to mention great wealth. He was paid in gold, riches, gems, women, and wine. It was a good life of rewards if you lived long enough to ride the victory horse home.

There was a group of young royals and elite bloodline soldiers who were drafted to be groomed in fighting for, honouring, and protecting Egypt. Adhim had no time for these well-kept boys. He'd laugh as he drank his red wine and joked with other soldiers over their role. The issue was not only that fighting heroes were well celebrated and admired, but that the wealthy, royal, elite soldiers were honoured to the highest level.

Adhim's position was threatened and fifteen years of battle scars felt compromised over these five brats, three brothers from one bloodline and two from another. A great battle was to be led by Adhim, across the desert plains where only the toughest and bravest survive. Even Adhim's skin was like a leather bag. Dark, parched, and permanent lines etched deeply into the skin. He began to plan and assess the situation well, and he decided he would kill all five. These kids were an embarrassment anyway and couldn't lead a kingdom. Adhim knew that his age may be against him, but his blood, his fury, and his motivation had no boundaries.

Adhim decided that he'd ambush during battle. He had many swords and weapons, with multiple blades. Some looked insignificant and small but very effective. He went for the two strongest first. "Ha! Too easy," Adhim crowed. "They were beside each other as I slay them, and they were all too busy in battle to notice who their killer was." Red, red eyes of panic and anger.

The youngest of the three brothers witnessed the callous murder of his two older brothers and charged at Adhim. With one huge sweep of his sword, the young soldier's fear and fury was no match for the power and might of Adhim. The young soldier was instantly beheaded.

Adhim fought on with the enemy forces; he could not reach the other two soldiers. He would complete his murderous task tonight. The evening came, and all who had battled now rested and attended to wounds in their tents. The two young soldiers lay together ready for sleep. Adhim approached the tent and offered wine to help them sleep, only within the wine was a powerful poison. Both soldiers died of poisoning that night. Adhim had freed a venomous snake in the tent, claiming and verifying the boys had been bitten and killed overnight.

Adhim had gotten away with these heinous crimes and remained as the leader and general of the army to protect his region in Egypt. The Pharaoh's queen was a healer and scribe, and she had seen what Adhim had done to her nephews and cousins. Shocked and extremely angered by this, she sought revenge. She released a venomous spider in his quarters, which bit him on the foot. Adhim died after a twenty-hour battle with a creature one-thousandth his size. It was the last battle he fought during that incarnation.

This past life has been cleared and healing has taken place.

Amen.

"This place has my favourite trees; they're falling strands of green branches and twine that flow so gracefully in the breeze. I sit and watch the dance of spring. The butterflies are enticing the branches to waltz. It truly is God's magic, and I love to make it mine."

Diana, named after the moon goddess, was a beautiful maiden. She lived on the edge of the forest and often visited it to connect with the nature spirits, the animals, and the elementals. Diana knew she was special even as a child. Her grandmother told her many things of a familial gift and a lineage of healing and magic. It was white and pure. Diana would sit wide-eyed and in full attention to every piece of information her grandmother would impart. Diana loved her grandmother very much. She would help to prepare medicinal herbs and resins for every ailment known to man. People would knock on her grandmother's door all the time to collect their remedies. Diana thought this was so wonderful.

One day, when Diana was around eight years old, her grandmother sat her down. "Dearest child, you carry the gifts of sight, healing, and the ability to perform rituals and magic. You are a little white witch, my dear!" she said with glee. Diana and her grandmother giggled like two little girls. They were in clear understanding of one another. Diana's grandmother taught her to be still and to meditate. It was important to be able to go within, and eventually she taught Diana to expand her energy field. She would be able to clear her energy bodies, to be guided, to invoke, and to pray.

Diana became a very gifted, powerful white witch. Diana was just seventeen years of age when she was faced with her beloved grandmother's passing. She felt honoured and blessed that she was able to conduct and celebrate the woman's life in ceremony. Her grandmother said, "It was just my time, my darling." Diana knew her grandmother would be with her after physical death, but still, she had to acknowledge some very powerful emotions over her passing. She would miss her physical presence, her hugs, and her soup!

Diana's grandmother was buried beneath one of the most magnificent oak trees in the forest, and Diana would visit often to sprinkle daisies over the grave. "I know you loved daisies, so here, Grandma. I love you!."

As Diana settled into her life living and practising on her own, there were a few covens who requested her presence and wisdom. Diana preferred to work solo, as her grandmother had; however, when she learned that a famous witch named Margaret was requesting her presence at the next coven gathering, Diana couldn't resist attending. Margaret was well known for her incredible psychic visions and prophetic predictions. Diana had enormous intuitive talents, but she was eager to learn to scry. Diana decided to attend this particular coven meeting, where Margaret was head of the committee and the region.

"Welcome, Diana. We are so sorry to hear of your grandmother Isabelle's passing. She was a very respected and loved Sister of the Hood."

"Thank you, Margaret. As you know, we are only temporarily parted." Both smiled and agreed. Diana was handed a goblet of mead wine.

The women chatted, and eventually Diana broached the subject of developing her intuitive sight. "Oh, but Diana, you already have the gift. You just need someone to expand it for you and give you the key to open it!"

Diana was so excited and pleased to hear that she was already gifted but un-activated, so to speak. Margaret agreed to teach Diana weekly lessons of psychic development in exchange for various herbal remedies and concoctions for herself and the congregation.

The deal was made, and Diana was very appreciative. She would make extra for Margaret, include larger bottles and additional gifts, and make soup and beautiful floral hair pieces for all the women of the congregation. Diana was a generous and gracious healer. She was a beautiful soul.

And so the psychic lessons began. Margaret was teaching Diana from a psychic perspective, reading and allowing information present in the aura, on the body, or within tea leaves. But God had another plan. Diana's third eye and crown chakras began to open, allowing information and images of everything she required to know to be channelled from her beloved Grandmother, Jesus, a high priestess, and a beautiful empress.

Holy night! This was powerful. Diana would literally glow, and anyone in the room would feel her vibration. Diana instinctively knew that she had to increase her awareness and earth magic to keep her rooted in, just like her beautiful and favourite willow trees she adored.

Margaret was pleased at first, but slowly became bitter and jealous. The coven was booking Diana for oracle readings and healings all the time. Margaret had lost her popularity as a healer and being known as the all insightful.

Margaret believed she had created a monster and therefore felt justified in an intervention. Margaret's dark side had foretold that Diana would develop an ego and greed influence, which would ruin the balance of all things. Of course, this was not true, but Margaret was capable of performing a very dark form of magic. She invoked all directions—north, south, east, and west—and out slithered lizards and snakes, shadows and spirits. It was not pleasant at all.

Margaret mixed and brewed, invoked and conjured. She burned a black candle and a white candle and created an ethereal vortex. This was etherically placed over Diana's third eye and sealed with a pentagram. She then invoked a black onyx bowl, placed it over Diana's crown, and sealed it with a pentagram. The black onyx allowed only certain information to come through; however, the opaque-black solid mass would certainly cloud Diana's vision. Margaret knew what she did was wrong, but she convinced herself it was for the best.

Poor Diana woke with a horrendous headache, almost unable to stand the pain. She mixed and brewed some of her very powerful remedies, but nothing seemed to work. Diana knew she was well. She could only read her tea leaves, as none of her previous intuitive skills would work. The tea leaves indicated that a curse had been placed upon her because of jealousy. Diana appealed to Margaret for help.

"Yes, Diana, of course we will help you. Best you stay within the coven, work and live alongside us, and we will protect and guide each other. Your sight and channel will return; don't worry."

Of course, it never did. Diana would appeal to her grandmother and God to help her, but all she could understand was, "All will be revealed and healed at the right time."

God, we now ask that this curse and the black onyx bowl be removed from Diana now.

Be aware that headache and/or dizziness may be experienced as the energy flow adjusts to your natural ability.

Thankyou Spirit; for this beautiful story and healing today.

Blocks: Head and third eye. Blocks have been removed and healing has taken place.

Amen.

Early 1900s

Jonathan was a very wealthy, highly successful merchant. He imported spices, teas, oils, and food items to England, America, and Europe. Jonathan had abundance and material wealth, and a very opulent mansion complete with golden and marble fittings, plush velvet curtains, and plenty of maids and servants. Cynthia was Jonathan's lovingly supportive wife. She was always constructive and had a good business mind, and she often conversed with Jonathan about expansion of their business and acquiring more wealth. The more money they made, the more children they had. Jonathan would laugh, "Every time I obtain another agreement, another baby is born! Damn kids, they can smell an inheritance, even from heaven!"

Jonathan was very driven and passionate about spreading the word about his business worldwide. He wanted to be the most successful merchant, bringing in the purest essential oils, flavoursome teas, and exotic spices, but he also wanted to expand to import handmade rugs, woven and beautifully patterned blankets, and traditional giftware from Lebanon, Egypt, and India, all of which were becoming quite popular and fashionable.

Cynthia had enough nannies and home help not to be overrun by domestic duties, and she enjoyed the evening dinnertime the most. Business was intensely demanding, and often Jonathan would have to force himself to retreat from his study to join the family for the evening meal. As a result, he would either bring documents to the table or rush through dinner and excuse himself quickly to return to his work. Cynthia would be slightly angered by such actions, as it was very rude and it was the behaviour of a commoner. How ghastly!

The business quickly developed into a corporation and was extremely profitable, sailing big ships at sea to import from the East and then by rail and truck from port.

But there was a dark cloud looming. Intercontinental travel, weeks at sea, and lack of hygiene brought about many diseases and illnesses unlike any seen before.

The Great Plague had just been identified and many houses in London and Europe were in lockdown with a black or red cross on the door indicating that infection may be or is present in that household. What began as a fairly controlled and contained outbreak quickly became a widespread and vicious infestation. People became very frightened, and rightly so. Once infected, no person was spared—no child, no woman, no priest or doctor.

Jonathan was increasingly concerned. At first, all of his workers at the wharf and some ships were under quarantine until checked to be clean and disease free. Disruption and dismay were all around. Soon Jonathan's neighbours, workers, and schoolteachers, all were struck down by this terrible illness.

One night in his study, Jonathan reflected about how and what could stop this awful disease. It must be the devil's illness! Jonathan sat and prayed for his family and for help. "God, is there anything, in my fortunate position, that I can do?"

"My son, you are blessed with abundance and plenty. With the love and concern in your heart, take your wealth and invest it into the needy."

Jonathan immediately took action. He felt a huge connection to this cause. His doctor friend had told him there was no more room in the hospitals and people were forced to stay at home, putting family members at risk of infection.

Jonathan immediately began to build a hospice. He started with an existing hall and an extension. This hospice was the size of two modern school gyms and housed two hundred beds for the very sick and the dying. Jonathan arranged for blankets, food, and paid professionals to look after them. He included many beautiful pictures of Jesus and Mary on the walls to comfort the sick. Jonathan spent many hours in the hospice, risking his life to talk to the dying. Jonathan knew that for all he'd worked so hard to achieve, for the children he'd fathered and raised, nothing was as personally satisfying or gratifying than giving back to these people who were far less fortunate and who were now leaving the earth plane.

Jonathan had to experience this aspect because there was already a future lifetime as a great healer predestined. The major difference would be that Jonathan would channel from his/her Christ lineage, which was already obviously streaming through.

Jonathan died aged fifty and rested with soul-family until the next incarnation was time.

All blocks have been removed, and healing has taken place.

Amen.

Apostolos (Paul) was managing the construction of a prominent temple in the city of Athens. There was political unrest, and two factions were arguing over the naming, size, and internal features of the structure. It was to be built for the Olympic Games, and so timelines and organization was important.

Paul was a very task-oriented man skilled in many areas of building himself, but he'd worked his way into a supervisory position, which held much more responsibility. He was particularly associated with many talented stonemasons and artists, who were given the opportunity to work on this major structure.

There had been disagreements in council about how some of the features would be positioned. Paul was getting increasingly frustrated that the project was suffering so many delays over some argumentative councilmen who thought they knew it all. Some of their complaints were ridiculous and can't work. Not in the time he had to build it anyway.

Paul appeared in the chambers once again after being called from the site. "With all due respect, your honour, I cannot absorb all these delays and decisions must be made and now! As the games are just eight months away, it must be completed by then. The king must not be humiliated by incompletion."

"You can continue, Paul, but I cannot promise payment for works that have not yet been approved by all members of council. This is the way our mighty city has been built. What if everyone just went ahead and built whatever they wanted? We exemplify democracy, Paul, regardless of the games or

Zeus himself. If it is meant to be erect this way, the gods will see it will be done."

Paul was frustrated but found it even more infuriating to waste precious time arguing. He returned to site where workers, labourers, and masons had gathered. He explained that not all details had been approved by the council.

"We can still begin, but risk non-payment if in the end what we've built is not approved." Only half of the workers remained after learning this. Paul picked up tools and began working as well. It was the honour of this great city and the king that pushed them to work at the risk of non-payment. Paul was concerned and felt it was unfair, but at least he was not alone and worked alongside a team in unity.

They worked night and day for long, long hours. Periodically, Paul would attend council to ask whether all twenty-five items on their list had reached resolution. Slowly but surely, more items were approved and marked off his list. Payment in gold was assured for these items. The men were happy and celebrated. They would be recognized and honoured for such amazing architectural and structural work when the world visited Athens in a few short months; however, they still needed to feed their families in the meantime.

Time was running short. Many men had not completed their area of work and left as they were afraid to continue on, in case they would not be given their final payment.

In the final weeks, Paul was left with only three others. They were practically enslaved, working day and night. Paul was so angry and tired, but he continued. He prayed very hard and asked God to please allow all works to be approved and to be paid for in full, and of course that the world would be witness to one of the greatest structures in Greece. It truly was magnificent, majestic, and monumental! There were sculptures and goddesses—a great white beauty indeed.

Paul had lost a lot of weight but had the drive and determination of a lion!

During the opening ceremony of the Games, an enormous crowd gathered, and thousands of people were in the square. There were flags, fabrics, music, and food everywhere. A huge fabric like a curtain covered the temple. The Olympic Games president spoke at a podium, announcing the unveiling of this grand structure.

The curtain suddenly fell, and the building was revealed. There was an enormous cheer, the crowd went wild, and the music began to play. Paul was exhausted but so happy and accomplished.

And did he receive his final payment? Yes, he did. And he also received a promotion to work within the palace of the royal family, supervising and coordinating royal structures.

Blocks have been removed, and healing has taken place.

Amen.

Layah looks out over the sunset: the horizon of the desert, the red sand, the wind cooling as the day's heat subsides. The red colour reminds her of her connection to Mother Earth. But she questions and is disturbed by the bloodshed of her sisters. "I will miss them. God, embrace in them in your care."

*   *   *

King Thulmut and his Queen Selma ruled in the year 500 BC. We began as slaves in the powerful and mighty kingdom, but even slaves have a hierarchy. And some of the top level have close access to the family, royalty, and household servants. Over time it came to be known that four females of the four-hundred-strong group of slaves were blessed with several gifts. These four women spoke to the gods, channelled healing energy, read crystals, and scribed symbols from the heavens to assist Egypt, her king, and secure one's safe passage into the afterlife.

Some years passed and the four strong women took initiative and earned attention for the king's and queen's guidance and medicinal needs. Two sisters were particularly powerful and well regarded, Layah and Oriana. They were gifted from childhood but grew up very poor. They were fortunate to work and be accepted into the pharaoh's court.

Layah was a healer and worked with medicinal resins, and she was also an oil maker. Her sister was an oracle and scribe. The two other healers were also very skilful and powerful in their own way. As time went on, the pharaoh, his court, and his queen would frequently call upon the services of the four women.

Layah was the quieter one of the sisters. Oriana was more vocal, and the queen took a particular liking to her. The other two healers were also quiet as they conducted their daily chores, prayers, and sessions of meditation with mindfulness and with connection to the gods.

One day there came news that the queen was required to travel across to Jordan. She would be away for some months. She was to take a healer with her, and it was to be Layah's sister, Oriana. Oriana would ensure guidance and safety would be with her, which was particularly imperative before and during political discussions with any leader of neighbouring countries.

The other girls and Layah wished Oriana well, but they also warned her. It had been noted and intuitively revealed that the queen was not encouraging of her king, and that she was planning to carry out her own revolution in the kingdom and take many lovers on the side. She was moving from spirit and heart into darkness. "Tread warily, sister! She will not succeed in her plot, and you may be entangled in something very unhealthy indeed," they warned.

Oriana acknowledged and thanked them, and then packed her belongings. "I shall miss you, but this is such a great opportunity. We've been so poor all our lives, and now I travel with the queen."

Layah smiled, but in her heart she knew Oriana was weak and could be easily misguided. The other two healers gave her a hug and wished her well. They then asked her to pledge a secret rite, one that encloses their healing modality and the herbs, resins, rituals, recipes, and secrets to remain within the group. Oriana pledged and left.

The healers looked at one another, but didn't say a word. They all knew she was a weak link who may become confused and misguided. Faith was the passion driving their God force, and now one of them was being influenced by riches and fame.

The relationship between King Thulmut and Queen Selma grew cold over the coming months. Messages were sent back and forth, and rumours of unrest began to circulate. The king called upon his favourite healer Layah to assist him. He was growing very agitated and anxious. "She is humiliating me with countless lovers and not even hiding it!" Layah knew her sister was involved in advising the queen to behave so inappropriately. The pharaoh became furious and ordered a message for Queen Selma's return.

The queen had no option but to return with Oriana. There was a fiery exchange with the king upon her arrival. The girls gathered to greet Oriana. Her eyes were darkened and cold. She had turned into something else. What had happened to her?

Thulmut was so furious that he was unapproachable for three days. Only Layah could go near. He was being told by his queen, "Please spare me, I'm so grief-stricken and sorry, but the oracle Oriana told me that your healer Layah and her two friends were plotting against me and our powerful kingdom, and that you, Thul-mut, were stupid enough to fall for it!" This was all lies; the opposite was true. But the king was confused and very dazzled by his queen's beauty. Deep down he loved her, but he didn't trust her. He actually trusted Layah much more. It was an icy palace, and how awful it felt since the queen and Oriana had returned.

Layah and the two healers secretly met and discussed the betrayal. The queen had convinced Oriana of untold riches and security alongside her if she helped overthrow the king, Pharaoh Thulmut. Layah was distressed and disappointed but knew it was true.

"I must tell the king and be loyal to his service and the gods. He is a pharaoh of the heart and will lead Egypt to glory on earth and in heaven. I must protect that for the benefit of all." Layah said to herself.

Oriana was aware that she had been found out by her sisters and soon too, the king. Oriana received the message whilst she was scribing in her room that night. She quickly told the queen, "They know! And they will ruin everything!"

Oriana had betrayed and was disloyal to her fellow healers, as well as their kingdom, forgetting she was also bound by oath to sacred knowledge.

The queen assisted Oriana in having the two healers killed. Layah was also charged with crimes; however, the king was still unsure and had her pardoned. The king was growing increasingly confused, as a spell had been placed on him to hinder and cloud his decision making.

Before the disloyalty charges could be heard, the two healers were found dead by attendees to their room. One had her throat slashed in the middle of the night to ensure she could never speak the truth of light and God again (as it was believed this would karmically travel to the afterlife, and Oriana would have to meet again her again one day; also this was done to lessen the chances of crossing paths again). The other healer was given a cup of tea before bed with poison in it. She squirmed, cried, and suffered for many hours over the night, vomiting countless times. She was found dead on the floor by a servant in the early hours of the morning. Poisoning was used to prevent her being a vessel of light for any future lifetimes and in the afterlife.

Layah mourned such betrayal and battled to remain in the stream of love and light, but she knew karma would allow the wrongs to be righted.

The queen was poisoned a few weeks after the king learned the truth. Oriana was slain by dagger.

Layah became the king's lover, mistress, and divine guide.

All blocks have been removed, and healing has taken place.

Amen

Nerod's Self-Gratification   22/8/11

Nerod was a priest in Egypt who worked within the Temple of Prayer and Invocation to the Gods. Nerod worked with the fire element and with this, he was particularly powerful. It was also associated with dragon energy, and his eyes shone red from self-gratification and the need for admiration and power. He had a successor who was his assistant. In his working and development structure, if the assistant showed growth, strength, loyalty, and will, then and only then would he become the successor if Nerod either left or died. But Nerod was living a life of two faces: one that held the hand of a suffering worshipper and handed bread out in the streets to the hungry, and the other that cast spells and served only for his own wealth and growth in status and fame.

He was ego-driven, concealed by a mask of faith. His assistant David was less vocal, but his belief and mindset was cut from the same cloth. It was quite interesting to observe that only men worked at this temple. Most people felt that the Sun God's resonance was present; however, there were plenty of hidden agendas.

Healers and priestesses associated with the feminine felt quite repelled as there was much ego and passion of a sexual nature. It was invasive and over-emphasised. Most women in the surrounds felt somewhat uncomfortable here as the men came to pray.

In the temple worked another man named Adeyah, but most people called him Adi. Adi was in his sixties, which was a sign of a very fit and healthy man for that time. He believed that the Sun God kept his fire alight within his spirit and that he

56

was healthy and well all these years because he'd served in the temple for thirty-two years.

Adi was a good man of pure heart and integrity. He ran the temple's prayer sessions, he cleaned, made candles, and mixed oils and resins for medicinal purposes and space clearing. He also performed general maintenance of the temple and its grounds. He never had a day off to rest. He'd watch the sunrise and sunset each day, or it didn't feel like he'd worked and served the gods with sincerity.

Adi had observed Nerod and was quietly questioning some of his motives; however, Adi would never make that known. He would be severely punished if discovered. One day David noticed Adi watching Nerod.

"I cannot read your thoughts, Adi," David said, "but I can see it in your eyes. You question the man before you." Nerod was at his altar praying and performing a ritual.

"Oh!" Adi exclaimed. "I'm sorry, Your Greatness. I didn't mean to stare. I didn't sleep well last night and . . . and . . ."

"Nonsense!" David exclaimed. "You are very transparent, loyal follower, and I can see your doubt, and you're probably not wrong. " David was becoming mysterious and unpredictable. David had learned a lot from Nerod and developed the same hunger for power and gratification. "What a sad time for this community and this temple, as it was once led by the Great Lion (as he was known), brave, virtuous, and faithful. He left the temple and led great armies to victory. Anyway, Adi, your eyes and mouth utter different stories. I can see and I feel; I am a seer, and I can feel your dividedness as well."

Adi felt a little more comfortable to speak. "Well, yes. I do question the integrity of this priest. I have seen many come and go, and none had his energy! The masses of men who flock here seem to get what they need from him though, and all their crops and businesses are very prosperous indeed. So, with the Sun God's blessing, I assume all is well!" David then began to open up about Nerod's plans to work his way into the temple clergy and to eventually have leadership in a number of connecting temples in the country. He had focus and drive, and he was powerful in his presence, which would influence and encourage the emperor. Nerod's passion and driving forces were power, wealth, fame, and women, similar to the emperor's.

Adi had a very close associate on the clergy; in fact, it was his brother-in-law. Adi felt compelled to warn his brother-in-law about this persuasive, self-gratifying priest who was trying to manipulate the system to serve himself. David was happy with Nerod moving on and therefore encouraged him! He'd share comments like, "You're bound for such greatness and glory, master!" Now, David realised and cunningly knew exactly what he was doing. David had aspirations, just as Nerod did, and with Nerod on the clergy, David could step in as leader of the temple.

David had already realised how observant Adi was. David certainly didn't want Adi snooping around him when he took over the temple. He told Adi about Nerod, knowing Adi would tell his brother-in-law, which would cause a bit of a stir, enough for Nerod to understand that Adi had betrayed him and therefore have him removed for the act of disloyalty.

This plan and circumstances followed precisely and without any adverse effects on Nerod at all, because the clergy saw Adi as jealous and spiteful. After so many years of hard work and service, Adi could never be a priest at the temple, and therefore such actions were justified as strong motives.

Without Nerod making Adi aware of his knowledge of the betrayal, Nerod prepared a spell and ritual that released a viper into Adi's heart. It severed his vocal chords as he tried to scream. It then released all of its venom into his stomach, poisoning him very painfully and slowly.

Adi passed away.

Nerod took position at the Temple of Egypt and became second in command of the clergy.

David took over the Prayer Temple.

There were dark days indeed.

Healing has taken place.

Amen.

Neos, Temple of Balance, Harmony, and Unity

In a time just preceding Atlantis, the temple's priestess had seventeen healers and physicians working in her holy space. People were a lot more aware of their energy needs and their body's health requirements, so the temple's healing work and medicinal products were commonly and frequently sought after.

Nephrite was teaching, mentoring, and conducting small classes to further educate and ready her next dozen or so healers in varying modalities. Nephrite would conduct classes at two most afternoons. This was the hottest part of the day, and most people were having a sleep before continuing their day at about four in the afternoon and into the evening.

Nephrite offered healings, energy balancing, scribing, art, reader/oracles, tea readings, massage, hand and foot treatment, crystal healings and readings, and palm and face readings. Her temple was very busy, and to meet demand, she had to ensure her healers were ready to cater to all situations and statuses. There were emperors, royalty, councilmen, athletes, artists, and politicians. They were wealthy.

There was a graduation announcement and ceremony about to take place. Healers had been working hard and studying diligently in hope they would receive a much-sought-after position at the temple.

Zian and Lydia had proven their commitment to their chosen healing modality, and they would often spend long hours assisting Priestess Nephrite in the clean-up and setting up for the following day. Zian and Lydia were peaceful, happy, and helpful. The other students and workers often passed comment on how they were trying too hard, or that they had no self respect, which was completely untrue. Their comments were derived from jealousy. The priestess knew that the girls' commitment was exactly part of the practice that bore great healers. They were able to disconnect from ego and engage with complete dedication. She watched them closely after months of training and made her own assessment. They had all of the elements required to encompass their role and follow the criteria of what she was famous for, NEOS: the temple of harmony, balance, and unity. Visitors would come from all across Greece and Mesopotamia and sometimes from faraway lands.

The gathering took place, and the murmuring of voices were respectfully hushed. Nephrite stepped onto a platform wearing the most beautiful purple gown, finished with a golden headpiece, gold belt, and sandals. She was a picture of light and a true goddess to aspire to. When Lydia and Zian were called to accept the ceremonial decree and their initiation, both women were very pleased. They had both come from poor backgrounds and had no support from anyone. They made their studies a pure force of passion and a direction without distraction. Nephrite handed them their golden wands. They were healing wands, which would provide protection and nobility from the gods, but they could also be used in healing clients, as well as for gridding and clearing homes. It was a beautiful tool and highly regarded, bringing great respect for its owner and her capabilities.

There was a group of students who were shocked and revolted. "How could they be awarded entry?" they said. "I can't believe it, what? No!" Many faces turned to them to hush the obvious disruption to the ceremony. These jealous students were questioning the priestess's decision, and they continued with their childish comments. "How could she allow such inexperienced young girls to be in a Goddess role? It's ludicrous."

The two main offenders were considerably older, and they had often made the younger healers feel inexperienced and inadequate. Whilst being loyal and working tirelessly for some years, these two jealous healers seemed to be forever in schooling while not achieving any certified or personal growth or goals. Nephrite acknowledged this, but because the two fifty-year-olds appeared to mentor and impart wisdom to the younger ones, she allowed this cycle to see its journey to reveal to her, as she trusted. Nephrite trusted in what was revealing and presenting to her always. She believed the situation was purely to develop and nurture the students and support the future of the temple. But on a personal level for the two senior women, the truth was they feared the responsibility and the required growth they'd need to embrace, if they were to be temple healers. Yes, they had maturity in chronological years, but lacked the vision, strength, and brutal honesty to assess the years of ignoring their personal issues and growth lessons.

There would be no more hiding behind veils. They would have to display leadership and decision making. In truth, they were terrified. They had developed an ego-based self-gratification, using students as justification for selfless service. Whilst receiving countless comments of greatness, strength, and wisdom, the ego was satisfied. To the young healers, the experience and knowledge of these women seemed endless, but in fact, it was stagnant, limited, and fear-based.

Lydia and Zian were given their accreditation, and finally Nephrite publicly acknowledged the less-than-favourable display by her senior students. When questioned, the women argued and became defensive, offending the priestess even further on her decision-making and intuitive capabilities. She was quite angered and now aware of the misuse of power by the two older women, as she had suspected for some time. She was no longer confusing loyalty and service with fear and self-limiting beliefs.

She banished them to an island off the coast of the mainland where they could work assisting in the construction of another healing temple in her name. The two women were unforgiving and swore revenge.

Thank you for showing me. This important clearing has taken place. Love and light.

Amen

Bridgette worked for the king's court as a spiritual nurse and herbalist extremely knowledgeable in the human body and diseases. Bridgette was an orphan raised by nuns until she was schooled and old enough to take care of herself. She stayed in contact with the nuns, loved them, and visited often. Bridgette was a natural healer and had a dream of becoming a doctor. But being a woman, it was not allowed that she work as a doctor. The nuns had nurtured her incredible ability to understand the function of the body and her philosophy that the earth and her seasons were God's pharmacy for all to use.

King Henry enlisted Bridgette's services for his staff, himself, and his queen. The queen was quite jealous of Bridgette's beauty and intelligence, but kept her displeasure to herself. Bridgette was beautiful, very smart, and connected to her faith. She also loved to spend free time in the forest connecting with nature, collecting ingredients, and looking for more ideas and inspiration from God's pharmacy.

One day the queen asked Bridgette to attend to an urgent matter regarding one of the generals in the king's army. The general had fallen ill with pneumonia and as this general was too important to the army to be ill, she asked on the king's behalf that Bridgette see to his medicine and requirements.

Bridgette recommended a steam bath with essences and oils from certain trees in the forest, including wildflowers, alone with lemon juice and ground herbs to drink. *He must sweat*, she thought. Additionally, she would send him a healing to address the problem energetically. She knew what the problem was. *A*

Fighter/Warrior archetype in this kingdom? Definitely 'possessed' from all the lives he's taken.

And so Bridgette prepared the medicinal tinctures and the steam bath essences. She was not permitted to enter his quarters, as this was considered an inappropriate and risky practise, in case she was infected. The general was quarantined, so a slave was sent in to administer and deliver the items with strict instructions.

The jealous queen stopped the slave just outside the general's door. "Don't say a word, you hear me? Or you'll be placed in the dungeon with rats!" And with that, the queen opened the tincture bottle and added a few drops of poison.

The terrified slave shook her head. "No, Your Majesty! I don't know anything, I didn't even see you."

As the story goes, the queen had had a rather steamy but short affair with this general some months back; however, he was the one who abruptly ended it as quickly as it started. She was extremely offended by this, so she saw no harm in exterminating him and getting rid of the very beautiful and charming Bridgette at the same time. Perfect plan. *Everyone is far too obsessed with that little witch anyway!* she thought.

The general began to die of the poison relatively slowly, first beginning to sweat, then eventually falling into a paralysed coma and eventually death. This process would take eight to ten hours. The king was alerted as the general was noticeably declining.

The king approached the quarters and looked from the door. "Your Highness, I will not live. I am dying. I have seen nothing but the imagery of your physician Bridgette in the room. In my mind, I know she has something to do with this. Wasn't she the one administering medicines?"

The king looked startled and then furious. "Of course!" The general passed soon after and produced a black tongue—the sure sign of poisoning.

"She murdered my general, but why?"

Bridgette was called to the high court at once. The king questioned her and then slandered her, yelling obscenities and accusations of witchcraft. Bridgette did not understand. She was absolutely shocked at his anger and felt the powerful emotion of betrayal.

The king exclaimed, "He felt your presence there before he died. He knew it was you! Why?"

Bridgette thought about the distant healing she had sent only hours before. *How did he know? I tell no one about these. How could this happen?* Too many thoughts and confusion blocked her messages from God. All she could do was sob and pray.

The entire kingdom was saddened when Bridgette was sentenced to public death in the central square of town. In a white flowing gown, in front of thousands, Bridgette was tied to a wooden pole. People were yelling, "Slay the witch!" The loving, compassionate nuns gathered to pray near her.

Bridgette looked at them, focused on God, and tilted her head to the right. She closed her eyes, and an image of Jesus was clearly before her. He was holding out his hands to embrace her.

The Knight's Bell rang, and a hooded man with a large knife stepped forward. There were rights being read out, and she was asked if she would beg for mercy and God's penance be given.

She kept her eyes shut and prayed, concentrating on the image of Jesus. One tear streamed from her right eye.

The call came: "Slay the witch!"

The hooded man walked up, and in a moment, a blink of an eye, he cut her throat.

Blood streamed down her white gown, her body limp.

The nuns cried in silence and prayer.

Jesus took her home.

Amen

Therese viewed Mother Superior with love and respect, but also with an ounce of envy.

The Mother Superior appeared to be in control and emotionally, mentally, and physically balanced. Therese wanted so much to be like this. In the early days, Therese was so very grateful for the care and nurture Mother Superior gave her. Being orphaned at seven years of age, in and out of broken and disruptive homes that were full of unhealthy energies and abuse, she was given the opportunity to be taken in by a convent at age eleven.

Therese entrusted that God had finally heard her prayers to be cared for and protected by another mother who would replace her own. At the convent, she had many. But her favourite and most loving connections were with Sister Augusta and Mother Superior. Mother Superior was so balanced and extremely intuitive. She knew Therese had come from a disruptive and impoverished past. So what better than to give the hungry food? What better than to give the shivering a blanket? This divine child would be given money to manage, money to learn the skills of budgeting and expenditure. Money is an item of exchange. It is a currency. Mankind has worked with varying types of currency for all of the ages. But some things remain consistent, and money inspires great power and need in most. Mother Superior felt that she could correct any damage done by Therese's early days of lack and empower her with great teaching and responsibility.

Therese well understood mathematics, the recording of figures, and budgets, and she excelled at making the money spread and multiply through good investments, donations, and returns through charitable work. Therese always put herself up for a challenge and surpassing the mark. However, she just needed to be reminded of boundaries in self-care. Therese needed to feel needed. She wanted to insure herself in a way, so that all she did was so impressive it couldn't possibly be done as well by anyone else. She was very afraid of being rejected again.

Once she turned twenty-one and was officially a grown woman, her displeasure in God and her faith grew. At first, quietly, she felt a rise of anger and bitterness inside herself. She felt God had let her down. How could God have allowed her early life to be so horrible for a child to endure? And just when she felt she was rescued at age eleven and placed amongst the nuns, those very nuns began to use her. Would they? Could they? Self-doubt and overwhelming pain began to surface.

They are overworking me and making me feel like I can never truly relax. I just might be replaced if I stop to rest. I'm worth so much more! God would see my worth. Why don't the nuns see my worth? Without me, the convent would not be so wealthy and giving! I need to adequately pay myself a little extra insurance, as I'm sure they will discard me before too long. Just like it's always been.

Therese slowly collected an amount of money, which she hid under the floorboards beneath her bed. Mother Superior had dreamt of the betrayal, but God had also given Mother Superior Therese's reasoning in it all. Mother Superior felt saddened, but she understood, as it was her past she was feeling victim to and chose not to heal from. Mother Superior could guide and nurture but could not force Therese to heal if she chose not to. Mother Superior knew that Therese was a good soul deep down and didn't want to create a big disruption. She decided to write Therese a letter, giving Therese a last chance at surrender to God and her healing. She asked her to admit to her crime and with compassion and love for herself and

Mother Superior, and that she ask for God's forgiveness if her heart truly wanted freedom and redemption. She decided to also offer a quiet retreat. Therese could exit out if that was what she wanted, to begin a new life elsewhere with a $200 head start, which was enough to live very well for quite a number of years.

And so she left Therese to decide.

Unfortunately, Therese ran away and was never seen again.

Mother Superior was greatly saddened, as it felt like she'd lost her own child. Mother Superior surrendered her pain to God.

Healing has taken place.

Amen

Many skulls on top of stakes are placed into a cave. This ritual was to lay to rest the dead, allowing the spirit of the possessed person to return to the light. The human skull had to be dismembered from the body, and the body burned.

The healers of this male-only temple provided an exorcism-style service. This temple was called the Temple of Fire and was run by a leading priest named Stolar. There was much evil residing within the community, on certain people, and in various places such as homes, businesses, and even temples and places of worship. This was mainly due to the way people lived. They were desperate times, and life expectancy for the people was very low due to war, invasion, or sickness. Greed, fear, and misused power were natural and commonplace. There was also a "lower dimension," a coexisting galactic region that had connected to our planet during that time. As low frequencies connect, they become more powerful, and so with every unloving act, a cycle develops and manifests in physical form.

As with all dimensions of time, humans and their soul being have always had choice and heavenly help. When placed within an unhealthy environment, earth angels and healers and all those wanting to experience healing within darkness would gather. The men worked in the temple, which helped to clear and eliminate demonic possessions from people, places, and things. The temple was decorated in black, gold, and green. The male healers were intensely strong and courageous. They feared nothing! Their experiences were graphic and often violent, as they dealt with the most mystical and darkest of energies manifesting into beasts, snakes, black clouds, and horrible stenches.

Angelina worked in the all-female temple, the Temple of Light. She had great respect for Stolar and his healers; however, she clearly warned him that it was imperative he remain egoless and was constantly reminding him to cleanse his temple. She had seen a dark cloud descend on them, destroying the love of God.

Stolar had a belittling attitude towards her, and whilst he knew she meant well, he was afraid of <u>nothing</u> and found her warning quite insulting. Surely she was just being a fragile female. "Leave the real work up to us," he said. "You just focus on your work and all will be just fine."

But Angelina knew it was not fine at all. She was convinced that some lower frequencies and energies had infiltrated and were affecting Stolar and some of his healers. This was a gradual breaking down on a very subtle level of their energy field to allow a greater darkness in.

One evening, the men were drinking wine and frolicking about in an unruly manner. Angelina had heard them but was attending to a visitor. The leader of the Ruling Council of the Temples, Chancellor Murak, was visiting her, collecting gold from the day's takings (similar to taxpaying), when the noise could be heard coming from the Temple of Fire. Angelina made it very clear to the chancellor that she had been quite concerned of late, and so he decided to accompany her to the temple.

Upon entering, two men guarding the front smiled strangely at them, clearly displaying entities and certainly creating an air of discomfort. The chancellor looked at Angelina and she at him. They were both thinking the same thing. It wasn't good.

Both had their minds racing, looking for a quick solution as to what to do and how they were going to resolve this problem.

It was an infestation of grey, very low energy. It was becoming hard to breathe, the air was hot, and the smell of burned flesh filled the air. Angelina felt sick, but they continued walking through the corridor to reach Stolar's chambers. Under normal circumstances, Angelina would not be permitted to enter the temple; however, accompanied by the chancellor, this was acceptable.

The noise became louder and louder as they approached the door at the end of the corridor. They proceeded inside. They opened it to a roar of laughter, the vision of a wild celebration, flowing wine, and naked women. Stolar put his glass down and looked at the princess healer with a pleased expression. "Well, well, well, what brings you out after dark, sweet princess?"

"We need to speak with you at once, Stolar!," the chancellor exclaimed. "It is a matter of extreme importance."

Stolar and his assistant rose from their chairs. Stolar clapped his hands. The music stopped, and the laughter and drinking quietened down. He extended his hand towards a door to the side of the room, through which they were to retreat.

The four of them proceeded inside. Angelina felt quite ill and noticed a beading of sweat along her brow. Her breath was quickening, and she felt very much on guard.

She didn't like the way Stolar was looking at her, as if she were a lamb. It was unnerving, but she kept her focus. A discussion began, which quickly developed into an argument. Angeline was insisting that Stolar and his healers had become blinded and were housing the very demons he spent his life clearing.

"Can't you see what you're doing? Look at your behaviour! Can't you feel the darkness residing here and within yourself? I warned you about ego and its alluring power!"

Her voice was raising and shaking now.

The chancellor spoke similarly, asking Stolar to attend a council meeting and allow the members to decide whether the temple should be closed temporarily to allow a full investigation to take place.

Stolar stood and began to yell. "Nonsense! This cannot be! You are the very demon she speaks of, as you threaten to disable the Greatest Conqueror of the Darkness! It is you who are the Deliverer of Evil. You are attempting to possess the princess as well!"

"No! No!" Angelina cried as the chancellor was knifed in the stomach. He lay dying on the stone floor. Angelina glared at Stolar, his assistant standing wide eyed closely behind. She could see the red glow in his eyes and a powerful fear came over her.

"Send the beast's body for burning," Stolar said to his assistant.

Angelina reached into her gown pocket and found the vial she was searching for. It was a sprinkle substance that caused temporary blindness, intended to be thrown in the face of anyone who was a potential threat.

Stolar was one step ahead. He grabbed her hand, and a scuffle took place. His rage and panic were explosive, as the light and dark within him struggled for power and supremacy. He became wild, and the possession entirely consumed him. He grabbed Angelina around the neck and strangled her until her life breath had been completely taken, until her body lay lifeless on the settee.

And to Spirit, Angelina and the chancellor rose.

Stolar defended his actions by claiming they had tried to kill him. He was pardoned.

Healing has taken place.

Amen

Little eight-year-old Nadia runs along the dusty street. She is clothed with a hessian sack, and a simple rope ties at her waist. Her face is very dirty, but underneath you can see a pretty little face. Nadia emanates a vibrant, positive energy, with her big smile and open expression.

She runs towards a house, knocks on the door, and hands over a bag of gold to a half-balding man. He thanks her. "Good work, Nadia." He hands her a piece of gold for her work. The man then collects many of these little bags into one big sack and leaves the house. He has to deliver them to the king.

He is collecting taxes. This man's job is tax collector; however, he's so lazy he gets Nadia and many other children to do the collection work for him. His belly is fat, as he's very well fed. The children are the opposite. They are frail and underfed and rely on the consistent work so they can buy food to eat. They won't let him down, and he knows it. It's like the smug cat who's swallowed the canary. He has a win/win situation. The man tells himself he's actually helping these children by providing them with an income, but the work can be dangerous and children deserve to eat without child labour. He receives extra bonuses from the king for delivering extra taxes or the taxes on time, which he does not pass on to his child labourers.

Nadia is a survivor, confident and healthy. She is not threatened by the tax collector, as she knows she is much smarter and faster than him. She knows that one day, the tables will turn and the canary will no longer be captive. She will fly once more. The other children were not so confident of this. They lived in fear of his constant threats of "No work, no gold." Nadia knew one day she'd be the empowered one.

Nadia spent the next seven years working and quietly observing. At age fifteen, she had developed into a beautiful young woman, attractive to all the young men who saw her. She was never far from the royal palace, and she dreamed she would somehow make it inside one day.

Her dream actually came true shortly afterward, when she was approached and invited inside by the king himself! He had noticed her outside the front gates and was quite taken by her vibrant smile and friendliness. He offered her shelter, food, and clean clothing in exchange for being one of his many food servants. He quickly grew to like Nadia, as she was grateful and gracious. Something about her allowed him to trust her, which was against his suspicious nature.

Over the next year, she was promoted to be his assistant in the "managing of the wives" and the educational program of both his children and his wives, having direct communication with educators and teachers of both. Nadia was experienced in various ways, including having strong survival skills and the ability to generate income honestly. The king realised the value in her. As much as her humble beginnings were very challenging, she held strongly to her personal ethics and beliefs, and she stayed positive and focused on her dream. Nadia had reached into his life and convinced him that everyone needs a job, task, or education to feel worthy, including his people.

Nadia became a valued and groundbreaking example of the king's popularity. He became known and loved as the conscientious king who cared about his people.

Nadia created a large school for children, and she eventually was responsible for having the extra bonuses for the lazy tax collectors abolished.

She devised that the extra wealth be put back into the schools and education programs throughout the kingdom. The collector lost his bonuses and the worker children, as a lot of them were now being educated at the school, which included meals whilst in attendance. Lots of the children wanted to become healers or wanted to work with animals.

Healing has taken place.

Amen.

Raja and His Sons   17/11/2011

How does a spiritual representative, through many generations of faith, hide from the truth? Act with such greed and be so ego driven? Surely he knows that the element of karma is active and is being magnetized to him. He was fully aware and formally educated in all of his spiritual practises and knew wisdom was always offered and delivered to him. But the ego will feed on what the heart ignores if it is allowed to.

The raja of this region in India had two sons. How proud he was to be doubly blessed. The raja was a very spiritual man who lived by the belief in and love of the gods. He prayed and practised, as did many ancestors before him, but he really felt his connection. He believed in the sacred and the laws of attraction. He lived a bountiful life and expressed much gratitude through prayer and meditation on a daily basis.

Human life has both karmic and learned criteria, and the raja was not exempt from this. From a young age, his younger son seemed so much like his father: gentle, grateful, spiritual, and with presence. The older son showed signs of impatience and frustration. He needed more time to connect to reasons and lessons. He had no ability to draw on his inner vision or gain clarity from it. He always needed assistance from his father to understand things and would often argue with him, especially about the issues that affected him personally: his plans, his scope for future endeavours. Raja attempted to make his son understand that what was presenting was always a sign to pay attention to.

"Acknowledge and learn; what is it that you're being warned about or being told?" Raja would ask.

Initially, his son's responses would be defensive and fiery. But through his love for his father and concerns over his position in the family, he'd eventually calm and listen.

The younger brother had none of these attributes. From a young age, he was a natural healer, connecting with nature, particularly the elephants. He was calm and clearly an old soul. Raja had many times noted how evolved his youngest son was and gave thanks for having him journey this life with him.

Raja knew his senior years would require him to step down from his duties and hand over the position and responsibility to a younger heir who would have the physical energy and vitality for the role. It was not a role that was filled lightly and without immense consideration. It also was not selected according to age order; rather, the One would be destined for the role.

The eldest son knew Raja was thinking of the youngest brother to fulfil the leadership. He knew that every time his brother displayed that solid, wise, and peaceful demeanour, he was getting closer to that golden chair.

One day, through his typical spontaneous, unprovoked anger and frustration, the older brother decided that he would stop his younger brother. *The heir to* my *throne!* he thought. He would ensure that his younger brother was no longer a contender and would be too physically weak and without enough mental strength to own such a position.

As usual, he acted impulsively. He went in search for his brother and as he did so looked out the window. He saw the great, grey elephants in the resting area, and also he spotted his younger brother once again connecting with the animals. They were enjoying each other's company, and the elephants were truly showing affection to him. *Well, well, well,"* the older brother thought, *You can hardly be a ruler, guide, and spiritual teacher with a broken back!Let's see who's got the strength, the wisdom, and the health to take Father's place.*

He took a rifle from his closet and swiftly moved through the corridors so as to not be seen. He positioned himself behind one of the pillars and took another look at his younger brother who appeared to be meditating amongst the herd. The herd was restful, with their bellies full. All was extremely peaceful.

The oldest brother took aim at the metal water trough and then hesitated. *No, the water will leak, and sacred is our water.* He then fired shots into the air—*Crack! Bang! Bang!* Within a second, the peaceful gathering was in a panicked stampede. Alarmed and flying up onto their hind legs, the elephants were and running into each other. The young brother could not be seen within the dust of all the movement.

The older brother was frozen in his spot, staring, looking, searching through the mass of grey-brown flesh. Then, suddenly, he could see a small figure laying on the dirt with no movement. It was lifeless.

The elephants had gathered their composure but were obvious in their tension and distress. One elephant began nudging the lifeless figure. The older brother hurried outside. "Oh no. Hey! I didn't mean for him to die! Just be stopped. That's all." But the boy was dead, trampled by the peaceful giants who had been made so afraid.

Their father mourned a great deal and eventually became ill. He did hold his older son accountable for the young one's death and never gave him the position to take his throne. He could not forgive him for such a callous, self-centred act. Many of the elephants became sick or died, since they mourned as well. The elephants displayed a strong dislike to the older brother from that day forward.

The Raja gave the leadership position, his wealth, and his respect to his nephew. The nephew had been very close to his youngest son and was extremely similar to his personality and energy.

The elephants wore a special headdress in memory of the young son.

Healing has taken place.

Amen

The black snake slithers through the lush green grass. It moves through, barely disturbing a blade, but it has one thing in mind: fresh water. Water to drink for survival. The snake his no other aim but to serve its thirst.

The painted face of an indigenous warrior presents. He is hunting. Is he hunting the snake? He is walking nearby. Closely following with a spear in hand is another warrior. These two tribesmen are not brothers. They look over one another as brothers, but their blood is not the same.

They make knocking sounds with their tongues to communicate. They are the most basic of version of man, socially similar to that of the apes. However, hierarchy in apes was selected by the strongest genes and those who were the most physically powerful. Within this tribe, dominance could be intellectually and strategically obtained as well.

As the first warrior appears to be hunting near the snake, the other appears from behind. Bound by their partnership within the tribe, the other would verify the kill, and then it would be received with honour. One did not hunt alone unless he had earned that right by way of being very brave and strong, fighting many battles, or being elected by the tribe spirits (via the witch doctor) to have special rights such as this.

The first warrior was always very eager, thirsty, and very alert when hunting, but the other patient warrior had more of a sixth sense. He would be extremely light-footed and able to hear prey where no one else could. One was all fire and fury, and other sensitive and agile. Two opposite and balancing elements was present in this hunting team.

The first warrior was jealous of the other's fine skill. He'd often wish he could be more still and cautious, and able to stalk as successfully. Sometimes the first warrior would burst out upon his prey too early and end up losing it, whereas the other would be patient, very still, and wait for the right moment. But when you're hungry, this can be very challenging.

"We need to work together as a team. We are not in synchronicity. We are wasting energy and time when rushing into the kill and then allowing it to escape."

The heat is intense, but hunting after sunset is too dangerous. The patient one is tiring from the heat, his body requires fuel, and he doesn't have the stamina. Fresh water is needed soon. The first warrior is feeling guilty and his ego is bruised, as they have lost two prey because of his impatience.

It's looking a bit grim as the sun is beginning to set. The men grow tired and weak from hunger. The patient warrior decides to look for berries; the other disagrees. They are two opposing energies together, relying on one another, but it is becoming confusing and destructive.

The sun is now setting, and they must head back before many predators come out to hunt them. Light footed and finer built, the patient warrior bounds through the thick jungle; however, the other is huffing and panting and cannot keep up. He's also making far too much noise. Suddenly, there is yelling and shrieking going on behind the patient one. The strong, powerful warrior has fallen in a hole. It is an animal trap set up by hunters.

The patient warrior looks down at him, knowing the night is closing in fast. He contemplates leaving him there. Annoyed, the strong warrior calls out, "Get me! Save me! Don't leave me here! I'll be eaten! I promise I will learn, I will become a better hunter and warrior, as I will allow you to teach me!"

This was a great honour to be given. Instantly, the patient warrior was raised into position of leadership between the two warriors. Sheer strength was no longer superior. He used vines to perform the rescue. When they arrived back to the rest of the tribe, the patient warrior was acknowledged and celebrated as proving he was a skilled hunter, a strategic warrior, and worthy of leadership. The strong warrior would now be underneath him in hierarchy and must learn under his direction. He could eventually initiate a student under him, but he would always be under the patient warrior's leadership. It was how the tribe lived in balance. They survived many generations and always would.

Healing has taken place.

Amen.

Jocelyn and Margarete   *29/12/11*

Medieval Europe—France

Jocelyn was a fine seamstress and would sew many garments and gowns for the French court. both noblemen and women. She was a natural with design and fabrics, using European- and French-made silks and finely woven laces. Each piece was an artwork, and Jocelyn loved what she did. Jocelyn's younger sister was just as talented but worked independently, as well as alongside her sister, particularly when they had many elegant garments to sew for a function or a special occasion.

When they would team up, certain baskets of work would take months to complete, and so proper preparation was necessary and work had to be steady and consistent. Jocelyn's sister Margarete was particularly talented with lace and embroidery work. She was proficient in delicate beading as well. She had extraordinary vision, being able to envision the finished gown or garment before it had even begun. Often, brides of noble families would come to see her before consulting anyone else.

Jocelyn's work was in demand as was well, except for one thing: Jocelyn was married to an angry, jealous, and suspicious man. He was a labourer by day, and yes, he worked hard to provide, but he expected Jocelyn to complete his food, service, wine, and chores by the time he came home for dinner. He was angered by Jocelyn's fine and calm temperament, her talents and success. He despised that all her attention was given to her work and not him. He'd verbally attack her and force her away from her work, making her feeling less of a worthy wife if she didn't listen to him. He complained that she should have married her sewing machine instead of a man.

Margarete would remind Jocelyn about the pressing timeline on some deliveries to the palace, and Jocelyn would show her distress. "I don't know what to do! He's so angry and fed up. He shall leave me if I continue. Margarete, I may have to give this up and have the many children he demands of a wife," she said sadly. "We will have much less money as well. He tells me that I'm greedy and the devil has lured me for fame and fortune!" Magarete was disgusted by what she heard.

"He's gotten worse! He's an animal!" said Margarete. "You were raised not only for breeding! You are a talented seamstress, a creator of beautiful fine pieces, and *we* are in demand. *We* are successful. I don't know what to tell you, my sister, but I know one thing: I will be forced to seek another partner if you cannot work with me. I'm sorry."

Jocelyn was heartbroken and torn, but she understood her sister could not give up fine the opportunities and pending success because of her own jealous and controlling husband.

Jocelyn had to resign. Margarete was forced to find another young, up-and-coming seamstress to assist her. Jocelyn had four children and lived quite poorly, just scraping to get by. Her controlling, angry husband drank too much and became a recluse towards the rest of the family. Jocelyn lived a very isolated, lonely life with her four children.

Margarete developed into one of the most famously known and in-demand seamstress and designers of the time.

Healing has taken place.

Amen

"Oh, Antonio! This house is beautiful! *Bellesimo*, darling! I hope, I pray, this is our chance to make it. Our children will have a much better start to life than us."

"God has brought us here, and God will bring us the money too, Angela. I believe that," said Antonio.

This home had many rooms, beautiful stone columns, and a marble floor. It was more space than they could fill, and luckily the furniture Antonio made would certainly suit the décor of the home. It was not free, of course. He would have to work for every piece, but it would be sold to him at a wholesale rate.

Antonio had to entrust in his boss, Mr. Bendino. Bendino had made numerous promises of huge contracts and record-breaking sales. He had asked Antonio "to just hang in there, brother. I promise you, when this takes off, you will never have to see another chisel or hand tool again! It will be all the latest machinery, and many, many workers under you! You will be foreman. Ha! A cushy, very well-paid job indeed. Just see it on the horizon. Boy, if you are loyal to me now, you'll be looked after like a brother. You are my brother. That's why I trust you, eh?"

Antonio relocated his wife and few possessions to Venice, all on a promise. But it was too good to refuse. If it all came through, they'd be set up for life. Angela could stay home and have as many babies as she liked. She could sew all the clothes that she liked as well. Antonio would be able to buy her mountains of fabric. He smiled, dreaming away and envisioning a promised new life. Surely it was just around the corner.

Mr. Bendino was a fast talker, very smooth, and he was a shrewd businessman. He was always impeccably dressed and was very convincing when he spoke. He appeared genuine. Antonio was hopeful for a new life, and he trusted in the promises.

Antonio would work, slaving for fifteen-hour days in heat, in cold, in quite harsh conditions. His own mind powered him forward. When Bendino would get anxious and appear frustrated that items were not being created quickly enough, Antonio would feel anxious and experience a rising bitterness. He would then try to see it as another challenge to succeed and listen to another round of inspiring comments and constructive criticism from Bendino. "Come on! Let's make this quicker! If it's ready by noon tomorrow, we lock in the deal." It was all on Antonio's shoulders. He felt like if he stopped, he'd be turning his back on the pot of gold at the end of the rainbow.

Antonio waited, and he worked very hard another six months. Angela would ask, "When are we going to see the money? Why is this taking so long? We have this lovely house to live in, but I can't eat the floor!"

Antonio snapped in frustration. Although he had never raised his voice before, he certainly let it all out at her that day. Angela ran into another room in an explosion of tears. All of her dreams of having babies and being well off seemed to be fading fast. She may not even have a husband before long! Antonio looked so thin and very tired. Antonio was suffering from severe headaches and had developed a sore back and right shoulder.

Bendino's promises finally ran dry. He began talking about moving again, and he would eventually shift operations overseas to Asia. Antonio and Angela went back to Sicily and moved in with his mother. Antonio spent his next years depressed, unable to really move from his chair. He was carrying humiliation, guilt, fear, and anxiety for both himself and Angela.

Past life fragment recovered.

Healing has taken place.

Amen

Hinaku was the medicine woman of the tribe. In Northern Africa, this tribe was one of the three largest clans. Hinaku was a mature aged woman and an initiated priestess.

The chief of the tribe called upon Hinaku to be aware that she must begin to pass on her teachings to a student, whether that be a young male or female of the bloodline. Hinaku received Mikaya's name in a dream on the eve of her sixty-sixth birthday, and so she knew her young niece (her brother's eldest daughter) would be the One. Mikaya was a respected member of the community. She was married and had two children, both girls, aged eleven and thirteen.

Mikaya was a woman of faith. She trusted in a higher power who was ever-present and guiding her direction within all areas of her life. She had a strong, natural ability to receive images and prophecies in dream state that were quite detailed. She often approached her aunt to discuss these images and prophecies. Hinaku would explain and guide her about its meaning, and if necessary, perform a clearing on Mikaya, particularly if she'd attracted an evil spirit, or entity, because she was pure and light.

Hinaku was a very strong, stern woman, and this was accepted of her as she had a leadership role and a large responsibility for the whole tribe. She would ensure enemies be kept away, voodoo cast be reversed, and the overall health and wellbeing of the tribe be assured, particularly for the chief and his family.

She began teaching Mikaya certain techniques and secrets. Mikaya also had to receive a large piercing through her nose.

It was a bone-like small spear. It hurt quite a lot, but she knew it was part of the initiation process and her passage into the role. Her children didn't like the piercing but said that they were proud of her and honoured that she would be the next priestess and healer. But, they said, Mikaya was "so much kinder and nicer" than their great-aunt!

Mikaya learned very quickly and embraced the practises and meditations with incredible speed. Her vision opened so quickly that it came as an utter surprise. She'd have flashes and images about a person just by touching them on the arm. She knew what was wrong with a sick person and why babies and children presented with rashes. She diagnosed a sickness in the belly that had circulated among a few tribe members and cured them within a single night.

She said, "I just knew what to do. They told me."

"Who?" said the chief, so impressed with her accurate skills and foresight.

"The mighty ones, great beings of the sun, the stars, the universe, the only power and light, which feeds us, loves us. He speaks to me," she smiled shyly.

The chief had a tear roll from his eye, which was highly unusual. Such emotion was rarely expressed by him.

"We see the prophecy fulfilled. A great healing goddess predicted she would come to our tribe. It is written by past sages. Her coming will call an end to sickness, war, and all pain and suffering. It is a great day indeed, and within my lifetime." He bowed before her. Mikaya was shocked. "It is done. You will be ceremoniously inducted into your position of High Priestess and Healer of the Tribe in three days' time, on the night of the full moon. I will speak with Hinaku. She is tired. She is best served by being alongside me in preparation for her last phase in life, that of wise one and teacher."

Mikaya was honoured and excited. She was unsure how she would fulfil such an enormous task, but she trusted and knew the great ones would guide her.

Hinaku was silent when she was told. Suddenly, a piercing pain went through her head, and she reached up to rub it. "But she's so inexperienced and young! There's no pressure as yet, and she won't cope with the duty. One must be mature, wise, level, strong."

"She is all that and more," said the chief. "She is the one prophesised to come. It is Mikaya, our Mikaya."

"No, it is not possible," said Hinaku, "The one prophesised was meant to be an orphan, no family, brought here miraculously by the gods."

"No," the chief said, "that was a test to see if we were really ready and trusting, listening and understanding our purpose— my purpose. It was meant to be from my bloodline! Of course! I will reign and move forward with the strongest, wealthiest, and most untouchable tribe in all of Africa. No more will we be threatened."

Hinaku realised her reign was over. She became angry. She felt used and thrown out before her time. She was convinced the chief was acting hastily. She stopped to consider her thoughts, which were growing more and more sinister towards the young priestess.

Mikaya felt Hinaku's pain and her rage. She reasoned with herself, *Surely, I must be safe. She is my aunt and bound by the laws we all live by, spiritually and physically.* But this was not to be. Mikaya was poisoned by the angry but justifying Hinaku.

As Mikaya lay in pain, realising what had taken place, she began to pray, asking the Almighty, the god beings, to heal her, to rid her body of the poison and allow her to live if she was truly meant to. Mikaya began to sweat profusely, leaking the toxins from her body at a powerful rate. Hinaku peered through the window opening and saw what was happening. In her frustration, she leapt inside the hut and strangled Mikaya until no life was left in her body.

Hinaku managed to convince the chief that it had been an attack by a member of an opposing tribe who had learned that the goddess healer had come. The chief mourned and was very confused and dismayed. He had no choice but to reinstate Hinaku as the tribe's priestess.

Mikaya's husband and children knew the truth. Her husband also knew she would soon come after Onada, their eldest child, who was very much like her mother. The chief was already seeking confirmation from the gods that Onada could possibly be the One and would be guided by her mother as her spirit guide. She would therefore be ready to initiate her full potential early in her life.

The lineage was continuing, and Hinaku was once again threatened in her position.

Mikaya's husband decided to take his two daughters and flee to southern Africa, as far away from Hinaku's pain and ego as possible.

He kept Mikaya's piercing, her small spear, in his hand.

That is all.

Thank you for presenting to me this lifetime.

Amen.

Oh, holy night, power and might, remove the blocks that cause me strife, allow free-flowing and clear sight for now and forever, power and might.

"What are you doing, Eadi?"

"Oh, hello Teacher! I didn't hear you standing there."

"What are you doing? Magic? You arouse forces you don't understand. It may have consequences only you will have to answer for."

Mena was the teaching healer in the Osiris Temple in Egypt. She was a senior healer who felt drawn to teaching, and so it was decided she would pass her knowledge to young healers and do great service in the name of Isis.

Eadi was a young student, only fourteen years of age, rough around the edges but displaying great power. The issue with Eadi was that she needed guidance and nurturing to utilise this great power from her heart, not her mind, which would enhance the her magic from outer dimensions and the earth.

Eadi had been orphaned at a young age. She was bitter and angry over her parents being killed in an unfortunate accident whilst working at one of the pyramid sites. Both of her parents were crushed by falling boulders. She would seek understanding and peace through her pain by reaching out to the gods; however, she still had so many unanswered questions about life and our existence. She was impatient and quick to give up when she couldn't understand or complete a task. Somehow she believed she was being punished in this life, and that's why her parents were taken from her. Through this heavy belief, she had a burdened and sad heart.

Mena felt sorry for Eadi. She offered a lot of guidance and exercised a great deal of patience towards her. Mena did not agree with the use of magic and invocation of energies to influence a particular outcome; rather, she believed in clearing and supporting the concept of "what is meant to be." She argued that whilst sometimes a seemingly good result presents, there is often a backlash when the placement of energies has been manipulated. It really reflects a lack of trust in God, and it supports only a partial angle from which you view the entire situation—from your ego's perspective. Whereas if all of your energy is channelled from Source and you work only from the heart, it is channelled and directed from the highest perspective and only the ultimate outcome, for all involved will manifest. There can be no returned energy and only an aligned path will prevail. The Source energy supersedes anything conjured from the ground or on a mental level.

"Trust, Eadi. This is what you lack—not of me, but of yourself. Your survival instinct has been in battle since you lost your parents at age seven. You are now fourteen. You have much to learn, and I am prepared to guide you through the ego's influence, which fuels the bitterness and confusion in you and keeps you from feeling the peace in your soul. But you must surrender to what you think is protecting you. Your aggression, your "control," is not control at all, as it will turn against you. It is not of love, it is of fear, and it cannot support the path of a healer, which is that of surrender and living with grace."

Eadi listened, but her mind was objecting. Her thoughts were strong to defend.

"You have no idea what it's like, the suffering I've endured! Whatever I do, I do to help myself stay alive and be clothed and fed. But I do hear you, Teacher. I am trying hard to overcome my defences. So, are we meditating this afternoon? How many will be attending?"

Mena replied, "Well, yes, I'd scheduled the session for tomorrow, but perhaps to assist your progress and shift your fear, we can connect together for a private session this afternoon. I trust that will suit you?"

"Oh yes, thank you, Teacher. I'll be there."

Eadi was unconsciously sending very negative thoughts, feelings, and energy towards Mena. Eadi felt that all her talk about love and hope and guidance was only for those who haven't truly suffered. *Who gives her the right to tell me? She sits so comfortably with her fine silks and freshly brewed tea.* Eadi was in fact cutting into Mena's heart. *Perhaps she ought to experience pain to understand what I actually go through.*

Eadi became more and more angry and bitter towards Mena's wise words. She rejected all of her higher teachings about healing via channel and through the heart. She was spiralling in negativity, and she actually wished Mena's heart would stop talking! *Then what will she do, when the heart no longer feels good? What then?"* On and on she went with negative thoughts and projections.

Suddenly a swirling grey energy began to encircle Eadi. She looked in surprise and began to pay attention to the mini-twister of energy that was conjuring in the room. She picked up a staff that had with a crystal on the end of it. She pointed it to the door where Mena had left just minutes before and proclaimed, "So as you feel my heart and its pain, I cast this upon you like pelting rain, a dagger point to bleed like me, to understand you will seek to be!"

Suddenly from the hallway came a rumbling sound. It was like a vibration, but not of the earth or sky. It was a cast from Eadi towards Mena. At that moment, Eadi realised what she had done. The entities that resided in her, the darkness, the bitterness, the hatred, had overcome her, and she had reacted with such evil intent. She was now filled with panic and fear. She raced to the door and ran down the corridor towards the meditation chambers.

She swung open the door to find Mena slumped on the floor. She rushed to her, exploding into tears! "I'm sorry, I'm sorry! Oh God, help me!"

Mena was dying. Her heart of pure light could not sustain or consume the darkness that had literally crushed it. "You did this? Why?" she said, with such little breath.

"It was my anger, my hatred, my fear. Oh Teacher, please forgive me! I have learned! I'm so sorry!"

"I forgive you, Eadi. It is not I whom you need fear. In reality, it is yourself and your own regrets, your unhealed issues and your refusing to acknowledge the lessons. These may plague you the rest of your life. I told you, it is all consequential. Blessings . . . child." And with one last breath, Mena died in Eadi's arms.

Eadi was never punished by law. It was made official on the death certificate that Mena died of natural causes—a heart attack—but Eadi knew the truth. She could not live with what she'd done. Eadi decided to end her young life, plunging to her death from a cliff into the sea. She hoped she may find her parents, and certainly Eadi to beg them for further forgiveness.

Both of them loved, accepted, and forgave her. It was Eadi who couldn't forgive herself.

That is all.

Amen.

David was the only child of a business couple, Dan and Milly, who were farmers and travelling sales people. They were from Arizona and would make a living delivering and selling their produce to towns. They would work their land to grow crops, then make bread flour, jarred honey, wine, and even lollies. It was like a convenience store in a wagon! They would travel across partial areas of desert and mountain ranges. It was quite tough terrain to get to some of the towns, but having been brought up in this lifestyle, it was natural and acceptable to them. Dan's parents had done the same when he was a boy, so he knew this very well. They'd earn enough to ensure the next year's crops and supplies and have a little to sustain their life as well.

David was excited because he was able to join them on this particular road trip for the first time. He had always had to stay with Grandma before. But Dan said in his South Eastern accent, "The boy's old enough now. We'll teach him as my daddy taught me."

This trip, unfortunately, was to be their last. Approximately halfway to their destination, Dan, Milly, and young David were swooped upon by outlaws, who happened to be well-known fugitives. They were wanted for various train robberies and a series of murders. These harsh men had no mercy. They robbed the family and murdered Dan and Milly, all in front of this poor young boy. David prayed with all of his might. He was crying as he listened to the fugitives arguing over what they were to do with him.

"He's seen too much!"

"Shall we spare him?"

"No!"

On and on they argued while David sat on his knees, hands tied behind his back.

"If he makes it across the desert with his hands tied, well, then he's a pretty determined little fella! Ha! Let's go. Come on." And they rode away on their horses.

David was surviving on adrenalin. Somehow, he managed to mount the horse still by his side from his father's destroyed wagon. He had to grip the trunk of the horse with his short legs, but he managed to secure himself well enough. The sun had already set, and he thought, *How will he find my way? I don't want to sit here looking at my dead parents; I have to try. I will leave here. If I die, I die.*

The exhausted boy fell asleep, tipped forward over the horse, who just continued on as if guided by an outside force. The horse appeared to know exactly the path back to the ranch.

At nightfall the next day, David's limp body rode back through the gates of the ranch where he lived. Grandma looked out the window and saw him slumped over the horse. She yelled to Grandpa, "Help! Help! Oh God!" She rushed to him, blood-stained and barely conscious, and she got him down. David was still alive. His grandma cried with relief and dismay. She still knew nothing of the fate of her dear son and his wife.

David lay in a bed, unable to speak and still in shock. Finally, after three days, he was strong enough to tell of his horrifying story. The sheriff was called, and an investigation was started.

David never fully recovered. He had no desire to live and go on. He stopped playing, and he stopped caring. He communicated only with animals, having lost all faith in people. He didn't trust anyone, except for his grandparents.

He knew they too were going to die and he would be left all alone.

David didn't live long in this life. He was shot and killed at age twenty-two in a bar fight.

God, thank you for the healing and soul recovery of this lifetime.

Amen

There is a violent struggle, and he has his hands wrapped around your neck. He dominates your strength, and his desperation and anger in winning fuels him further.

You are in a room, up in a tower of the castle. There are stone pieces and a table. The area is minimally furnished, apart from a few wooden items: a chair, mantle, etc. The castle is huge, with many rooms and corridors, and it's likely the servants and his father are in the main wing.

Father had not been well for some time. He had lost his passion for living and for succeeding on a material level. He had always been furiously competitive, analytical, and power-driven. He'd built a family estate and wealth, not to mention status and power, over a twenty-year period. He'd come from quite humble beginnings but knew the right people and executed dealings at the right time.

My mother was his absolute mirror. She drove him further with her emotions and her enormous desire to be living the high-society lifestyle, adorned in jewels, wearing the finest French lace and Asian silks. There was an understanding between them. They may not have much passion left for each other, but they certainly shared a passion for power, money, and status.

Mother died of pneumonia over eighteen months ago. Since then, Father lost interest in most things. The castle became a cold place to live. He finally admitted that he missed her so and that her presence filled the rooms. Now with his life partner gone, there was no one to accompany him, no one to please, nor impress, nor argue with. His reason to live was suddenly at the forefront of his attention.

Being one of two sons, myself the younger, I was always more attentive to my father's needs as a family member, and to contribute and learn. Whilst we were wealthy, my father and mother had nothing handed to them; it took hard work and persistence, and a fair dose of attitude and education. The circles in which they socialized were of a high regard in power and wealth, and Mother and Father loved it. He'd always say, "Your hands have the ability to shape and make what you want in your life, but to exceed your skill and reach further, you will need to use a greater tool. It is your ability to think, analyse, and outwit your oppositions and opponents that will pave your growth to success. Talk less, watch more."

Words of wisdom, no doubt. He was a prime example of this philosophy. I listened and learned from him. My brother, on the other hand, had an inferiority complex. He always felt entitled and acted aggressively and dominantly, especially towards me. His position within the family had a clear advantage, as he was the eldest, and family responsibility and power had an order about it. But instead of honouring this and learning as much as he could from Father, he was gallivanting with loose women and consuming copious amounts of liquor, nursing ill feelings, selfishness, and chauvinism.

My father knew well that I was the most like him. I was calm, reflective, and decisive, and I was a creative. He knew it came naturally that I nurture growth rather than squander it, as my brother did.

Father's failing health and disinterest in life led him to speak with me about being left in charge of the family estate when he dies. I was rather surprised, being that there is a usual age order to follow. But he was making a rational business decision, not a blinded one.

Little did I realise, at the same time, my brother had been delving so much in women and liquor (since Mother died) that he was becoming even more angry, depressed, and irrational. He was clearly possessed by evil. He was abusive, unreliable, bitter, and failing. There was nothing I recognised of his former self.

Father handed me a wax-sealed document outlining the details of the will, which putt me completely in charge, with a clause that I would do my very best to care for my brother and his health. Failing that, I was not to squander or waste excessive amounts of time and money if he was not willing to redeem himself. Rather, I was to allow him the journey of collapse, if necessary.

I was shocked, but Father said, "I am not willing to carry him anymore. If we continue to accept his destructive path, we denounce self-respect, and he'll destroy everything I've built. Once we lose ourselves in blood, our emotions will see no end, and we'll stop at nothing to save him. It is not the way, to give that power, that we become lost in the darkness to rescue another, no matter who he is."

Meanwhile, there was a servant, a maid, who had been listening to our conversation from behind the door. She had been having a secret affair with my brother for six months and was hoping to improve her life and status by capturing his restless heart and marrying him. She also worked as a spy and quickly notified him of my father's intentions and everything she'd heard.

A few hours later, he came back to the castle in a drunken rage and instigated an attack on me. He reeked of liquor, and

I remember seeing the red, evil fury in his eyes. As I struggled to free my breath, I realised I was losing power. The more I struggled, the more energy and breath it took from me. I couldn't fight anymore.

My last glimpse was seeing the maid approach the door behind him, wide-eyed. She was waiting for my death so as to stage some sort of alternate crime scene.

They had not pre-planned this; it was spontaneous, ridiculous, and desperate. My brother was drunk and stupid, and now the two of them would have to set up a false crime scene, one that would convince Father that an intruder had murdered me. *This is crazy,* I thought, but I couldn't care anymore. I wanted to cough, but it wouldn't come out.

I'm losing the ability to think. It's all white. I surrender.

That is all.

Healing has taken place.

Amen

Chapter 3

Genetic Healings

Equal strands of red-and-white-coloured energy pillars extend vertically then intertwine, blending and moulding together in a dance, which infuses a union.

It is the encodement process of one's DNA. This process finalises the physical and the emotional and mental beliefs. Through the soul's desire to encompass and experience various healings (genetic and karmic) during its current lifetime, the relevant predisposition to certain ailments and diseases such as depression, anxiety, addictions, weight issues, behavioural problems, emotional imbalances, drug and alcohol abuse, stomach ulcers, heart conditions, diabetes, gall and kidney stones, disc and skeletal problems, cancer and arthritis, anaemia, migraines, menstrual and fertility problems, and all other physical, mental, and emotional presentations, will be accessible to create and heal.

The underlying root for a soul to agree to undertake a genetic predisposition for any disease is always and only for the reason to heal it for the soul self and soul group/family. The infusion or manifestation of all imbalanced physical health begins on a subtle energy level, and it is always the case that repeated warnings of infusion and manifestation are taking place. If this goes unnoticed or ignored, or the subject believes they are highly likely to become ill, then the actual disease is given access to the body and it takes root. Once a disease has manifested, it has in fact existed and been accepted on an energy level for an extended period of time. The energy of such ailments always comes from the exterior, which may or may not be genetically pre-disposed. Rather, it may be karmically desired.

The difference being that when a disease is karmically attracted and it presents in its energy form, we intuitively repel and accept it simultaneously, causing a push-pull feeling. On some level, we already know that what we are about to experience is going to be a corrective re-balance, a recovery, or a surrender, which is likely not to be easy. We feel its intensity and intuitively prepare for a rocky ride ahead. Yet we continue on, knowing it is pre-desired and part of our evolvement process. The more we accept and release the need to control, the better and quicker the outcome.

When it is genetically predisposed, the body accepts the frequency more readily and easily, fully embracing every element of it. Unconsciously, we virtually invite it in. We confirm through our behaviour and thought forms how this negative frequency is fully acceptable to own because of familial lineages and/or medical history. There is therefore no greater challenge and opportunity than to eliminate genetic encodements. We can and will choose to fully encompass miraculous healing through a change in perception, matching our thought-forms perfectly in their opposing force to re-create an environment that no longer supports the disease.

Accompanying the new DNA stranding is the revitalised thought-forms that support individuality, health, and vitality through an independent and renewed source and sustainability. In this adjustment process, we can utilise powerful affirmations such as, "I no longer choose to carry the belief that my body mirrors my that of my genetic relative, nor can I actively heal him or her through the undertaking of his or her disease."

It is not uncommon for an incoming soul to engage in the discovery of "wanting" to experience the awakening of not being able to heal generations of their family diseases and dysfunctions. Their human incarnation still requires control and the experience of powerlessness. Love is always, in its pure sense, unconditional, and therefore the elimination process must mirror that to be authentic and truly healing.

It has been a common practise for individuals and their families to believe, "We must sacrifice ourselves so that another shall live." This is the greatest distrust of love displayed through a false belief and action. It does not in any way convert to loving compassion or empathy; rather, it is martyrdom, control, and an ego-based conditional existence.

It is now, in this time, that we understand a great deal more about our lifetimes and the issues we choose to learn and evolve from. If we are all swimming in a mud pool together, it is impossible to see clearly and wash ourselves or each other clean. One must choose to leave the muddy pool and discover the many bodies of water, rivers, oceans, and streams to cleanse in. We can swim to clearer waters and choose another way to cleanse without disassociating or being unloving to one another.

Slowly we are making choices that are not so laden with guilt. Wanting to better your life and health and choosing this as your reality, regardless of your loved ones who choose not to, is the answer to true self-empowerment, personal happiness, and creative manifestation of unlimited choices. It is the freedom of all involved, and it illuminates the path for those who are watching and learning by your example.

(Energy God light used to heal DNA/Genetic Encodement are pink with gold and blue with white.)

Channel complete.

Thank you.

You walk forth this day, 2 September 2011, to begin a month of plenitude. It represents number nine.

Oh Mother of God: Mary showers you with the colours of peacock feathers, blue, green, gold, purple, black, all glistening together in the light. The imagery is an intensely beautiful and vibrant glitter in energy form. She showers your energy field entirely and you glow, so pleased, expressing gratitude. Mother Mary shows you a white door and beckons you to go forward. The vibration here is very, very high, almost like you would feel at the altitude of a mountain top. The emotion is pure joy, and she smiles lovingly for you walk through.

A kaleidoscope of colours is present, and then a stairwell leading upward appears.

You are now weaving a white robe gown, and your hair is long. A gold belt, an ornate gold head piece, gold sandals, and many gold bangles adorn you. You are a highly regarded Egyptian priestess. You worked exclusively for the family of King Tutankuman, and as you had access to infinite wealth, there was no need or desire from the material world. Surrounded by gold and riches, foods, the finest of rose-scented oils, frankincense, and myrrh, you had everything one could desire. You were extremely grateful for being so fortunate in your respected position, as these great and powerful men and women entrusted in your guidance and healing recommendations. As a symbol of this gratitude, you did not seek payment for your services; rather, you relished in the light and believed you were a great servant to the gods. You would accept donations and gifts but never relied on a formal payment. "What for? I have everything I need and more. When the day arrives that my heart is weighed against my wealth, I will be awarded entry into the afterlife and beyond. I have seen many future lifetimes, and I know who I have been. I now relish the freedom of wealth acquired yet fully enjoyed whilst serving our king and the gods."

And so we see where this living, creative aspect was born. As a powerful, respected priestess for a wealthy, powerful king, everything was provided for and so you did not require payment. Your generosity was acknowledged, and you were loved, respected, and admired even more. You believed that your service was enough because in your highest truth, your wisdom and ability on earth were gifted to you. The same Source that provided that gift would also ensure that all of your needs were met. And they were.

Now, this pledge or belief is carried forward from many lifetimes past as a blueprint within you and once again surfaces in this current reality. Whilst you will always have a generous heart, as this is part of your soul, it is required that there be balance to create the natural cosmic and universal cycle of giving and receiving. Agreed payment for services rendered provides a healthy cycle of giving and receiving. Clients are highly responsive to this cycle of balance, as it inspires self-respect, self-love, responsibility, and ownership of one's health. It also acknowledges the natural respect for the service, the education and acquired wisdom. Their commitment further stimulates healing and ongoing learning. It is the reality of today that allows you to receive abundance and reward on all levels. It allows you to build on the precipice of creating your vision—an advanced, unlimited, educational, heart-led, and inspired healing centre that services many thousands of people per year.

Amen.

*   *   *

At the top of the stairs is a door with a blinding gold light streaming from behind it. You open it. An intensely pure white light penetrates all existence. There is no here, nor there, no me, nor you.

"Is that you, God?" you ask.

"My child, you have asked, and it is time to receive. You have pledged in my name and opened your heart, and with every moment in time you lived, you gave of yourself and lived a life in service to those who were asking for help. Through being you, you assisted in guiding the awareness of healing among countless souls on many creative and multidimensional levels, including earth. Channelling love and peace, your vibration, your vessel, and its healing capability have transcended, and so has your energetic bank account. The time has come to allow payment of your services so that all may develop and grow, balance, nurture, and love so much more.

"To allow yourself to receive is the golden key to unlock unlimited wealth. We do this through believing we deserve to receive unlimitedly. You will always give to those asking for help, and now it is yourself."

Your face beams with an unimaginable delight, and this is just the beginning.

Thank you, God.

"No, thank you, my child."

Amen.

The Illusion   5/9/2011

What actually crucified our Jesus Christ? Fear, misunderstanding and misuse of power, judgement, denial of love, of tenderness, of vulnerability. Blocked were the disconnected men as they used force to deny their fear. Within their self-gratifying laughter, the truth of humanity's direction was already being pre-paved. Christ transcended death, and no one could understand this. He was thousands of years beyond current humanity—and so he had to be to embark on the most profound and compassionate journey of earth life. His mission was to teach, to reveal, and to present to each and every one of you the path with heart.

Currently you experience the mirroring of doubts and fears that were felt during the crucifixion of your father. As you lay in your mother's womb, your passion was ignited but also a fear in the injustice of earth caused by its people.

How could the greatest man of all time be exposed to such suffering, all because he loved? The arrogance, the ignorance, and the existence of harsh human practises and beliefs all contributed to it. Very few people had a higher consciousness that they were willing to expose and live by. Your tiny body squirmed and jolted within the womb. You listened to your father's intuitive messages that all will be alright. Your mother's adrenaline and sadness pumped through your tiny body. You wanted to protect and nurture, as was your natural instinct.

Your genes remember and carry this aspect. You feel, see, and hear a vibration as you experience the sensation of feeling cornered. The memory returns on a subtle but encoded energy level and you think, *My fate will be the same as my father's, to be*

115

crucified for all to see! The genetic encoding has triggered the memory of pain and fear, but it is no longer accepted from this day forward. It is no longer a desire to allow it to surface and live in the present as this aspect/memory served for that time, place, and purpose long ago, and it is no longer existent nor my reality.

We know that at this pinnacle point, the intensity of opposing forces feels large and intense. Turning back on itself, it implodes, and the toxicity dissipates along with any presence. We must not give the entity/vibration power. We must keep the vibrations high.

Money in its physical form slows the progress; however, as has been shown many times before, believe the situation is light, free-flowing, and prosperous, and prosperity will come. Why do the rich become richer? One of the main reasons is that they don't doubt their creative ability or their wealth. Allow the release of concern and focus more on manifestation of abundant flow. Allow God the freedom to select the way in which it will be delivered without erasing any possibilities. Protect and guard your vision and your energies vigorously, keeping a positive and happy outlook.

This is for your awareness only; this is a past event or scene: I see a female, extremely angered and jealous of you. She is very threatened and holding a curved-blade knife with the idea to cut your throat. You openly express and speak God's truth. She will not succeed, but darkness is a challenge of life on earth until all inhabitants have evolved beyond ego. So having an awareness and intent to protect yourself, your vision and goals are vital. In truth, these lower energies cannot stop a God-led path, no more than Christ could be eliminated from the hearts and minds of all humanity.

Genetics that link your lineage to your current incarnation and family have revealed an aspect, which we clear today.

God, we ask that you love and support, protect and guide this heart-led, innovative, courageous, prosperous healer that she is, with no further genetic interceptions, from this day forward.

We thank you, God, and know you're ever present and are guiding us on a path with heart.

Scarab beetle presents.

Forever more.

Amen

Laughter abounds. How structured and self-limiting the human race is! You believe that the measure of your success is based upon linear time. You continuously lose your power and happiness based on this measurement. Even light workers are doing this. My goodness!

Time is of no essence and certainly not a qualifying factor when it comes to being a healer!

Now let me see. You've been doing this for five thousand human years or so? That makes you pretty qualified indeed! I do apologise; I do not wish to offend. But my humoured self has a little chuckle every now and again as it is these little rules and false beliefs in which humans contain themselves that require the reminder of an illusion in your midst. Wisdom can be obtained in a blink of an eye and certainly does not require years of long, arduous struggle or endless qualifications for validation. This belief is not from God or your higher wisdom.

The most enlightened and free-flowing channel is a baby. His receptivity is unlimited. What then of chronological age? In history, we may have referred to someone as "a wise old sage," but beyond its fairytale value, this phrase marks no relevance to human existence today. We have surpassed this outdated expectation and belief.

In particular, we acknowledge that the human genetic family, along with its history, had attached this mindset and enforced a belief that all women, and particularly young women, would never be successful of their own accord and certainly never without a husband.

We are embarking on a union of a trinity energy for empowerment, which includes 1) nurture with strength, 2) creativity with direction, and 3) intention with confidence.

In truth, all known or well-documented Lightworkers, healers, and Masters of Love on earth, both ascended and incarnated, both male and female, emerged with their gifts and evolutionary ideals from a young age. The first to lead the modern procession was our Lord Jesus Christ.

We need not say any more.

Empowered and strong, creative and open to all levels of seeking growth. The ever-changing and expanding existence that is you is now aligned to this. Past conditions, beliefs, ideals, misconceptions, judgements, and expectations are now eliminated. All preconceived ideas that qualifications and deservedness are validated by age, height, weight, and dress code are illusionary and eliminated.

Amen

Creative Force = Manifestation, and the Opposite Is Also True   14/12/2011

Italy, 1930's

A little black Fiat travels along a dirt road. The car stops. A female in her early sixties gets out. She's wearing an apron; her hair is tied in a bun. There is farmland all around. A basic post-and-wire fence divides the properties. She tentatively holds a post and climbs up onto the fence, getting a higher perspective and view. She looks into the distance. She looks and looks, and then she climbs down. She hops up again and climbs over to the neighbouring property. Now she looks again into the distance. She is looking towards her property from the neighbour's side. She appears unsatisfied. What is she looking for—or at? She hops on and off quite a few times. She can't be sure she can extend herself. The dollars. The taxes! The money she pays for being a landowner here. In any case, we slave away our lives to give to our children and keep others at bay.

This lady is a female blood relative of our client's mother; likely, she was a great-grandmother. This enslaved and limited choices mindset was passed down in the genes, along with a large dose of guilt. Being enslaved and then feeling guilty for being born into a family that suffers just to keep you fed and alive is a very heavy and unhealthy price tag indeed.

She was predisposed genetically (and certainly energetically) to this aspect, and it manifested fully on the physical body at age four. At this age, our client also fully realised that his life had this genetic equation: life as an adult equals hard work and unavoidable pain, since hard work equals little gain and whatever is acquired is for your own children to ensure the continuing guilt and complete self-sacrifice.

Life also equals being aware and looking over your shoulder, suspicious of everyone. Expect to be betrayed, ripped off, or hurt in some way at any given moment. There is no trust, no spontaneity, no joy, no love. This is why our client lived in a fight-or-flight position and was ready to go into battle at any given time. And there is extreme caution with change. He doesn't trust change or anything new, whereas his partner embraces change and anything new. You can see the clash.

At age four the sacral energy centre received damage at this layer and with this particular aspect. It visually presents as a dark black hole.

We request this illusion he had of his life be healed and the soul fragment returned and reinstated with his energy body, aligning and reactivating all chakras now.

This was a life record playing over and over through many generations in all lifetimes and with many different scenarios. It was their mantra. Allow healing of this illusion to take place and reality to be reinstated.

Thank you, God.

Amen

A perfect baby born, a being of light made flesh, with ten little fingers and ten little toes, a vision of grace and the infinite power of our creation.

We take too much for granted.

In their minds, the proud parents are already envisioning colours of outfits, from pink and frills for girls to blue and trucks for boys. The nursery will be decorated and accessories influenced purely by gender and its expectations.

Whilst gender is an obvious inclusion by the sex we've chosen to incarnate in, we ponder the societal influences and dominant role playing we project on our brave recruits. When we mix our preconceived ideas of what each sex should do and be with genetic and karmic encodements, we are co-creating a preconceived minefield of possibilities, some of which are unnecessary at this level of human evolution.

Why must girls be the pretty pink princess playing in the kitchen, mixing up a batch of cookies whilst changing her babies nappy while her male companion of equal age roars and runs, collapsing into the sandpit with the airborne truck touching down with an explosive impact?

If this is a creative or a natural inclination, we are witnessing the free expression and exploration of role playing that children display through the art of mimicry brought about by being exposed to actions and behaviours of their parents. It is agreed that this is healthy and educational, provided it is a healthy and educational role model and environment. Secondly, we must acknowledge how many children's behaviours are discouraged, i.e., a boy who would like to feed the baby or a little girl who indicates that she would enjoy playing with a train set. Children's play in role modelling will always be a part of their learning; however, it should not exceed or eliminate creative play, as this would indicate an overexposure to adult environments and behaviours, particularly if the environment is intense or unhealthy.

Encourage an unlimited exposure to all arts, paste, paint and clay, sports, and all activities that are completely gender-free, allowing the spirit of the child to integrate with the physical body without limiting beliefs about his or her abilities. It is a pure body experience of the joys of physical life.

By age four, upon the entering into preschool or kindergarten, the influential encodements are complete. Whatever the child has been shown will have a lasting effect on what role they play emotionally and mentally throughout their life. The parents represent exclusive teachers to a child, forging a clear example of what the child understands as their major influences and role models and what that actually looks and feels like.

Many children being born today are quite different. They bear with them a new consciousness, a new awareness of their immaculate self. They no longer need to prove their worth through what they do, as they know outside approval is irrelevant for their evolvement. Children will always want to please their parents, but many will require less conditional nurturing and will seek genuine connection to their parents through unconditional love. They will already show a security with self and a natural ability to self-soothe, as they understand their purpose and their evolution. This is very good news. The insecurities and injury of past generations of self-love lack will be eliminated.

Old patterns of unhealthy gender role-playing, which led to gross imbalances in all levels of abuse, control, sexual misconduct, aggression, jealousy, obsession, and violence, will be dramatically decreased, in the next generation. These former three-dimensional expressions and manifestations are not supported in the higher vibration of the new earth and her incoming souls. This new consciousness is self-sustaining and honouring in varied beliefs and cultures. It encourages respect and love. It embraces new ways of trade based on fairness, sustainability, natural resources, and the natural balance of the earth.

Sounds like Eden? Well, in fact it is.

Thank you.

A few moments before the eleventh hour on 8 February, 2012, this healing marks an ending. Jesus stands before me, both children huddled in at each side of him, and the words "seek shelter" can be heard.

They are very safe and protected, and are choosing a path of light. They have seen and experienced much darkness, like yourself, in many lifetimes, and whilst being reminded and certainly touched by grace (as she/he are grace anyway), they have experienced fear through circumstances created in their young lives.

We will not allow our children to be terrorised. That is not our intent. But their souls, with their unending wisdom of God and all of existence, understand her quest. She is prepared at birth and has all of the related energy information encoded with her. From any point in time, relative to their emotional and mental maturity, they will be shown and guided. Opportunities are always presenting whilst they move through their life experiences and situations, allowing them to make choices. They have a very finely tuned guidance system, which tells them what feels "good" and what feels "bad."

We cannot and simply do not want to eliminate life experience through our limited thinking. That would be of no use to an evolving soul. Some experiences may appear too harsh or tough, but she/he wishes to experience, release, and conquer all false and limiting beliefs of fear. Provided it is understood that love is always supporting and within them, they will healthily succeed, and if not, they attempt once again. It is an endless cycle. The very nature of us, our true essence, has no concept or understanding of failure. It is illusionary and based in another belief of fear. So we therefore continue on, driven forward by the very force we are made of, pursuing our desire to be completely unified in peace and love.

All of our human experiences, no matter what drama or story prevails, depict that we have chosen to believe that we are surrounded by love or fear. The soul yearns to abolish all levels of fear from her life experience so that she truly and only ever experiences love, joy, and bliss in her life. She yearns to create this example to show her brothers and sisters as well.

"On earth, as it is in heaven" is the ultimate aim. The two, sister and brother, have made a pact, a soul agreement together. They must experience these shifts, which are concurrently matching their own environment, their family, their community, and their nation. There are multiple shifts occurring on extended levels, which are assisting the transmutation and elimination of low frequencies (emotions) and behaviours that are no longer desired to be experienced and sustained across the globe.

Symbolically, the underworld rumbles and stirs the serpent's long tentacles. She reaches up through the ground to expose herself from time to time. She only does so because the frequency above her awakens her, and she anticipates a feeding frenzy. If love resided consciously, continuously, and unconditionally, the serpent would never awake. It would lie dormant, sleep, and dream. Eventually, so undernourished, it would disintegrate and return to her true mother, nurtured within her womb forever and always, until a union of creative force in dreamtime replenishes the ashes with love and new life begins.

Ashes to ashes, dust to dust.

Mother Earth, in all of your beauty, creative power, love, and energy, please anchor and sustain the frequency of light bodies now residing and descending to earth. As more and more are coming, many more thousands are healing simultaneously.

Home is the kingdom of heaven we share, and you are its pillars of light.

With much love,

Jesus

Turning Twenty-One Years of Age   8/2/2012

My darling son, my first-born, you carry within you a key to all you know. You see, my sweetheart, my heart and yours connect to the frequency of God and all that exists in this time and space. My heart explodes with love as I acknowledge you. I see a strength that comes from my genes—my fire, which has sustained you well throughout challenging times. But now we have arrived at a great destination, a time that is so significant and symbolic. You are about to enter a passage in your life that explores true growth and development.

Turning twenty-one is the beginning of a nine-year journey of creating all that mirrors and produces your ideas, which forms your identity and a passion for self.

Twenty-one is the point at which you receive the key that unlocks the door to all you wish to develop, experience, and learn. You will decide who you wish to become and whether that matches who you really are. At the end of this nine-year cycle, you will reach age thirty, where you will be and experience all you have created internally and externally. A new cycle continues, but we will discuss that on your thirtieth birthday.

During this nine years, you will decide what you wish to do, how you wish to live, with whom, and what significant life lessons you have already encountered and ingested to help reach you maturity and continuing life path of wisdom. These really are your preliminary years before you reach full maturity, years of encountering so many enriching life experiences in your creative process.

Your soul speaks very clearly to me. I acknowledge your journey thus far and its impact on your personality self, which sometimes displays confusion and pain.

I completely and lovingly say this with all of my heart. Your journey, my beautiful son, is just about to begin. You are making your pilgrimage to the mountain. Your soul's yearning to feel and experience a union of body, mind, and spirit is your quest and goal. This is a time of discovery, an embracing and celebratory time in your development. I know and I trust you will make it so perfectly well.

As you embark on the days to follow, I ask just one thing: that you stop and think, feel, and reconnect to your inner wisdom before you make final decisions about anything. Sit quietly and ask the question. You will be receive the answer in your feelings, in your body, and within your heart. Trust the wisdom, my darling.

And so I excitedly, joyfully, and so lovingly celebrate your special day, which represents a rite of passage.

For you, my child, my first-born, I love you.

Mum

Genetic Family Healing   3/4/2012

From her heavenly home: a message from my mother

Patrizia, my darling, I look at you and send you so much love. Your unending compassion and belief in God will allow you to create what I could have never done. You sow the seeds and allow the fruit to ripen in your life. And so it is; this is a path of heart, not one of ego.

My child, your soul and your quest in this lifetime inspires healing, both karmically and genetically, for your entire biological family. Without your strength, persistence, and sense of justice, it would not be possible. Each family member, express your gratitude and take a deep breath in relief as she paves the way to assist you all.

It must be acknowledged that for now, you are the last female of the family, and it is meant to be that way. As you stand in the centre of time, you have healed our ancestry. You have firmly placed your heart at the centre of all female genetics in our lineage. The intended feminine members will be very different woman indeed. You have begun this now. Respect, honour, choice, and leadership had been synonymous with our male counterparts only. Why? The females were background support, lacking self-direction, value, and choices in their lives.

This is now changing. You are experiencing it in our family and certainly within your clientele and all those around you. It is a new consciousness and an awareness that is far-reaching and being experienced across the globe. The young women of the world must continue to strengthen and act upon this equality with love and encouragement. There is a unification and a new understanding of the sexes being created and born. There is a true partnership that has the potential to be so magnificent, in balance, and self-sustaining that it may last a millennium. It encourages individuality and unity for all people, inspiring further generations of both sexes to be equally creative, innovative, valuable, encouraged, nurturing, successful, and loving, all within the realms and natural comfort of gender and its roles. It is fluid, free-flowing, and open to creativity within a personalised structure. Today, our women are making changes and acting upon them on a conscious and physical level. Our mature, aged women are no longer choosing to live subserviently and are realising their greater potential. It is now and it is very good.

Your father was afraid of my potential; this is why it was never allowed. I was to live within the perimeters of what was understood a woman should do, and that was all. To be able to go out and meet people or have fun would allow me the feeling of joy. It may have allowed me to have fun and experience the happiness he could never provide. This would make him feel vulnerable and afraid that I might leave! How destructive the thought forms that allow fear to initiate the ego. Now he goes out; let him go. I do not care.

A lot of men are experiencing rising fear as they struggle to understand the current changes in women and their own adaptability. Some ask, "Where does that leave me? And how will I cope with a woman who cannot be controlled anymore?" If your energy expands and your self-empowerment to match, where does this leave him? He does not yet see or feel the deliciousness of sharing life with *his equal,* his feminine match, his yin of yang, no better, no worse—just perfection.

Genetically and certainly karmically, you attempted to take this on for me through the way you lived your life. You did this compassionately and lovingly, and mostly unaware. But of course, when we do this for our parents or loved ones without the realisation and courage to make the changes, we only continue the story. And it needs to stop. I am in joy now. I see you courageously proceed with faith, overcoming many obstacles. I want to tell you how grateful I am and how much I love you.

Continue with your plight. Do not give up. What remains with you will be there and what falls away will do so, all within the progression of you and your life, and that is perfection.

Trust that all is as it should be. You are hearing your guidance clearly, and you are actively making choices that support your goals.

She hands you a bright-yellow flower, a marigold.

Love,

Mama

In a sea of candles

The panther prowls, overseeing his territory. He knows the path he's come and wants to ensure the path along which he's going in order to survive.

The restlessness, the tentativeness, the alert nature of this animal makes it a fine predator. In the dark it becomes a chameleon, melting into the landscape with only its golden eyes visible, viewing his surrounds with extrasensory, fine vision.

The panther has a great deal riding on each hunt. Success or no success, the hunger is great, and energy resources run low, which makes it hard to hunt. He is all the more desperate to succeed. The pain of emptiness draws saliva to the hungry animal's mouth, and each of his senses are intensified as he stalks his prey. He can smell the prey from afar and must plan his execution. Unfortunately, the panther succeeds with only a third of his attempts. With every attempt and vigorous chase, pounce, and catch, enduring the intense pain of hunger and depleting energy, he actually gets the satisfaction of ingesting his kill only once in three times. This leaves a sense of desperation in him.

This fine, stealthy killing machine with all of his power, speed, and strength should provide success on every attempt. But this is not the case. Disappointment, concern, and emptiness already infiltrates the mind and body of this beast, disallowing his confidence and passion. He just survives, only just.

Today this genetic panther, this symbolic generational animal energy, must be laid to rest. This man can be passionate, energetic, and successful without him. This powerful panther no longer influences him with expectations of disappointment, failure, and fear of survival.

I am being shown excavation work associated with building sites. There is a reference being made about "bottom feeders" working with the "crap," "the rubbish," and it has a negative, dirty, unvalidated belief and energy associated with it. This filters through to those who would be paying for this service, who then undervalue the work and the importance of this work being done properly. Additionally, if the very beginning of the project and the foundations are not firm, clean, and adequate, the rest of the project will lack. So we are being shown today that the belief that this man's work is associated with lower energy is an illusion and can be reversed by acknowledging the importance of solid foundations to create success.

A golden light streams into the ground where the excavation is taking place and the machinery is performing the work. The entire site and all of the workers are being filled with the abundant, golden light, and it is simultaneously filling every person with positivity and self-worth. Feelings of value and respect reflect to supervisors and accounts departments who are paying the workers.

Consistency and self-value are also root issues here. The invoices must be submitted to make the payment possible. We eliminate the flighty, anxious, one-third successful, desperate panther and only incorporate the abundant, golden energy to encompass and filter throughout this man and his company.

From the ground up, as above, so below.

Suddenly the image changes and the panther is seen captured, speared by a native. He is speared through his torso at his ribs. His skin will be utilised by the native hunter. As the panther lay panting, thirsty, hungry, and now humiliated, the native feels a brief moment of guilt. He hadn't killed the cat to eat it; it merely represents a skin. The native is aware of the panther's battle to stay alive each day, never in peace, experiencing each day as a contest of skill, strength, and determination to survive.

Healing has taken place.

Amen

My attention is brought to an old Wild West scene. An outlaw sits perched behind a horse-drawn carriage. He is a wanted man pretending to be a trader, and he's riding into town. This man has stolen and taken a life or two, both without regret.

He's a bitter and hardened man, and he doesn't care what he needs to do to get his way. He plans to steal again and remain on the run. It's the only life he's known. His father was a big drinker and gambling man, and he's modelled after him.

It took four hundred years to allow this ancestry an opportunity to heal. Our client George was a well-read, scholarly individual, but he unfortunately carried an energy aspect of his forefather and was experiencing an unexplained guilt for it. It is true that his feelings had no rational or logical reason, but he nevertheless found himself carrying a heavy weight, which was burdensome. He never truly celebrated his achievements nor his value. He was a self-confessed perfectionist who viewed himself as not quite good enough. In his mind, he was not educated enough, handsome enough, or successful enough. But in reality, he was all of these things—extremely educated, thorough, considerate, talented, admired, and handsome. He was passionate about books and found great excitement and joy in learning. But he was lonely.

He rode a bicycle to work each day. When he arrived there, he would organise and arrange typed pages in order, ready for formal printing. Beginning with notices and community news, he gradually expanded his machinery and size to offer a printing service to companies and authors of books. Over the next thirty years, his company grew in popularity and size, mainly servicing authors, and it went on to become one of the most popular self-publishing companies in America. His eldest son would eventually take over the reins and continue the business.

But there is a depleting energy in him that still exists today. This has occurred because of the perfectionism outweighing and eventually exhausting the creative and expanding process. And with that expected residue of not worthy and not good enough, the attraction of those who don't expect worth would be delivered.

In those days, delays were of an expected nature. There were no laser printers, typesetters, or computers. The energy of slow production supported the slow and cumbersome outcome. He had something to prove. He was a kind, educated man with no association with unlawfulness or crime. His outlaw ancestor was not him; however, he always felt a connection, a guilt associated with his bloodline, further enhancing his need to prove himself.

The outlaw who was George's great-great-great grandfather. He didn't live a long life and was eventually shot by a sheriff in the centre of town. He'd been with a show girl very casually for some time with whom he'd had a son.

We see an old-fashioned lantern on the street corner buzzing as though it's voicing its voltage. Light streams appear then move forward at an unimaginable speed. Within a few seconds, the year is 2012. Jesus stands behind the building, larger than it is. He extends his hands around it, as if to hug the building. He clears the attachments that appear like an infestation of outer roots, strangling the exterior.

We see them fall away and disappear, and the slow, stagnant, energy dissipates.

We give thanks.

The original founder briefly presents and gives thanks, then fades.

This founder has connections to France from the female side.

Amen

Mother Mary

There is no love on earth like that of a mother to her child. It is likened to the love you all receive from God, from all of us in heaven, as we shower our pure unconditional radiant love upon you.

A woman's body when she becomes mother allows her spirit and body to unite directly with God upon earth to create a vessel of love for souls. There is great appreciation and love for this sacred, beautiful gift. Is there truly a greater gift?

There is an opportunity to embody love, to experience, to learn and create, to coordinate and swim with your entire soul group and all of humanity in a collective energy and frequency within a universal sea. Mothers share a passion, one that is unique to them. She prepares her body lovingly, she prepares her mind for the strength she will need to meet the earthly challenges of sleeplessness and fatigue. She carries a unique and undeterred persistence to overcome any obstacle for her child. It is intrinsic. Its unimaginable power drives her passion and patience forward, and she is rewarded only by a sparkle in her baby's eyes. The mere glance from her child, smiling and outstretching those little arms, bonds her forever and instils her natural instinct to protect her greatest love manifest, her self-like creation, her awareness of her connection to divinity.

Such awareness of our sacred selves gives truth and recognition to our immaculate creation. Our being of flesh is the most holy of expression, fuelled purely by the essence of God.

Today we give thanks and reverence, awareness and great love returned to all mothers, all who represent mothers, our holy mothers, and our God Mother, she who always showers us with her nurture and love and offers her gentle embrace whenever we ask.

Without you, Holy Vessel of Light, our existence, our choices, our evolvement, could not be experienced.

With the solemn acknowledgement of your grace, we love you.

From all children,

Amen.

England, 1050's. It is a time of intense spiritual pressure. The people are following an earth-based religion and faith, based on the cycle of the seasons, with God as the overseer. They were esoteric and often considered a threat to the strength of the early church. People were forced to embrace and practise early Christianity or be executed. Simple. Even before the pagans, the fundamental belief was in God who governs all in the universe. I walk through my lifetime with questions I seek to answer. I am creator and I am God example, in flesh.

Timon was a young boy living in a small community fifty miles southwest of London. He was an only child who lived with his mother, a well-respected herbalist known by some community members as a physician of God. She was a widow. Timon's father died in battle defending the community and his family during one of Rome's orders to eliminate whoever refuses the book of the Lord.

Timon was very angry about this. Having lost his beloved father in this way forced the question, "What sort of God would allow such atrocities to occur to the innocent?" He was only fifteen years of age, but he knew his time would come when he would be a man and fight as bravely as his father did, and have the opportunity to seek justice.

Timon protected his mother, Hilary, with an eagle eye. He was inseparable from her. As she brewed and gathered medicinal ingredients, which she grew herself, he worked outside, always keeping a watchful eye. Hilary was very beautiful. She had a peaches-and-cream complexion and wavy, long, red hair, and looked magnificent in her green velvet dress. "I love my mother so much," Timon said to himself. "She is a gift from God, and I will never let anyone harm her."

Because of her herbal and medicinal practises, Hilary was actually on an arrest-and-detain list from the palace, being accused of being a witch. The community knew the soldiers would be back, given that her husband had been killed. The people were supportive and sympathetic towards her.

And soon enough, one cool autumn morning, the soldiers rode into town. Hilary took to hiding. Timon instantly became aggressive, yelling at them, "What do you want? Get out! We don't want you here, you scum!"

The older men tried to stop him and calm him. "Be quiet, boy! The last thing you should do is attract attention to yourself!"

One soldier had enough of Timon's bantering and, from the height of horseback, hit him across the back of his head, causing Timon to fall to his knees.

Hilary witnessed this entire scene through a crack in the door of a barn. She lost all her concern for her personal safety and came running out. "No! Please stop! Not my boy!"

The soldier's plan was successful as this was exactly how they wanted to coax her out.

Timon never recovered from the horror of what he was forced to witness. The soldiers made him watch the slaying of his mother. They cut her throat and, as she bled to death, tied her to a pole, scalped her, and cut her hair to bring back to show the king that the witch had been slain. As it was, this was also a firm warning to show people that the pagan ways were to be no longer tolerated.

Timon spent the rest of his short life so saddened, he became insane. He ended his life by drowning in a local river.

Amen

It is the power you enforce with the beliefs about your future that prepares you for every relationship and event you experience.

You are gifted and passionate, and certainly destined for good things.

Aren't we all entitled to an opportunity? Why of course. It is up to you.

You have all the corridors open to lead you to various rooms. Each represents a journey. You must apply yourself with unwavering faith and let nothing obscure your dream. Look at the example of your Spiritual Mother. Unlike her, sometimes the events and particularly, the people in your life can create pessimism, but we urge you to use that buffer you sometimes call upon, the one which filters the fear and the self-doubt, and use it now.

You are more than intelligent enough, and you have shown courage and independence in taking the first steps to disconnect from what no longer serves you. It was time and you listened. Now listen again. Seek nothing else, much less another's opinion of your life. You know what you want, now seek that only.

What if I told you all things in life *are* guaranteed? What if I said to you that your mere intent was enough to manifest your dreams? It would seem too easy and perhaps even take away the thrill of the journey. Humans have an inbuilt high-maintenance button. When it's activated, we expect an arduous journey. We expect it to be tough, and we expect to be more celebrated when and if we make it. Learn to practise and accept your journey as not only your rightful place and choice, but also one that flows in simplicity and synchronicity, effortlessly. We apply the energy required to achieve our best and celebrate the joy in our achievements, but we don't begin the journey to Mount Everest wearing shorts and a t-shirt.

On every level, you prepare in your quest to achieve your goal. Apply your desire, creativity, and prior knowledge with positivity. This is the key to success. You are not afraid to achieve, and you don't expect on any level not to get there.

Whether you are accepted for a scholarship or not, it makes no difference, as any opposing forces to your achievements and success have nothing to do with money itself. Money cannot buy faith, hope or joy.

Stay true to who you are and what you wish to achieve. Move away and shield yourself from those who tempt to diminish or squash your dreams. We clear the way to allow all possibilities for synchronistic and aligned events to allow this course to be affordable and attended.

Thank you, with love and gratitude.

Hallelujah, hallelujah! Some of the most powerful realizations come from observing your close circle.

There is a core to this. Your kindness and service to those in need are your virtues; however, you may also attract the individuals who challenge your truth and your faithful surrender, and this root comes from your birth mother.

Your mother lived a difficult, service-orientated life. She didn't ask for anything for herself other than to see her family live well and be in good health. She unfortunately did not experience much peace, love, respect, or appreciation, and whilst she was incredibly strong in the face of her own personal torment, it eventually took its toll. How many individuals repeatedly took from her? And at what level and how much did she allow them to do so? What did she truly receive in her life? Her life was experienced as a sacrifice, and this is not God's desire or loving intent for any of us.

At age four, you absorbed and adopted your mother's heartache. You decided to physically and emotionally share the load by performing hard work. You took too much responsibility by working long hours through tiring circumstances in hope that it relieves the burden from Mum a little bit. The men of the family were certainly not going to do it. Their selfishness and ego surpassed any love or compassion they could have felt or exercised. The dominating belief in their nature was to view females as a possession and utilize them as workhorses for the betterment of the whole family. There was no consideration of another's feelings, needs, or desires. What a powerful implemented energy, from both perspectives, for a young child to absorb and for this child to grow into womanhood, particularly if that child was a healer.

Today, the ego has presented again. It is just in another form. It pushes itself as a force and has an intent to dominate; however, the opposing factor you present, which is the desire to deliver healing and compassion and bring the light of peace into the hearts of all people, is the hope and the love you ignite within them. You see their recognition and realization that to live in balance and happiness, you do so with self-love, choice, and acceptance, even when others may not approve.

Today we acknowledge this truth, and we sever the response to instigate rescue. Each individual comes out of her or his free will to heal, and with that intent, you will serve as educator, healer, guide, philosopher, storyteller, and one who leads by example. If one refuses to feed from the food you offer, leave their plate and walk away without any loss of nourishment for yourself.

Healing has taken place. Thank you.

Chapter 4

Ascension Healings

Master Teacher: Mass Healing Modality

Master Teacher: Mass Healing
Modality   *1/7/2011*

....

The eye of an eagle, the intellect of an elephant, the spirit of the dove.

Your thoughts, in which you are considering a path of teaching and performing mass healings, are intuitively received. Yes, this needs some clarification for you. Please remember that adjustments to the plan along the way are healthy and are always an indicator of growth and development.

Your healings and adaptability for greater understanding are because of your lineage and your light body, which now functions in a fifth dimensional reality. You are at the forefront in knowledge and experience, which serves to help and heal so many. You have your own signature healing techniques that are unique. These teachings can be shared and taught at a practitioner level only, and you will know who and when the practitioner will be ready to embrace their journey as a healer. Obviously they will have sought many healings and much personal development to be able to understand and guide a person on their path. But you are best served with the masses.

It will be your choice whether you continue to work on a one-on-one basis with certain individuals. It is always personally rewarding, connecting, and beneficial.

The mass sessions are an extremely effective healing modality. They are also quite unique, and it is time for you to fully embrace and utilize this as an energy healing option for people. It is not without its integration and energy adjustment reactions, so therefore an allocation of post-healing sessions for clients is necessary, educational, and self-empowering. It will serve to educate the individual about the healing process they are undergoing and what that may look and feel like. It will give them support and understanding, which is in itself a safe place for those who find themselves wanting to heal and renew their lives with little guidance or tools. It is necessary for them to experience an ownership and acceptance of it, likely for the first time in their lives. This is unknown territory for some people. We will encourage, educate, and guide. It is has progressive levels and layers with each person and subject, depending also on their awareness and personal development work already undertaken. All people are eligible, no matter what their circumstances. All people are able to heal from their current ailments, whether they be physical, mental, or emotional. Healing is obtainable, sustainable, and successful for all who commit to it, for their lives and their soul's union with their ultimate self incarnate.

Level 1: All similar persons presenting. No age restrictions. Beginners with little or no personal development work undertaken. Three separate categories of general health: family/ children, relationships, and creativity/work/abundance.

Level 2: Includes persons who have previously completed some personal development/energy work. Includes those who have an awareness and an understanding of mirrors and the universal laws of attraction. It will include those who are beginning to recognise total responsibility for their own life and the power of choice to make the change. Categories will include physical health, fertility, anxiety and depression, relationships, family/genetic healings (including children), karmic healings, past-life aspects, empowerment development, female/male power, prosperity and abundance, work and creativity, and creative flow in business.

Level 3: Includes persons who are actively and consciously taking charge of their lives and circumstances and are willing to release old patterns of behaviour in the physical, mental, and emotional bodies, as well as all genetic encodements, all karmic encodements, all oaths, contracts, promises, and attachments. This is for those individuals who are healing and evolving with awareness, trust, and complete surrender, as well as those who have previously invested in one-on-one healing sessions and/or additional group sessions. Categories will include all physical health issues, depression, marriage/relationship issues, twin flame/soul mate attraction, fertility healings, advanced genetic/karmic healings, past-life healings, life purpose healings, male/female power advanced, prosperity and abundance at work/home advanced, and corporate and entrepreneurship healings.

Practitioner Level: Involves energy work and education at Level 3 and additional study, plus one-on-one practitioner training.

*   *   *

There is much to offer the individual on the mass-healing scale within the varying categories and levels of experience and evolvement. The categories of healings and education sessions/courses, plus additional techniques and tools, will empower you with the choices to create your life from the inside out, unlimited and healthful, expansive and abundant, and full of loving purpose.

All healings, courses, and workshops that enrich your personal development and life allow further progressive teachings and philosophies to be created and delivered for the masses. Listen to your instinct. It must resonate with you, or else the knowledge and understanding will not be encoded. Again, we remind you that you all have the answers you seek within your heart. Your readers have access to the knowledge and guidance at the Level 1 with your first book, *The Healers Journey.*

These healings and courses, sessions and workshops will run at and be immensely successful in The Ascension Centre, Melbourne.

Amen

Have Faith

Lay your hands upon me. Let me feel your familiar and loving embrace. I've missed you so. If God was to have one true desire, it would be that we be happy, joyful, and live meaningfully, and that all live with an intent to acquire higher learning, growth, and evolvement.

Like many candles burning brightly, your warmth and light fills a room, and so do the ones gathered for the healing. The earth is continuing her shift in consciousness, moving forward and beyond the fifth dimension. Humanity no longer sees through a square-pegged hole. There have been many physical requirements, mental aspects, emotional tendencies, and social conditions that influence your daily lives. However, the least has been faith. Courage in your ability to carry and utilise faith is a gift that provides unending treasures. Having faith allows for your body, mind, and soul to relax into the energy "in flow." It gently allows doors to open and others that are no longer required to close.

Archangel Gabriel: I come forth to assist all light workers and creators to connect with faith, which is in truth every single one of you. You are now living in a time where one can speak of beliefs and true feelings without ill fate. Do so with joy and nobility, do so with passion and reverence, and the more you share that energy, others will join in with relief! They no longer fear to be silenced. To acknowledge by speaking and celebrating your belief in an Almighty God is your anchor and your sanctuary onto earth. It balances your existence as a light body residing with your physical being. By living as a type of energy conductor, receptor, and transmitter, we utilise this energy and allow further miracles and gifts to present. Fear is always the mask of rejection, and those who refrain from utilising full faith dare not, as they fear if it were not true, they'd be left truly devastated. How can one fear so much? What is required is to release, to clear, heal, and acknowledge karmic lessons and soul quests or contracts? Today, we call upon the power of God and the healing angels of light unto all humans to assist you in severing any doubt, to eliminate the fear, to speak the Lord's name, Jesus, God, or any ascended master, prophet, or angel, who assists you along your journey.

Jesus: Speak my name and know me as thyself, Jesus. Love as I do, believe as I do, care as I do, be as I am.

Emerald-green light surrounds the planet, and as I look, a concentration of light directs towards the polar cap region of Antarctica. Extremes in global temperatures, along with evolving energy shifts, have our mother under some intense pressure. Like children from her womb, we also feel the physical, mental, and emotional pressure. Honour, release and connect to the joy growing within you.

Amen

Swinging joyfully on a flower-laden swing, you see the ropes hang from the Tree of Life. The ropes are flowers, all in pastel colours. The fragrance is so very sweet, and it is visually abundant with the beauty of large blooming cottage roses.

"It's so lovely up here, I feel the freedom and the joy of all that I am, but when I step onto the ground, a part of me feels fear," the young woman said.

This is not a very big issue; however, it is significant enough to create discomfort and reaction. It is part of a family belief system and partly a genetic encodement. This encodement tells us women to accept victimization, when they are truly powerful. We wish to abolish this now, as there is no room for this belief in the twenty-first century on earth and within the ascension process.

The trunk of the tree stretches down to earth, and this lovely girl begins her descent from the branch and her swing. As she touches the earth, she notices a podium within an amphitheatre nearby. "I will speak there," she says. "I will impart teachings in that space." She walks into the centre of the amphitheatre, and then walks towards the podium. From an archway on ground level, she sees her father enter. He greets her with a proud smile, and his arms outstretch to warmly embrace her. Their relationship is now stronger than ever before, but he also views her as his equal, no longer the apprentice, no longer the child who needs his loving guidance.

He nods to her indicating its nearly time to rise to the call. There are more details yet to be revealed, and that is part of the exciting, joyful, mystery of life. If we knew it all before it occurred, we might react with doubt, or fear, or likely interfere with the divine timing.

"My beautiful daughter, such majesty in your presence, which beams from a pure heart. For you to educate and heal many, many people, you must express love, emanate strength, and have a clear intent. And all of those elements exist within you.

"Your time grows near, and whilst your connection to me can never cease to be, remember who you are. You have the ability, the knowledge, the faith, and the love to inspire change and teach all who seek. You are no less than any of the significant healers and sages and prophets of our history. You do not require a special cloak; your lineage exists within you."

"Thank you, Father. Your faith in me drives me forward each and every day, and I know this to be my path. I trust in this awareness completely, and I know you are within me. I hear you, and I love you, oh so much. When it is time, I will rise to the call, and I will not fear. I know who I am. I know she is great. I know she can heal. I know she can teach with sincere and humble intent, with endless gratitude, compassion, and peace. I thank you."

Jesus begins to move into the distance and fades.

Blocks presented: sacral and base chakras.

All blocks have been removed, and healing has taken place.

Amen

Welcome! We've been waiting for your arrival! You understand now, don't you? You had to allow this to develop in your own time and upon your request, permission, and intent. We are so happy to work with you!

Huge double golden doors open up into a large ballroom. A pathway leads up the centre of the room, and on either side, there are awaiting light beings, all looking towards the direction of the huge doors. There are ascended masters, deities, and angels, all gathered for the arrival. As we walk slowly up the pathway, we stop and acknowledge all the smiling faces, the huge vibration showering such joy around us. We understand now that we had to come this far in our soul's evolvement to have the awareness and experience of humility, respect, love, honour, and the gift of working with these beloved beings, masters, and healers. Their identities will be as profoundly unique as their individual messages to us, as are the healings, teachings, and insights they impart directly to the third eye area.

At the front of the hall, Jesus stands with his clasped hands together. He has the most beautiful smile. It's a smile that comes from his heart. It is shining through his eyes and radiates from his whole being.

We reach the top of the pathway, and he turns to wave behind him. Suddenly where was once a wall and window appears an open landscape! Unimaginable beauty with colours so vibrant, it is most certainly unearthly. It is a natural scene revealing many thousands of miles of display trees, flowers, birds, rivers, oceans, grasslands, mountains, and rainbows. It is gradually unfolding like a moving picture carrying us forward within it. From the depths of the landscape, a Merkabah symbol suddenly comes floating towards us. It is glowing white, and it is tumbling and rolling closer. As it turns and glistens, it is so undeniably perfect. I watch in awe.

The moving scene stops and a mist clears. The scene reveals a pair of golden gates that lead into—or more accurately towards—the dimension containing earth. There is a bridge is before us now, and the connection of alternate or parallel realities grows finer and closer.

This energy healing today bridges a gap.

Our guides, masters, angels, and deities will present at any moment we call upon them and request assistance. They will impart guidance for embarking on the path of the heart. We validate and accept our self-mastery through all we are experiencing and learning so that we can emanate that frequency to encourage and assist others to encompass self-mastery.

An energy that is undoubtedly a love frequency is now in sync with us, in accordance with our loving request.

Blessed are we.

Thank you.

Where the Road Divides   9/8/2011

Thousands are walking together like a huge wave of heads moving forward. It's a pilgrimage, one that is taken by those of faith. People have always been aware of their inner light, that divine spark that ignites the soul's passion into the awareness of the mind and the body.

The approach of uncovering root causes of illness in the body and then utilizing that wisdom by initiating energy healing from a self-empowerment perspective is a very different approach from that of Western medicine's philosophy of diagnosis and treatment.

From an energy perspective, a *dis-ease* manifests after a negative emotion or low-frequency energy has already fully integrated into the aura and/or chakras, allowing entry into the physical body, and resulting in cellular dysfunction and mutation. At its origin, it is not a clinical condition at all; it is a frequency. Therefore one needs to draw on recuperating, rejuvenating, and supporting the area of body (and chakras) where the energy "leakage" or temporary malfunction has existed. We utilize an energy healing source of love and connection through our own Source, which heals all.

So how does one scientifically explain the method or the experience of a miracle being performed? How can one experience the unifying of the heart, mind, and limbs within a sterile environment that usually radiates fear and disempowerment? We are alive, magnificent beings and need to be healed and respected as the most awe-inspiring, miraculous beings on earth! And that we are.

Whilst there is a need to consider and learn from the analysis of illness through symptoms and cell behaviour, etc., it is only part of the entire picture. This data produces the resulting diagnosis, giving us only a limited perspective and solutions of a pharmaceutical or surgical nature only. Alternatively, identifying and treating the root literally eliminates its power source and ability to hold onto its host. Everything has an origin, and its exposure is dependent on healing and recovery, whatever that means for the individual.

Practitioners and individuals who bring forth reaction may be fearing tremendously, and by their considering this truth of human health, the fear of the actual act of surrender and trust sparks a vulnerability that initiates strong defence. Send them love and offer gentle reassurance and guidance always.

Verbalising their fears is an extremely effective release for some individuals. When done in counsel and with guidance, with the intention to identify the root and clear it, it allows for a powerful way to release old patterns. Affirmations also work extremely well to support the mind and body. We offer some suggestions:

1) I am God made manifest; I have the power to heal and I graciously deserve and accept all good things into my life.

2) I am a strong, vital, loving force who only knows perfect health, peace and well-being, today and always.

3) I am releasing all former negative beliefs and completely embrace the power within me to create everlasting peace.

4) I commit to the freedom of my spirit, who only knows love.

5) I am peace. I am bliss. I am love. I am.

Practitioners who enhance energy healing therapy and their counselling/communicative therapy with suggestions of affirmative statements for a client to use will find a great amount of positive feedback. The use of positive affirmations actually changes the dynamics of a person's energy field from the first word. Repetition may be required to fully embrace the words and their soothing effects. It relaxes and harmonizes the emotional and mental bodies in particular.

It's a road travelled thus far, and with great appreciation we view the highway ahead. With grace, respect, and friendship, we hope to bridge the gap of understanding and allow the expansion of possibility and of open mindedness to entice a curiosity in people and practitioners alike, so that we can aim to unify in love and provide the most profound awareness, solutions, and healing to all, without division or ego.

We continue the work, the learning and collection of healing data, and we are grateful to be led by the greatest healing source of love and light.

Those in the dark only need to know where to find the light, so guide and heal them.

Amen.

I see you, arms outstretched, light beams emanating from your entire body, most prominently from the third eye, your physical eyes, throat, heart, hands, and torso.

This is now a significant level. Light filters through you and your body and has assimilated the frequency through the cells and the flesh itself, as well as the chakras and auric field. This process invites the energy through as a conduit to be used for healings. This new frequency and level is a little bit like a radio tuned to the correct station. The dial is set, the reception is clear, and there is no interference.

Mt. Sinai

You now stand on a grassy patch of slightly wilted, golden grass with scattered wildflowers all around. There is a slight wind. Wearing a white short-sleeve shirt and a white skirt flowing in the breeze, you are relaxed and smiling. Jesus stands before you, relaxed and happy. This is a gathering for an informal ceremony with close ones present. We overlook an ancient city and it feels as if time has stood still. Much has surpassed us.

I notice as you turn to him you are wearing a white Jewish cap. Mary Magdalene walks up behind you and places a red shawl around your shoulders. You lovingly glance back and smile at her. She moves back and sits beside us on the grass.

The Ceremony

Jesus looks up and announces, "It is time." Like the sun poking through the clouds, light streams begin to shower down. He then takes the shawl from around your shoulders and places it gently over your head. Your hair is gently brought forward. With his left hand he signs the cross over your heart and asks you to raise your right hand. He then touches your right hand with his left hand. Palm to palm, you are the mirror image of one another. You smile lovingly at him with awareness and immense gratitude. An energy stream from the heavens beams towards Jesus and through his heart into yours, then from your crown chakra upward back to God. It is the sign of the pyramid—a perfect, divine light-created pyramid.

It is the initiation of the crowning of consciousness, of God consciousness, which has now been received and accepted.

You have fully embraced your journey and accepted your path to heal yourself and others with compassion, dignity, equality, respect, love, and freedom. This releases any past or current blocks. Genetic and karmic obstacles are eliminated. All you choose to heal, you will. You are a God vessel, and forever more this will be so. You have completed the human agenda of lessons and karma, learned and inherited from all lives. This cycle is now complete. You are operating with a higher vibration, and your existence is about to change. You will need fewer things or items around you and will wish to simplify life with basic requirements, which enhance grounding and God connection.

You will notice changes to your physical appearance. Your skin will be lighter and brighter, the same will be true with your eyes, and any weight issue will balance. Dietary requirements and tastes will change. Peace and laughter will be what you require. Materialism or items of human lifestyle will exist, but your desire for them will be lessened. It is just part of your world—no more, no less.

The pyramid energy source turns from white to rose pink in colour and then starts to fade. The sun comes out, and the ceremony is complete. It is a joyous occasion, and joy is the expression of bliss.

Source is from God, and God is interconnecting within all realms, dimensions, realities, spheres and subspheres, elements, galaxies, and throughout the entire cosmos. The earth is yet another realm, one that requires ascension. This process is inevitable and occurring now. There is no religious or societal belief, cultural system or government, doubt or fear that will prevent this.

Do you all know who you truly are? You have existed and believed you were limited by the physical body. You actually live within a multidimensional reality with an energy (God Source) connecting to everything all of the time. Those who are healing, clearing, and growing will connect powerfully, and when they do, with full consciousness, they will experience it as a phenomenal awakening, as they will connect directly to God.

In the name of God, love unto this planet.

Healing has occurred, and energy transcended.

Amen.

My beautiful daughter, how pleased I am to see you stepping into your role as the successor of my healings and teachings. And whilst compassion and goodness flows from your heart, mind, and body, you now know that many will embrace the miracle whilst others display fear of freedom. As always, the universal law of choice and free will is always adhered to. Your healings and teachings can only be felt and heard from those who wish to listen, release their burdens, and learn.

As one who has been healed and continues to heal, and as a student, you have listened and learned much. The support team forming around you, consisting of fellow healers, writers, oracles, and intuitives, will continue to walk alongside you and be aligned with you. Trust that after many lifetimes, karmic, and genetic healings and lessons, you are ready to unite and embrace your purpose together.

You attract that which you are: the faithful, the responsible, the creative, the passionate, the loving, the respectful, the trusting. You will understand the identification and the amplification of energy as it flows through you. You actually never stop healing, as I didn't; however, it transmutes and changes in form, depending on the intent and surrounding circumstances.

Teacher you are, as it is natural to you. It is also natural to some healers alongside you. As did the Apostles, the current group gathers. As the twelve come, one by one, you will know who they are. There will be a rush of excitement, and it will be unmistakable. Trust the signs you receive. Your heart will be expressive in this knowing. We set the past aside, and we give thanks to its wisdom.

With every lifetime, each and every experience you have had creates a defining soul story, just like a puzzle when pieced together perfectly paints the picture of your purpose on earth. Your external, visual signs are the stars, a rainbow, birds, butterflies, and rays of light through clouds; the beauty of the world is your home.

I am here, I am within it all, and you connect to me with each acknowledgment of this truth. The individual souls aligned to you now have the same passion, love, and purpose as light workers. It has been a long-awaited destination (in human years) to be incarnating on earth at this very significant time. As you know it is the beginning stages of the ascension, and there are so many wondrous miracles to experience ahead. Keep your faith, embrace God in everything you do, and just observe the multiplication of everything. Flow is freedom, freedom is flow, and we are naturally aligned within this stream.

A beautiful, flowing, emerald-green river presents with flowers of fuchsia pink, yellow, turquoise, and purple along its bank. It is a vivid scene, with various species of birds and butterflies dancing in the air—a vision of joy and abundant nature.

This is your home. It is the magic that's within you every day.

I am your father, I love you, I guide you, and I show you the way.

Christ lives within all of your hearts.

Healing has taken place.

Amen

Narcissism

So help me God, I must release this. I completely surrender to you to eliminate this from my energetic encoding on my cellular, physical, atomic, auric, mental, and emotional bodies and all chakras.

Ascended masters Jesus, Lady Nada, Quan Yin, Djwhal Khul, and Mother Mary present in file, one behind the other. Jesus raises his right hand and places his palm on my forehead. *Crack!* The sound in my head was loud! My third eye immediately opens and activates to see the truth. Narcissism is not our truth. Such behaviours were genetically encoded into human society many thousands of years ago from an intergalactic race. This race physically incarnated with human inhabitants and had much to advance upon at the time. They mirrored our evolvement within our history and certainly at this moment universally.

The ascended masters and all light beings, come to our aid and assist us in this final severing. We no longer require this aspect to learn from its lessons. Our level of evolvement recognizes and acknowledges that we no longer need to experience narcissism on any level.

We awaken all four chambers of your heart as part of your healing today. The heart is your true being and all-wise. It is your perfect internal guidance system. With your heart, you acknowledge and feel me, you love me, you sense all that is beautiful and gracious and all that brings you joy and fulfilment. Like four blossoming flowers, a bouquet of roses, lotuses, or lilies, open to your inner knowing that love is all there is and rest in this sacred space of peace.

We may not have always experienced this peace, as we had fallen into an illusionary aspect of fear and control. Such manifestations need to be dealt with as part of your learning and release so that you may guide many others and lead by example.

All is revealed to you as you allow yourself to grow and clear past debris of all kinds. We are your guides, your True Mother and Father. By the very nature of yourself, you may nestle gently into our arms and know you are home, completely safe, and so very loved. Your biological parents, your children, your grandparents, are all our children as well. They are no older, nor wiser, no greater than your equal. It's like a play, a theatre production with actors and scenes, plots and storylines, all within the landscape of what you set out to experience and learn in this lifetime. For yourself and for each other. Be not aggressive or unforgiving of these souls as they are fulfilling soul quests on their paths, which have crossed with yours with your full permission. Offer compassion and understanding and release both of your from any burden, as it is not meant to be carried.

We love you, nurture you, heal you. Always. The scene is a united embrace. Enormous wings enclose us all.

White/electric blue Archangel Michael energy showers upon us, and simultaneously Jesus approaches the solar plexus chakra of all people. This huge, bright-yellow energy wheel requires rebalancing and sealing. I see the glow on his face as he places his hands upon the chakra. The experience is so calming and pacifying. He is removing entities that appear in a greyish colour. He then infuses pink and green energy, both hands cradling the yellow energy centre, which is balanced and joyful.

Immense gratitude.

Three days integration time is advised; rest and recovery is advised.

Thank you Jesus, Lady Nada, Quan Yin, Djwhal Khul, and Mother Mary.

They each fade off into the distance. Healing has taken place.

Amen

For thousands of years, people have surrendered and prayed in their darkest hours. People have such a diverse range of spiritual needs. However, we have always known that we are able to seek the guidance and assistance of our priests, spiritual counsellors, monks, rabbis, and imams within our communities and holy places of worship when we are enduring personal hardship in life or experiencing pain, confusion, sadness, or grief.

It is at the point of surrender, when all else has failed, that people seek the imagery, guidance, love, and strength of their God representative. There are many great prophets and teachers who have graced us on the earth. Jesus was a master of surrender, trust, and faith. Upon the cross there was no greater power than that of surrender, as it truly connected him to his unending existence and a greater understanding of his role on earth. Jesus showed us this symbolism, which was not to imply guilt and remorse and certainly not out of self-pity or self-gratification, but as an example of our greatest power and gift we all house of the transcendence of an almighty being. No level of violence or rage, hatred, threat, fear, or dominance has any true power over the love that is our existence, and it can never be destroyed. Ever. He survived this torment with his heart full of love, compassion, and reverence for all involved.

Our healing capacity, our releasing and clearing capabilities, are no different, yet we often choose to see our death as an end, igniting all kinds of fear and doubt. It is marked as a conclusion of an experience, but one that represents a birth as well. This end, which truly allows your transcendence, imparts an understanding on many levels and ultimately the surrender and release of pain.

The church into which we enter has heard much desperation within its walls. There is much to write about this, but we will keep the focus on a person's desire to be "rescued." A house of God or place of spiritual refuge is not a place where an actual rescue takes place. One must acknowledge, strive, and desire to change their life with awareness and responsibility. Any house of God invites your soul to reconnect and reexperience a refreshing breath of fresh air, as you may have stifled every breath of love and peace with fear, doubt, and loss. Tears are often released, which allows the shedding of negative and relentless mind chatter, toxic feelings, and self-sabotage. These individuals have lived in overload and overdrive for some time. It is like a bubble bursting; it can no further stretch beyond its capacity. The question beckons: why do we wait until our situation and life course is so critical that we can hardly breathe? Stubborn or blocked behaviour, along with the acceptance of external influences to self where the boundary between where you and another begins and ends is fluid, eventually forces even the most resilient to their knees in a last ditch effort to be set free from illusionary binds.

There has existed an expectation with most structured religions that sets a standard of behaviour and with it an unfortunate egotistical ideal of better, lighter, wiser, more worthy, more valued, and closer to God position for our priests, rabbis, imams, healers, and readers. The old expectation or belief was to heal the sick, the poor, the hungry, the broken-hearted, and the disappointed.

Centuries of "Oh, help me please! My life is out of control. I beg you!" affirmations have engulfed our genetics with expectations of being rescued by something outside of ourselves. The new earth and fifth dimensional consciousness requires nothing but a willingness and a conscious decision to heal, with the responsibility of the individual and her connection to God engaged to allow the dynamics to begin shifting and the process of healing to be continued.

Entering the house (which is symbolic as well, as the house resides within you) requires a firm decision to change current course, to acknowledge oneself, and to recognize your relationship with God.

This centre, and the Ascension Centre, provides a heart-channelled, guided, and nurturing haven with a team dedicated healers, teachers, and counsellors who will deliver and awaken you to your inner wisdom to begin your ascension process.

Choose to align yourselves in unison with what created you. Be conscious and gratefully aware of the great universal jigsaw puzzle in the brightest constellation imaginable that you are part of. It would not shine half as brightly without you. Find your inner light and begin to acknowledge that every step you have taken thus far, every occurrence, every tear shed, and every opportunity that has presented was created within you, for you, to be you. You can create perfect harmony and self-love in your life. Responsibility and the ambition to love your experiences will be the force behind the power to heal, upon your request, via the help of earth angels, angels, guides, and light beings, those who serve him.

The Tree of Life is shown in the middle of a field, wildflowers abound, and the breeze is blowing softly allowing the reeds to dance and sway.

She is walking through the wildflowers, across a grassed paddock, towards the tree. It is far more magnificent and larger than I can ever illustrate. It is huge, its branches outstretched and supporting the air around her, embracing the atmosphere with a grand statement of gratitude, love, and purpose. Each colour and indentation in her trunk and branches represents a life experience and the wisdom earned from it.

Suddenly, the tree begins to shape and shift; it shows an ethereal image of two beings emerging from it, yet still part of it. The image becomes clearer to reveal Jesus to the right side and Mary Magdalene emerging from the left. The subtle imagery is of both joined together within this holy Tree of Life. They await unification. And whilst they have blended in this way for some time, they are now including their daughter. This induction is necessary for the next level of healing she delivers. She can call upon or activate the unification when she needs to for assistance on a personal level.

She finally reaches the tree with its trunk solidly in front of her. She outstretches her right hand and touches the trunk, expecting a hardened, rough trunk, as it appears to be. But it is translucent, and her hand flows through it! Suddenly, there is a small screen to view on the trunk, which begins to show the image of a flat; it is vacant. To her surprise, she touches the screen, and it appears to be liquefied with flowing energy. "Wow, it looks so solid," she says.

Suddenly, Jesus and Mary come forward, stepping out from the tree to appear very clearly standing before her. They both measure at least nine or ten feet in height. They look down at her like proud parents of a baby. Opening their arms to embrace her, telepathically they are all understanding of the process of unification for this healing trinity.

As they all embrace, she is gently pulled into the tree and blends with it. Her structure changes molecularly and cosmically. She walks through to the other side. It is a dark room, a space or void, with a light up ahead. The darkness has the peaceful comfort of a womb. There is a lovely soft and low humming sound, but otherwise it is quiet. This space is sensorially stimulating. She does not sit and rest, however. She walks forward into the light. The light whitens the entire surroundings, completely engulfing any matter, shape, or colour. Even she is now the light. Everything is made of this light. She is aware of herself still moving forward, as though she is swimming through a sea of white while still part of it. Suddenly, a faint image begins to present, which leads her into a familiar glimmer of sunshine and into the beautiful paddock laden with wildflowers. She intuitively understands that this porthole has allowed the integration and adjustment of her light body to heal at this new vibrational level. Her experiencing and travelling through these dimensions and through the light of consciousness was in fact a symbolic birth.

Mother Mary presents in all her glory. Magnified and infused by the DNA that created her, the Holy Trinity is now infused as one.

More messages will be imparted, clearly and consciously. Heaven's touch is a mere millisecond away.

In reverence and eternal love for humanity and our divine purpose.

The Tree of Life now stands more vibrant and magnificent than ever. Each branch appears thicker and stronger. The entire tree is has a golden aura, followed by green, pink, blue, purple, white, and magenta, and mother of pearl.

Absolutely beautiful.

Thank you.

Amen

Intended Creation 3/10/2011

At what point did you disengage from your power, your belief in yourself, and simultaneously, me? You are a being who holds incredible power; you can and will create any desire you wish, provided your message and your intent is clear. The moment we begin to absorb someone else's drama or emotion into the mix and adopt it as our own, the outcome will be unsatisfactory and have confusing results.

Your dreams in sleep time house important messages as Spirit watches the unfolding of events that create and support more and more negative emotion. It is time to stop and use your natural ability to regroup and refocus. We are the captains of our own ships and our own experiences. If another has the ability to penetrate your thoughts and positive vibrations, it is because something has triggered an awakening of that emotion in you, whether it is doubt, fear, vulnerability, inconsistency, or any feeling that causes you displeasure. This you will clear today; however, it is important for you to take the lead in your own life and recapture your sense of self in all her magnificence. Remember very well that thoughts of doubt are only indicators that those around you doubt themselves.

Energy filters are effective, but ensure your filters are conscious as well—energy filters, body filters, and mind filters. Affirm to yourself, "I no longer allow others' opinions of me to influence my life and its outcome. I am strong, vital, and on the path of my personal aspirations and soul life purpose. I recognise and appreciate the differences in others and acknowledge their fears; however, I offer their freedom, and I expect the same in return." This is truly the path with heart. Another very important thing to consider is that there are multiple things occurring in your life at any one moment. Dedicate an amount of time to acknowledge each item and think about the ideal and desired outcome of each issue.

Manifest your desires frequently and passionately while in a calm state. Multiple issues all swirling around unattended have only a like attraction of non-resolution and confusion. So when the primary focus or magnet is you, it is imperative to separate the issues, visualise the desired outcome, feel good about it, and then let it go. Your outcome is just as you wish, provided the heart and soul of the desire still outweighs and totally supersedes someone else's doubt. Choose your thoughts and intentions with wisdom, but most importantly with your heart. Your heart is all-knowing and all-wise and will always guide you to truth. If it feels good, it is good.

The more we pre-empt a situation and infuse it with fear and reaction, the more our powerful creative abilities will manifest and ensure that outcome.

Refocus on your every desire with excited passion. Visualise it to be true, and expect results to show you now! Most importantly, know that you are love. With that truth, anything inauthentic must fall away.

Know that you deserve all good things that you wish for. An abundant and creative universe cycles rhythmically and delivers continuously in so many ways. It is often our own belief system about what economic level we are valued at or deserving of, or perhaps what we believe to be true about wealth, that blocks the forthcoming flow and opportunity for change and creativity.

Set your sights to a new high beyond the limits you've set for them before. Feel the success of your dreams, as they are not far away. They are here now. Any apparent distraction or delay you experienced was just that. See it for what it is: an example of how easily one can become embroiled in another's fear and make it their own. You don't need to affirm your goals to anyone else, just yourself.

We are always here to guide, love, and support you. All you have to do is ask. You are part of a group of earth's leaders as healers, teachers and guides, who are so importantly assisting, educating, and inspiring all to their potential future.

Call upon us. We are listening and waiting to help.

God

Commit to Your Life Today   **21/10/2011**
....

Golden stairs ascend before you. As you look at them, you can see they represent your growth and the level of your new standing point. This is essential to review, and it is spectacular in its awareness and revelation.

If one is instantly tired when viewing the stairs before them, it shows that there is a lack of confidence or uncertainty in the creative process in some way. Perhaps it is within the goal-setting and the commitment itself, or exhaustion over doing too much single-handedly. We know that energy is a force that creates movement and matter. Acknowledging this allows us to question and seek to understand the subsequent effect this has on us all. When we accept that energy is powerfully present and that we have the choice to respond to it, it creates conscious movement, inspires the law of attraction, and allows opportunities and further decisions that we are free to explore.

You well understand this consciousness and even the most subtle of energy dynamics, which exist within and around us. It is like web of interconnecting energy that reveals simple laws of cause and effect. All things in the universe are connected and affect one another on some level.

It is now a choice of the depth or the level you wish to create. It will also correlate with the level on which you wish to educate others as well. The level of your personal understanding and development will bring forth the required evolvement for those you are guiding.

Be it that you wish to see.

Be it that you wish to be.
Be it that you wish to create.
Believe it is here today!

We are to not separate or create any divisions whatsoever, so allow flow in communication, education, and simple understanding.

If we experience reaction, confusion, or fear, allow the feeling to be experienced, identified, and then released so that a creative and free-flowing energy can resume. People are ready to take responsibility and reveal their highest possibilities to themselves and explore all opportunities. It is a gift we have always had. Many are awakening to this gift and will feel a strong yearning to learn more from you.

You are earth angels and powerful cocreators! Relinquish any illusion of human limitations now and all will be revealed to you.

Amen

Dark vs. Light   14/11/2011

As it has always been, our existence is about evolving, expanding, and utilising our creative power correctly. Low, darker, or negative frequencies have always existed throughout this process. In fact, their presence has been a huge part of our evolvement. We know that where there is threat, there is a cause and there is fear. Fear allows our light to be penetrated. It is the ego that feels threat and responds with disempowerment or fight or flight to defend. So what are we defending?

The truth is, light cannot be destroyed, but through a negative self-belief, lower frequencies can be absorbed and integrated.

Awareness and acknowledgement of a stepping-out perspective is the key to viewing the situation and the rising emotion without spiralling into fear. Once we are aware of what triggers within, we can work with it.

Additionally, be conscious and aware of each choice you make. The shifts in the earth are causing some profound personal challenges. Emotional and mental housecleaning requiring active life changes are surfacing. Our decision-making is more liberated as we desire to live with heart and in balance along with creativity and prosperity.

As your choices are to clear to heal yourselves, and you are making decisions that bring you closer to your God self, and opposing forces may present themselves. Whatever is left within you that still functions from the ego-self will react. The ego-self feels threatened and fearful, and we can often confuse this inner reaction with how the world appears to be reacting to you. It is not the outside world—it is your inner world and its walls collapsing.

Your higher being, your soul, knows that this is your greatest challenge. Reward and acknowledge yourself, as you are doing very well. This challenge reminds you of and shows you the ultimate polarities.

But know this: you react to and fear only what still connects to you, or what you believe has the power to on some level control you. You need to literally take the attention away from this force, sever and disallow its infiltration. Upon acknowledging its presence, create a force field of light, either together or individually, and ask yourself within the safety of the light, "What is it that reacts within me?" The area of the body—or most specifically, the auric field—affected is at the mental and/or emotional body layer. It presents as a hook or hole or gash and simultaneously feels uncomfortable in the same area of the physical body.

Acknowledge this presence and firmly say, "I have acknowledged this frequency, which does not serve me any longer. I therefore dissolve any hook, thought-form, belief, or presence from myself and my environment. I disperse and hand it over to God to transmute. I ground and reacknowledge my connection to God and Mother Earth powerfully and safely. I know I am completely cleared, loved, and supported now."

The more light we infuse and consciously use upon earth, the more it creates. The Eden that will exist upon earth and in all dimensions it mirrors will fertilise the birth of nirvana.

Negative energy in its current form on our planet attempts to control and manipulate as a way of survival, to invoke mankind to act unlovingly and dishonour one another. Our shifts in consciousness and energy will not sustain such acts in the near future.

You are at the forefront, part of the ones leading the way. Spread these words of awareness. Allow your example to teach others, and inform them that they have a choice, as the time is at hand. The more you remove yourself from darkness, the more you acknowledge and render it powerless. Fill your life with light and love, and you will dissolve it entirely, until one day it will be no more and we will attain heaven on earth, as it is written.

Amen.

Note: Like a river that is polluted and begins to cleanse and regenerate, the water, the animal life, and plant life collectively support one another in this process and join to proliferate together. It begins with one action. When the light and clarity is infused to support life, it regenerates and recuperates quickly. Choose health and happiness now. Support and create your positive visions now, without delay. Everything you choose to connect with will present as you powerfully create your reality in every moment. When you feel the pull of modern life, retreat to nature—a forest, the ocean, a riverbank—to look, feel, and connect. This will help to bring you clarity and positivity always.

Thank you.

Amen

God's Hands   15/11/2011

We are walking along the aisle of an international supermarket. Feeling so positive and joyful, we view all of the available produce on the shelves. Laughing and loving life, we want to share in the prosperity, to share in the luscious selection in all of its abundance. These doors are open; we are welcome to enter at anytime.

We begin to connect to God consciousness. A beautiful electric-blue light permeates the image. The supermarket disappears behind the light, and only the light is present. It is vivid, electric-blue with white.

The power of the light emanates an intensity that relates to the speed of physical changes and manifestation. We are setting this vision, as it is so, today.

Huge hands can now be seen. They are God's hands;, palms facing upward in a cupped position, as if ready to hold pouring water. A glittering light pours forth into the cupped hands. Flowing and pure, it is a beautiful image. It represents an energy of flow and creation. It is strong and dynamic but also as loving and tender as a mother with her baby. It is so luscious and real. The feeling expressed is "plenty for all." It is God's love in the flow of creation and prosperity. The glittering, abundant energy pours down from the heavens, overflowing his hands and pouring downward towards the earth and towards us.

Bliss! It's like the most beautiful heavenly rain within a stream of love—white and glittering but solid and quite thick in appearance. It now flows in through the roof and all over us! It is incredibly beautiful.

An aerial view from above takes my vision towards the direction of The Ascension Centre site. Inviting and warm in all of her magnificence she stands, beaming her love and ready to embrace all.

Know she is there. Trust. The beautiful, glittering, white energy flows forth.

There's so much love here.

Amen

Perhaps one thousand metres above ground level, upon the edge of the clouds, I am on a magnificent, white, winged horse, galloping in full flight. I see mountaintops clearly, as though they just out of arm's reach. The air is so crisp. The wind is blowing moderately. I cannot help but be taken by the view.

These enormous mountains, statements of beauty and grandeur are testimonials to the energy of life on this planet. This huge structure has the encodement of the earth's structure for millions of years, maintaining hundreds of thousands of life forms. Every cycle and season, from snow and blizzard to summer heat and tropical rain, come what may, it always remains. The closer view brings more detail of the huge trees that have grown there for hundreds of years. Look closer again, and the magic begins to reveal itself with a magnified view of the various species of birds and insect life sustained within the trees. The forest floor is prolific with animal and insect life again, along with plants and flowers of the most beautiful variety.

Food is abundant in colour, variety, size, and taste, and all within a delicate ecosystem that functions perfectly and independently in a cyclic balance of seasons. There are no banks, doctors, or sports cars here. There is no requirement for human classification here. People have no contribution with their monetary injections here. Life here is self-sustaining. It is absolute perfection. It has all the power it needs to co-create and abundantly exist forever more. It is the undisputed. It is pure energy. It continuously streams enormous power. It is nature. It is God.

The symbolism: there rests a delicate butterfly upon the trunk of a five-hundred-year-old great oak. It is a powerful existence made up of the purity of life essence in two different forms. It is the energy of God, so both the butterfly and the great oak are of equal divinity, equally existing and created from the same light spark. It is God in varied states of being. It is the living statement of "I am that I am." I create effortlessly in the light of my Creator. I do not think it into being, as I am it. It is perfection, it is ongoing, and it is intentional from a force within the self. It comes not from ego, but of love. It comes not of dominance, but of survival with the quest to create balance. It comes from the inner knowing that my existence is part of a whole that serves to create further the bliss of knowing all that I am. How much I love and yearn to be that? It is perfect; as it is God in full expression.

Look to the mountain, look at all she holds lovingly and powerfully to her body. She creates unendingly, as do you.

If you understand the significance of the leaf that shades the forest floor, sheltering some plant and animal species, cooling the roots of the tree to allow the fruit to bear, which feeds the birds and further pollinates and fertilizes more growth, which sustains other life forms in the endless cycle of perfection, you will understand the meaning of life.

Your houses, your cars, your possessions and your jobs are extensions of you and your creative process. Rather than offering them power for your security and sustainability, offer more power to your creative life force, which sustains you.

The way to co-create poverty is to have a desperate dependence or fear over losing or not obtaining these items. The rabbit does not concern himself over lack of food. He is thoughtless in the process. He does know lack on any level as he expects to find his carrots. Rather than functioning on the level of working to sustain a lifestyle or comfort or thing, view it as irrevocably there and expected to manifest without question, no matter what the challenge.

The mountain sustains all life forms abundantly and without question. Trust in the process that God has the ability to sustain an entire universe and it's cycles, and that same force will sustain, support, and give to you easily and unquestionably.

Thank you.

Amen

"I'll never understand women, mate! God! I don't know, I tell ya, if you don't keep 'em in line and let 'em know whose boss, they'll ruin you, mate. They'll take everything. Can't be trusted. Their stupid, just stupid, no logic at all."

The Healing

Pure, blinding-white light with a low humming sound can be heard. This energy frequency and sound is wiping out this low vibration.

This is a testimony to your strength, but decisions must be made.

Jesus: My daughter, I come to you as I hear your call. You are in need of support and guidance and I give you that, for an eternity. You are being shown the ferocious side of the human ego. Mankind has wiped out entire villages with the same fuel. But this behaviour does not coincide with your beliefs or understanding. As you move forward towards your goals and you build and create others, you do not wish to have this battle wearing you down. Your strength must be used wisely. You left the Roman arrogance of the time, many, many years ago and many lifetimes ago.

The beauty of this era is in the creative opportunities, the consideration and absorption of new ideas, the free thinking and choices, and the ability to learn and deliver guidance in a modern way to those who ask this of you.

Many share a resistance to the concept "Let go and let God." It inspires a great deal of fear, as it appears to be asking to relinquish total control of one's environment. It is important to realise that choice and your belief in that choice are the key elements in all you achieve. If your choice is to move forward with commitment and positivity, your creative process will begin and certainly manifest, regardless of what another believes or says. It is your choice to allow external influences to infiltrate and taint your vision. The more you're able to view the situation, person, words, or beliefs as an outer perspective separate from you rather than a personalised attack or restraint, the easier you will find it to depersonalise the experience and be less affected by it. This is a revolutionary skill to learn and implement, and it will change your life.

A man can still feel a sense freedom, even within his jail cell, by utilizing his freedom of creative thought, word, and action. His ability to expand the self and grow is actually limitless, as the restrictions of the physical body are only a small portion of his potential. It is also true that a man can believe he is a prisoner even within his own home. It the state of mind and its domain—unlimited, expansive, creative, with the potential to reach far into the self—that is soul and the soul mind. If you fully encompass this truth and practise it, you will surpass much human drama and unnecessary ego influences.

This is true even when it comes to those closest to you. Allow your loved ones to be as they choose to be. Cast no judgement. But give yourself the same choice and freedom. The experience of interception, interference, imprisonment, manipulation, and bullying are all limitations of the mind placed in fear by another's loss of control of you and your choices. Nothing, and I mean nothing, can truly harm you.

I am eternally here supporting you, loving you, and touching your heart in the endless dance and endless flow of the divine, the delicious consciousness we are connected through. This is all you need to trust in. Your vision is your creation, and no one can stop what is not theirs. Only you have that power. The eternal cannot be broken, prevented, or tampered with unless you allow it.

With bliss.

We embrace.

I love you.

Jesus

The Best in the World:
Your Hidden Treasure   29/11/2011

The best news! Spread the word, spread the awareness, and spread the joy! Awaken to your God-self, that eternal spark of divinity within every human being on earth. How exciting it is to introduce you to this way of living! We are here to offer the way to perfect health and balance to all people. All that you desire, including peace, love, prosperity, and abundance, is within your grasp. We say, "Here, we have an option for you. It is not a big secret, and it's not only for some. It is available to all, and it lies within you. We intend to help you reveal your hidden treasure."

Truly a profound awakening, as you have orchestrated your entire lives, including making all major decisions, choosing careers, marriages, likes and dislikes, based on what you have or have not acquired. Material possessions and financial security have reigned in the number-one spot, and yet the heart can feel penniless. There are those who are extremely wealthy in material terms but desperately unhappy in their personal lives. The beauty of this is that no one is exempt, regardless of apparent poverty or wealth. Whether it be the stockbroker in New York, the winemaker in Italy, the perfumer in France, or the miner in Australia, the people behind the business or behind the issue are all living, loving, eating, creating, and sleeping, just like everyone else.

The unquestionable and united desire of every living person is happiness and love, regardless of their current life status. We seek to experience joy through a series of life events and relationships, inviting positive emotion and desire to achieve fulfilment and contentment. It is so wonderful, because once the creative stream of inner joy is flowing, one does not want it to stop it. We express it through passion and excitement, fuelling it further to ensure the process keeps moving forward and evolving.

And so, for the first time in history, we enter an era of conscious awareness to equally unite faith and intent with physical action, identifying aspects and blocks that require healing. We provide the key to giving the power back to the people. In truth, you have always had the power within your choices but were often unaware of it, or were blocked by fear-based beliefs.

Our aim is to awaken, encourage, and educate as many people worldwide as possible. Our healings, our teachings, and our books aim to educate all people, from the entrepreneur to the artist, to the banker or shop assistant, to the teacher, to the stay-at-home mum or dad, to the nurse and engineer working in any industry, at every level, across all countries and continents of this planet. There is no one exempt from this education or who cannot benefit from it. As we anchor and deliver these teachings with light and passion, they are infused with positive intentions and love.

Welcome to your awareness of self through healing, education, and conscious choice.

Opposing Forces   1/12/11

The force of the electricity, which is in fact intense static energy, is multiplying. Disperse it, relieve it, and breathe. Step away from this energy so that we can view it from an external point.

A family residing healthily together must be united in a collective energy for the protection, growth, and betterment of the group. Each member, however, will still be creating in their individual directions. Sometimes opposing or negative energies can infiltrate from one to another and purposely affect each other, especially if one is intent on dominating, controlling, or opposing another's choices. Whilst one person may recognise and take positive action to consciously disperse unhealthy energies, another may use the method of wanting to bulldoze them. They intend to be stronger and tougher than the opposing negative force. This in fact drives further attention to it and creates more of the same destructive pattern. It becomes a battle of titanic forces, each trying to outdo the other. Energetically, this is like a massive tidal wave crashing down over the an enormous fire, then a huge explosion surpasses the previous blaze, so a larger tsunami is created from the earthquake erupting beneath to wipe out the huge flames, and so on and so forth. There's no end to the destruction—until one surrenders or dies!

We acknowledge the need for calm and centring. We acknowledge the need for self, as well as collective, assessment. Some people do not learn easily by previous error; rather, they wish to push harder to erase the error. One cannot learn and change direction and therefore create a different outcome without assessing the experience and their part in it. If we do not take at least half the responsibility in all that we experience, we are missing a vital clue. As hard as this may be to hear, this is completely true: no matter what the circumstances and creation are around you right now, you are half of the equation and the result. It's interesting to note how that realisation feels in your body. Have you noticed that it takes the emotional peg down somewhat when we stop to think about our part in it all? It's like a cooling breath on a potentially heated finger-pointing blame fest. Stop, breathe, and assess.

People will continue to experience this in one way, shape, or form until they relinquish the need to control others. You can suggest, guide, offer, and lead by example, but you cannot control or make another do as you do, no matter how much you believe your truth feels right for someone else.

As a soul, lessons of the body are chosen pre-incarnation. Other people play a huge role in your life, each coordinating and cooperating in the experiences of one another out of love and compassion for your individual goals and further evolvement. Wouldn't it be wonderful for us to remember this when we are attempting to stifle, control, or manipulate each other?

How true the words, "We can lead a horse to water but cannot make him drink it." The ultimate choice for others, like yourself, is theirs, leading to their desired experience from that choice.

Putting a type of self-management in place may be helpful. These are considerations or choices regarding how much you will exceed a personal boundary to accommodate another. But ultimately, we choose our own experience of everything, and this again would be another choice with consequences.

Even if we acknowledge the force of two individuals working together on achieving the same experience, there will still be a different experience and consequence for each individual.

Various mental and emotional assessments, likes and dislikes, will individualise the experience and its outcome, regardless of how you may think it would be the same.

An intricate and ever-changing web of the law of attraction, cause and effect, karmic and genetic influences makes for a very complex and perfect reality for all people.

We honour and allow the energy process to support us in all ways.

Two powerful words to remember in a power struggle: let go.

That is all.

Dear God   *14/12/2011*

Dear God,

One of the greatest healers of our time is with us. Please strengthen, refine, and develop her expansive energy and provide her with the understanding of what presents on a client to best guide and heal them.

Today we acknowledge another step in the evolutionary process and an initiation that is an expanded level of incoming healing energy into the crown, heart, and hands to equally receive. In the process of healing and clearing the energies of a person, the heart and hands equally expand to a higher level of consciousness and understanding. The crown has opened further, in both volume of light and in higher frequency. Within this frequency is an intricate web, a matrix of energy lines that represent and impart important information to help understand the issue at hand. This information, when broken down and viewed in finer detail, holds the story, aspect, past life, or theme of what the soul wants to heal. It has a direct link into the akashic records of that person. To have access to these records holds a very high honour, a sacred right that can never be misused.

People are now able to heal and understand the many aspects that have been holding them back. It is no longer a case of "bad luck" or that they've been given the "hand that has been dealt." This is a coordinated effort, and our responsibility is to educate and allow the person to choose again. At a soul level, the individual always chooses. However, a united perspective of both personal and soul-aligned awareness allows healing to be very fast and powerful.

Miracles and joy will be experienced by all participating because they are purposefully clearing and lovingly in unison with their highest good. It is life changing. If this is yet to be fully embraced, you will know when you do, as all of your preparation and years of life experience have led you to this point, and it will most certainly continue and develop further. The unification of your vessel (body) with your clairsentient and clairaudient messages will provide a balance, allowing a very clear understanding of what you are working with and what needs to be cleared and healed.

Jesus: My child, you are perfect and you are whole. Do not doubt. As your path is laid before you, you step one foot in front of the other. Listen and learn, as it is all given to you. Whilst you love and participate in life alongside many souls, in truth you need only to listen to the God voice within yourself. I am communicating with you, and I ask you to trust this. Your body, mind, and emotions are being prepared. This is ideal as a teacher, as you must be student first.

We are working and living directly from a dimension of service. You have ascended energetically, and others on earth have joined you.

Your body has changed extensively, allowing a more concentrated light and frequency within. It's nourishing and replenishing you. You may feel the shift in your cells that will extend out to your flesh. It will appear like an inner glow, and it truly is. Be aware and honour this. Take some time to acknowledge this gift by giving yourself food nourishment, fresh air, meditation, touch, and beauty.

We are on the edge of the new world reality. There is an expanded consciousness that is held with the wisdom of the heart, and all of humanity can take refuge and find love and peace here. My heart sings, I love you all so much.

He circles around you clockwise extending his left hand out to you as he exits.

Rainbow explosion of light.

That is all.

Male leadership has been an accepted part of our history, and men have always had control, particularly as the dominant sex between male and female. Women have been natural healers and nurturers and unquestionably connected to their spiritual existence. The very fact that they bring forth life through their bodies as vessels of life and light, being the bridge for souls to descend to earth and experience their human purpose, is a profound creative expression.

A human in balance, whether that be male or female, unites their spirit with mind consciousness, acceptance, honour, and wisdom to a physical expression of life. And he/she knows this is the greatest gift.

Women have naturally initiated and practised the concept of women's intuition, and it has been widely accepted across both sexes. It is a timeless part of our genetic encoding and soul blueprint when incarnating as female. Many divinely related titles have been created and referred to within feminine context, such as the Divine Feminine, the Great Goddess, the Mother of All Creation, and ultimately Mother Earth.

Every part of being feminine and having this perfect vessel to bring forth creation (not just on a physical level) is an expression of evolution, growth, birth, spirituality, and life. Those women who are unable to conceive or choose not to are no different. All women exist in a powerful cycle of energy, in that their very bodies are naturally magnetised to the gravitational pull of the earth and her cyclic nature. Her energy, her very existence, is part of the larger energy of the feminine, whether her body is used as a physical vessel or not. The nurturer, the great huntress, the teacher, the goddess exists in balance of all life, in the ebb and flow of the oceans and moon cycles, and in the creative force of any manifestation of anything.

In our recent history, we have not been the best at honouring the feminine. In fact, it had been mostly considered a threat in need of controlling. We have seen evidence of this imbalance in all organised religions, institutions, educational facilities, businesses of all industries, places of worship, health, all areas of leadership, across all countries in varying degrees, in countless societies, and into many, many homes.

Today, we see evidence that this is shifting, but it is important to acknowledge that whilst we are experiencing much needed change, it is imperative that the roles of the feminine and masculine are not confused and made to challenge one another once again for supremacy. Otherwise, we achieve nothing. As many modern societies have been making positive and appropriate changes, we as a people have gingerly approached the transition and have been attempting to redefine our roles.

In response, females have engaged and exercised over-masculinity in an attempt to regain power and position. Males have responded often with confusion, doubt, and fear, either retaliating with chauvinism, passive aggression, or becoming the submissive in an attempt to counterbalance, none of which is realistic, productive, or healthy. It is important to reach back into the intrinsic beauty and power that each sex naturally resonates with and holds. We must reconnect, accept, and understand that we are the perfect opposite of each other but magnificently in unison with one another. Feminine energy, anchored strength, vitality, fertility, creative flow, and greater wisdom requires no masculine power whatsoever. And masculine energy can rest assured in his solid, protective, but nurturing strength of creative action, which does not require submissive behaviour compromising his strength in physical leadership.

Each encompasses gifts, and this has a strong impact on how we embrace this wonderful opportunity to graciously rebalance the earth and her human children once more.

In greater understanding of attraction, when people gather together, the subject matter will be the focus of interest and attract likeminded people, not preconceived expectations or gender. We will appreciate the individual gifts each person has to offer, and within them the expression of the feminine and masculine can flow forth without restriction. It will be joyful in this new age, with past misconceptions (including karmic and genetic) being long outdated.

The information will be delivered, and the creative process will be unfolding, flowing effortlessly, with every moment. Experiencing and learning is as wonderfully simple as that.

Let go and allow.
The new way is coming.
It is welcomed indeed.
That is all.

Galloping in on a fast moving chariot, led by a magnificent white horse, is St. Christopher. He halts the chariot before us and announces, "The path is clear!"

The whip cracks, and immediately an energy stream of white light forms a pathway. This pathway is the road representing our vision, and it is clear. The energy surrounding its purpose far exceeds the resistance by negative forces to obstruct it.

This situation is not a contest and certainly not an issue that will have any impact on your plans. Putting certain actions in place now is a wise pre-paving. The rest will fall into place. You are hearing guidance clearly and accurately. Expansion, which has begun with you energetically, is now streaming and coordinated with your physical being. A strong anchor is able to root in the ideas/creativity/passion, allowing production and manifestation on the physical plane.

Energetically, you must resonate at the same frequency as your desired outcome so that your outer world matches you, and you it. In truth, you can create anything, anything at all. You just have to believe that it is viable. The universe has an endless supply of energy available to you at your request. The vibration you give out and the extent to which you believe your dreams to be forthcoming is the key to manifestation. Aim as high as you wish, and do not allow others to taint your vision. Doubt, fear, or scepticism is only present because you still hold a belief that doubt or fear is real to you and has the ability to prevent the outcome. Learn and release this, as it is an unnatural position for you to embrace. It has no validation in a universe which aims to create, embellish, and proliferate.

You have chosen this task and certainly the perfect biological family to experience such challenges so that you could learn these skills and impart the greater teaching to others. Be not threatened or tired from this experience. Embrace it and watch it unravel excitedly as a child does, with all the wonder of a miraculous discovery!

When you absorb at every level of your being that you are the creator of your life in its entirety and that nothing and no one can stop your evolution besides yourself, you will then truly be the captain of your vessel. You will able to shift gears to cruise through and travel unbound anywhere you wish to go.

You have surpassed much, and your faith and strength is the glue.

One dream in action follows the other, as the physical plane moves into alignment with your vision.

We are here. The path is clear.
Have love and gratitude in your heart.
Amen

Jesus sits at a banquet table surrounded by his closest, including the Apostles.

With his beloved by his side, he gently touches her cheek. He has a love for her that is eternal.

We are gathered here today to celebrate the return of a heart ministry. Many earth years have passed since the days we were all together and united physically on earth. We now joyfully celebrate those who step forward to sit in these seats, we acknowledge and we love them as they give, heal, and teach as we did, pray as we did, trust and believe as we did, lead and love as we did.

Compassion and service runs through their veins, and they are adorned in cloaks and crowns of knowledge and wisdom, as gifted and accepted from heaven. They are today's healers 2012, led by my daughter in soul and flesh. Walking the path with faith and determination synonymous with my bloodline provides an example for all of humanity to follow, as was always the intent. We are all brothers, sisters, mothers, and fathers, and in truth all part of a universal bloodline of love. We are naturally creative and desire balance and healing. We are born to light the way for all people who are wanting to completely embrace and love their lives. This time on earth is undergoing and experiencing a fifth-dimensional shift that requires guidance, education, and unconditional love.

Over thousands of years, the purpose has been the same. Each time you all incarnated and contributed to one another and the collective, it brought the learning and ascension, the evolutionary purpose, closer, consciously and lovingly, within our grasp.

In a parallel but coexisting realm, another table appears with yourself seated at its centre surrounded by twelve others, six to each side. There is much joy, laughter, connection, and love. Some reside internationally, but celebrations bring forth a unified gathering from time to time. When the group gathers, look beside you diagonally (at approximately five feet above ground level). The original banquet table will be gathered as well.

Amen.

The teacher will attract the student, and the student the teacher. It is perfection. And so it is the healer will attract those in need of healing to create health for all. It is law.

* * *

Those who are hungry, step forth to feed. There is plenty of food. We acknowledge, however, we cannot force you to eat or consume it for you.

* * *

The past is a kaleidoscope of colour, experience, and wisdom. The wisdom is what we bring forth within us to teach and then learn and expand on once again. It is an endless journey of soul. Ego has no negative power over the humble, as being humble is empowered. Therefore, be humble.

The knowledge and the vision of who you are and who you wish to be is the pinnacle point of attraction and therefore your self-perception. Stand for no less than what you admire in others, other great ones who taught and healed before you. You have surpassed much, but it is important to keep your focus forward. Those who have an agenda or karmic lessons to experience will do so, as it is their creative and healing process to partake in. As a teacher you may witness this, but we must always allow them the freedom to choose.

Your sensitivity will be heightened considerably as you continue to assimilate further increases in energy and awareness. The reality is, as much as we wish we could wipe away the tears from every person in pain, this would not support the greater process of an evolving soul. If this were all that was needed to eradicate all the pain in this world, wouldn't God have done this ten thousand times over by now? We understand that every person and their spirit is a much-loved divine child of the universe and she/he is always protected, guided, and nurtured every day of their lives. There are many, many light beings and angels who are illuminating your darkened way towards a new light. We trust in this and thank you. As co-travellers, we offer loving compassion, faith, and hope for each one of our brothers and sisters who walk this planet at this time.

As for you, your quest has begun. Those who are coming forward are sent to help you create your vision.

Remember, if you release the tightened grip and allow your hands to be open and relaxed, there is room to grow and expand. Be open to the unexpected and the element of surprise. It makes life so exciting!

Love you eternally,

Mary Magdalene

I love and honour thy vessel. It is an instrument of peace, of healing,
of love towards myself and every man, woman, and child that I meet.
I know this is to be true, unto my home on earth and beyond.

It is vast and clear, the atmosphere so thin in this dimension. It has an oscillating vibration that is not measurable.

There are rings of light in a frequency that support this environment, and it is surrounding me. I have lost the sensation of my body. I am the frequency, and it is me. We correspond together in a dance of vibration, in colour and blissful emotion, in unison, moving, shifting, and matching one another then expanding and moving again.

There is no preference between night and day in this dimension (even though it does exist); however, the evening provides a darker, cooler, undistracted energy that brings forth messages in a theta state, inspiring dream time and soul travel. My soul rests and rejuvenates. In alignment with my growth and expansion, this frequency is light and expansive, eliminating anything that spins slower.

For centuries man has been aware of the laws of cause and effect. The brain correlates and understands that an action causes a reaction. This is accurate on every level.

The biggest concerns for people are the reactions that they don't understand and therefore fear. Reactions feel painful when our basic survival instincts are threatened. At this point on earth, we are not ready as a species to completely eliminate basic physical survival instincts, as we still require food, shelter, and warmth.

Very young children are experimental with touch in learning from their external world. As we develop into adults, we have experienced much about cause and effect, both in our physical world and with relation to the relationships we have with one another. Our actions and behaviours will affect those around us, and we learn to anticipate this as we mature. To practise consideration and compassion, empathy and good faith in people is part of being a balanced, loving human being.

We need to turn down the volume on an over-stimulated and over-aggressive society. Our television, entertainment, gaming, and social media are all part of that stimulation, which depersonalises conscious responsibility and moral ethics.

Pain doesn't always have to represent a negative. It is our internal guidance system that alerts our attention. It is an important part of life and our growth. What's important here is that we approach pain with a new perspective. Rather than avoid it, we can embrace its message and implement appropriate action. A desensitizing world will retract and medicate against pain. But we are in the process of rewriting a modern age. Discomfort and pain are present as our spirits voice to embrace learning and implement necessary changes within. Once our internal world heals and changes, our external world mirrors that.

We are part of an earth community, and we understand that those who choose to journey and heal alongside us will experience the same. Resistance, reaction, emotion, and yes, pain are all part of the necessary shifts. These reactions express that clearing and healing are taking place, and there is no easier method or medication that will alter or quicken this process. The more we own it and release into it, the quicker and easier the integration and the joyous acceptance and celebration of strength we will have.

We ask for a gentle integration and an understanding of the process.

We pave the way for future generations to experience.

With gratitude, thank you.

Divine Conduit   12/1/2012

It is with gratitude that we acknowledge that we have access to divine guidance through those who are highly intuitive, refined readers. We all have this gift, with various levels of understanding and ability, but we usually doubt the messages we receive. And so we may choose to seek guidance through a reader, an intuitive, an oracle, or a scribe. How wonderful that even in our heaviest and most challenging times of doubt and fear, we are able to seek the wisdom and unlimited source of wisdom through the invisible dimension of true love and guidance. In this way, we are accessing a divine Mother and Father, no matter how old we are chronologically.

God, the Divine, Buddha, the Universe, or however you wish to refer to our Source, has an unlimited array of choices in materials, modalities, courses, people, music, and images to assist every single individual on our planet in all ways. It doesn't matter what nationality or background you are from, whether you are wealthy or not, female or male—there is no criteria or position where anyone is exempt. You are all part of the divine embrace, and you are never, ever alone during anytime of your life, no matter how you may think to the contrary. The messages are always being relayed to you in various ways; it is often the case that you simply miss them.

In whatever fashion the message is delivered, always give thanks. Gratitude is an important life practise, no matter how loud or silent you wish to state it.

Make your gratitude a continuous attitude.

The block or challenge you may face comes when you are expecting to receive your message or guidance in a particular way. For instance, if you expect guidance to only be received after attending church or the synagogue, then you will be missing out on a great deal more! The messages are continuous and in all ways all around you.

Imagine that your entire life is a painting that is alive! It is an ever-changing landscape of images, colour, and texture, with God or the Divine Source helping you paint it. If you understand that you can choose each colour, image, and texture to create the picture you want, and that your spirit support team may suggest various ways to paint it, offering a large selection of brushes and sponges to use, you will then begin to get an idea of how your life is and the potential that it has. It truly is a magnificent creative process; we just have to fully embrace it as such. Most of us currently use the minimum resources available. Consider this a moment of change and begin to really look around you. You will be amazed at what you see.

For those of you who still require to work with trust and heal self-belief, you may be more comfortable and feel secure in seeking the direct guidance of a reader. He/she may present to you as a medium, a channel, an automatic writer or scribe, a tarot or angel card reader, an intuitive artist, a clairaudient, clairsentient, or clairvoyant. All are available to you, and you can always use your inner guidance system to help you choose a person who feels good for you. You will know, so trust this.

All guidance and messages are unrestricted, given to you at any time of day, in any place. We must allow guidance, love, and wisdom to come forth via any channel that we are willing to acknowledge and listen to.

Restriction and fear exist only to show you that you hold an unhealed aspect or energy. So if your fear feels overwhelming or valid, it is only because the human ego is engaged and healing is required. Step away from your need to control or suffer and ask for guidance. You will automatically begin to experience an altered awareness, a change in energy, when you surrender and ask for help.

Our true soul being only wants to support our continued evolvement and open all doors to a happy, fulfilled, creative life of continued opportunities. So let it be.

With gratitude, thank you.

Freedom   14/2/2012

....

I see you, each arm held in chains that bind you. You plunge forward furiously, ferociously, expressing your anger at being bound by something that does not serve your evolvement. Lunging forward, the metal cuffs tear at the skin. You do not feel the pain, or you simply don't care if you do. Freedom is your goal, and the pain will subside.

Snap! You are momentarily shocked at your own strength! In amazement, you look at your left arm, now free. Only the right is still enchained. You use your left hand to fiddle with the lock; it is tight and secure. A big deep breath, and the frustration is calmed a little. You stop, concentrate to regulate your breathing, and stand perfectly straight and still. The room darkens, and only a spotlight shines above. You take your free left hand and place it over the right cuff lock. A slow motion movement, and *clang!* The sound rings out as the cuff drops to the floor. You rub your grazed wrist. You begin walking in a circle, anticlockwise. Then you stand facing forward. Your arms outstretch upward and towards the light above.

The scene brightens, and suddenly it is daylight.

It is an open field, a natural setting of grass and trees with a soft breeze blowing. It is calm and light. It is a place of rest, of reflection. You choose a comfortable place and sit in the long grass. The trees are nearby; the temperature is warm and comfortable; birds fly across in the clear blue sky; and you are at peace. It is time for you to rest and rejuvenate. You lay back in the grass, and you're aware that you are somewhat hidden from the world, as this is your time. How lovely that feels. This is your time to create and regain the balance of self. Within

219

this peaceful space, you can explore and check in with your internal guidance system, which is accurately tuned to your highest and most joyous goals and desires. A soft, relaxed smile comes over your face as you connect with the true you. There is no one else here wanting and demanding. Just you and your visions, your dreams, and your purpose.

You are well aware that the dramas of life have been able to penetrate you, drain you, and affect you, and on some level, you have allowed this to occur. But ever so lovingly, you accept this and forgive yourself. You realign your intentions and goals. We are coexisting and travelling alongside our soul families, entering this world with our unique input and output to create and experience all that we wish for our evolvement.

Do not be influenced by fear in any shape or form. No one else but you decides and creates your experience. We occasionally need to remind ourselves about our intent and instigate action, sealing it with faith. Our feelings are our guide. Trust in the awareness you feel and truly understand that your creation has no limits. It is your experience to unfold.

But as coexisting relationships influence one another, we must recognise where we consciously or unconsciously hand over our power. It is not unusual at all. Families are the perfect example of this. Mother to child, husband to wife, brother to sister, friend to friend.

This is the time for retreat, reflection, reenergising, allowing your freedom and your creative power to be reinstated.

You are responsible for no other but yourself.

Let no man, woman, or circumstance instil an illusion that your life is held back because of external beliefs or ideals. This is an obstruction and a lie. Recognise it for what it truly is and continue on your path.

Lay within the long grass for as long as you need.

Healing has taken place.

Amen

God-Force Healing   15/2/2012

The healing energy you now channel is a phenomenal force.

Vision: A large mountain. There is an explosion that causes a momentary blackout of daylight and a large shadow to thump against the mountain's surface. This causes the trees to bend and wave back into position.

You have asked to be able to perform God-force healings. This is your evolvement and the level at which you want to work and heal. The receiving of that level of energy in its condensed version is filtered to a point. Each body will receive the same frequency, but as it integrates with them personally, it will respond in a manner that is fully owned by them. In other words, it is a digestion and processing, a birthing that will be undertaken at their own speed, regardless of its intensity.

Each individual has an intention, and Spirit listens closely to what he/she has asked for. The healing frequency will be the same regardless, as that's your intention and purpose as a healer. Those who desire a slower integration and a gentle journey will filter it through at their own pace. Free will and choice is truth. For those who are ready, whether they are fully conscious of it or not, the healing will create the shift at the level that the person needs. The changes and shifts will be significant when a person really wants change. It is important to understand that our world is changing quickly. The ebb and flow of existence will have low and high tides. We cannot escape it, as the earth beats to a regularity and cycle that all life grows and flows with.

There are times that we need to retreat into quiet, positive prayer. Integration is happening on various levels in multi directions. You don't need to do anything other than trust in this knowing.

Every person is feeling the huge planetary shifts now occurring. It will pass. Like labour pains, the contractions come and go, and birth is evident.

Thou shalt not be afraid nor falter,

I am with thee.

Big deep in breath, and exhale.

That is all.

Who Am I Becoming,
and How Do I Know It's Right?   *6/3/2012*

Your whole life passage has come to this point.

There are some issues you ponder and questions you ask.

Am I energy healer? Am I teacher? Am I wife? Am I mother?

We are never just one element or identity. Like a flower with many petals, we are multifunctional, multiskilled beings. So in truth, you are all of these things, but we know that wherever you set your passionate focus upon, doors will open for further development.

In the past, when you wanted to spread the word from your forest cottage, you invoked and concocted elixirs, incenses, and resins aiming to enhance your knowledge by practising natural medicine and earth healing. You were well known within your local vicinity but wished to inspire followers from afar. You were frustrated with the low number of people you could treat and teach. Hence, after ten years, you decided to pack up and move to the great city of London.

Living within the seclusion of a forest was quiet and safe, as the commonly hunted and executed were witches, whether they be white or otherwise. But the desire to discover and seek overrode the risk. You solemnly believed that if it was God's plan for you to die in service, so be it. You no longer feared those consequences, as that low vibration of fear belonged to the fearful, not you.

How far do you persist in obtaining something that is depleting you? If various methods and attempts have led to the same block and unpersuasive result, not another second of your time and energy should be spent on it. It is a waste of time. We all have challenges in life that are designed to create definitive choices, and there are challenges in life that you persist with because you fear the outcome of a choice once you make it. You already know that challenges are remarkable teachers. They extend your boundaries, flex your muscles, and exceed your comfort zone. These are healthy challenges.

Challenges also stop you in your tracks and allow you to check in with self and reevaluate your motives. Does it serve? Will all this effort get you on track to your desired goal and wisest understanding of the journey? Once you answer yes or no, you will confidently sense what feels right for you and what does not. Wherever there is a situation that entraps you, denies your freedom, stops growth, is uncreative and manipulative—these are prominent warning signs, and it is time to change direction and reassess your reasons to persist. These environments and circumstances will never be supportive of your growth or your creative endeavours. Freedom is always the key issue.

From this perspective, we can understand that when one lives, loves, and works in creative flow (with freedom), there are no restrictions to the creation of any form or manifestation. This environment has all doors open, all of the time. Communication of your creativity and leading by example to inspire others through your representation adds further creative power, through an act of service.

Pleasing results come forth without interruption or interception. However, if a fear of another matches yours, it will be a block in your plans, or it will simply be a flag for you to reassess how important you find another's opinion to be regarding your development. In truth, we do affect one another; how can we not? Particularly if our loved ones attempt to intercept or stifle our growth through fear and dominance.

This will be of the highest tests for you personally. How far will you allow another to control your life, your path, and your development? When will we all decide that enough is enough and mean it?

All people make a difference to each other as we collectively contribute to the energy shifts of the planet. But as individuals, the single-most unholy act we partake in, the greatest misconception we hold, is that we have the permission to stifle, control, or interfere with another human being's desire to love and live their soul purpose in flesh.

Let it go if you cannot decide nor see your destination clearly at this moment. Swim away from the wave that attempts to wash over you. Allow the waters to shower and disperse. Don't worry, you will still be standing. Look ahead to the distant shore. There is something you already know, but we will remind you: you are never alone, nor unsupported. There is always tomorrow and every opportunity available for your highest good. This is guaranteed.

We are always by your side, showering our love, protection, and guidance towards you. All you have to do is ask and it is given.

Collective light beings of God.

The river runs red, and its flow is swift and strong. It is of blood, its life force travelling to unchartered streams. The element of surprise is at hand. As much as we insist on planning our lives, some things are:

1) left up to the divine force, which supports our desires, and

2) the subject of creativity, which is ever changing according to choice.

There are so many elements to consider as we try to adapt to the ever-changing energies encircling us. These changes relate to the enormous global energy changes, which people are feeling in their personal lives, as well as the many issues affecting them on a local and international level.

These changes are also initiating releases and spontaneous healing in people, which may have lay dormant for a long time. The releases are patterns of energy that no longer serve the current state of evolution. The body no longer matches the exterior vibration on the planet and therefore sparks an interior revolution! The soul wishes to forge forward and progress. It only knows this. It only responds to this. Release and experience it with openness and gratitude. Globally, this is occurring with all people of all countries. As inhabitants of a planet that is healing herself, our shifts are inevitable.

The work of the healer is positioned at the forefront of this experience, as she/he will also be experiencing these effects but will need to be guiding and educating those who are seeking to understand what is happening to them. There are very sensitive people who will be feeling the impact on their bodies most intensely. We recommend these people create a quiet place, a safe haven of comfort to ground themselves. Then they should gather as much support and guidance as possible. All people need to reflect and assess, but mostly practise self-love and nurture.

The disarray of energies may cause confusion and doubt. Do not be swept up by their uncontrolled spinning. Quieten your mind, connect to your heart, and reaffirm to yourself that this period will soon pass. Tiredness and fatigue may be strongly experienced as well. Allow yourself to rest, giving much nurturing, love, and understanding to yourself and each other during this time.

The voicing of your thoughts and feelings is an important representation of your inner experience. Allow the free-flowing release and ensuing wisdom to channel through you. As light workers, your old programs will need release for the transition to occur within you and allow you as teacher to lead by example those you guide and heal. Do not fear the uprising emotions and thoughts. Acknowledge them as you release and be aware of how grateful you are to have come this far. Commend yourself for your courage and fortitude.

"Need" is all around you. People "need" answers, "need" clearing, "need" healing, "need" help. The *needing* energy must be transformed to that of *choosing*. No one is exempt from help and healing; therefore, "need" in its desperate or limited emotion is not required. Choice, on the other hand, is required by all. Without making the choice to release and heal, one cannot fully integrate and enjoy the relief of change.

Need as desperation creates more desperation. Many who experience this turmoil will not understand why their lives are in such chaotic disarray.

We encourage you to cease the internal chatter.

We encourage you to quieten your mind.

We encourage to sit quietly and allow yourself to feel the emotion and identify it.

Ask for the presence of an angel, guide, or God to be beside you.

We encourage you to ask the questions, and we encourage you to listen for the answer.

It may sometimes not be the answer you expect, but nevertheless it is the answer you will hear.

We encourage you to know that there is no such thing as failure or loss.

Continue to dream, to create, and to believe in what you are creating. Allow the time to meditate on it undisturbed for fifteen minutes daily. Set forth the intention of your desires and goals. You are the creator, and you have no limitations other than those you set upon yourself.

Look outside of your usual comfort zone. This is when we utilize a formerly unexplored energy field of possibility. There is great power in this.

Allow all forms of opportunity to approach you. Trust you will be shown and guided to the right path. As each new opportunity presents, you will know what to do. Focus on now, as the past only reflects a former position and energy that no longer exists in reality.

There is much love surrounding and encompassing your tremendous gifts. This is part of the growth needed to realise your goals.

Hand on your heart, step forward today. Begin with positive action and belief of your potential, which is truly unlimited.

Amen

A golden waterfall of light with a brightness and beauty I cannot completely describe showers down over us, over the earth, and over all of humanity. It is the Christ, the purest of love for the earth and her inhabitants. The only desire is to be in bliss. We experience this state between incarnations and sometimes with alternate incarnations; therefore, we do know it. We are at a pinnacle point of change on our planet. Human incarnation is meeting an extraordinary challenge. But you can do it. You embark and travel full of light, love, and goodwill into an existence of resistance.

Prior to now, the surface vibration approximately twenty feet from ground level was completely infused with a type of resistant energy, partly because of the nature of material things and gravity, and partly because of the heaviness of the physical body, which also emanates a vibration of the spirit/emotional/ mental self. A combination of unhealthy and dysfunctional actions and behaviours, such as consuming drugs or alcohol, smoking, violence, pollution, and negative thinking (to name a few) additionally creates a thick blanket of energy smog.

Those of you who are increasing in your sensitivity will be able to feel such energy quite intensely. Fortunately, through the personal shifts and global awareness of many individuals, a mass cleansing continues to wash this energy and its density. This energy is thinning and supported by global shifts in energy, both energetically and physically, in people as well as Mother Earth, to assist in dispersing it further. As a result your light bodies (auric and spirit bodies) are releasing and clearing. Many of you are working through your karmic and ancestral clearings quicker with great awareness, and are no longer inviting unhealthy situations.

You may feel it like an impact on your upper body and head. This may appear in the form of a common cold or flu (as it needs to clear from the cells) or headaches. If you are experiencing these, this is your signal to clear and release and practise self-nurture. You are quickly acknowledging with awareness and learning. As we experience these sometimes intense physical and emotional changes, it must be understood that as a collective energy, the mass of people residing here on the surface will be pushing, enhancing, and revealing the required clearing and changes simultaneously.

We are assisting you and overseeing your progress. We support you with love and comforting energy to assist you in these times of change and challenge. Breathe deeply and know this is a time that must be experienced and allowed by all. No living thing is exempt, not even your animals. Nurture and love more than ever—everyone, each other, even the ones who challenge you as they are all experiencing the fear and doubt. Many have forgotten their divinity and the choice to be here at this time. Remember, love conquers all. Love eliminates low vibration. Your prayers and intent to shift density helps a great deal.

See the energy lifting and dispersing, and envision the ground level infused with light.

Creatively, you will seek no better time. Your creative energy will manifest quickly. Just allow and accept movement at this moment. This is the bridging gap or transition.

Remember to breathe, and use your breath as a tool to outflow and release.

Breathe in to energise and regenerate.

Set an intention to clear every day.

Channelled with Patrizia Trani

Let nothing of your past hold you back. Your past is gone and irrelevant. Today is your unfolding present.

Then give thanks for this knowledge and awareness.

God

That is all.

It is a sunny warm day, and I am lying on the sand of a beautiful beach.

As I lie resting, I am happy and calm. I am aware that I had been feeling exhausted, but I rest well now. From the shoreline a figure approaches. I know we must speak, and I wait. It is a man wearing all white. I don't know him, but part of me recognises him.

"I am Germain," he says, smiling at me. "You tire? I understand that you have carried. Burdens are, by nature, too heavy, but we persist through the discomfort and continue to carry the load. Why? Because we aren't sure whether it is a challenge needing to be met and learned from or an exceeded boundary and misunderstood responsibility.

"Your incarnation is of an experiential nature. Sometimes only learning the lesson and accepting its gifts occurs in hindsight; however, it needn't be so difficult. Alter your perception to include awareness and clarity before making your choices, and include the question, 'Does this lead to inner peace?'"

Germain continues, "We look at the equation A+B=C. Let us consider and find C, which represents your true heart's desire. Then you can identify how to best manifest A+B, allowing your path and this magnificent earth and her dynamics to bring you fruition.

"I'm here to help you fully discover and accept your role. You have been a bit like an ostrich placing her head in the sand! You are aware of your appearance and presence, but when you're overwhelmed and unsure, you hide away into a dark space, hoping that's enough to disguise you. There is no need to hide your beauty, your offering, your love and wisdom from yourself or this world, as it is very needed indeed.

"You are part of a glistening, diamond-lit sky in our cosmos, shining with so much light. Take this time to rest and rejuvenate so that you can recommence brighter, lighter, and with the inner peace you desire."

I respond with such enormous gratitude! I feel the lightness, the weight of burdens lifting from me as I lay in the warm sunshine.

I reply, "I understand all you have imparted. I will rest and replenish."

"The time approaches where you will not need nor desire rest," he says, smiling.

I say, "You look so real!"

"I am!" He responds, and we both laugh.

Lying back, so relaxed on the warm sand, I watch the birds flying high in the bluest of skies.

I look at Germain, staring up at the sky next to me. He looks back at me and smiles.

We are completely content to allow this time in quiet enjoyment. His eyes are such an intense electric blue colour.
I am inner peace.

There is a beautiful pink heart made up entirely of pink roses. The roses are in full bloom. It truly depicts the beauty of love in all of our senses.

All women are great. Women have a natural power owned only by them. They have the ability to bring forth creation with such an enormous capacity to love that one draws a deep breath in awe and in appreciation of them. A woman's ability to survive, gather, protect, and gently nurture all at the same time has given her the association, title, and mentor of Great Goddess.

Women have unfortunately seen a much harsher reality on earth for the last two thousand-plus years. During this time, our female counterparts struggled to survive, were rendered unholy or untrustworthy, and were seen as possessions.

Thankfully, we are now in a time where false beliefs and principals are no longer tolerated. This is not exclusive or only on a personal level within families, but across every area of life in our businesses, educational institutions, and spiritual institutions, on all karmic and genetic levels. We acknowledge and welcome a new age of empowerment for the enlightened view and appreciation of the feminine. The shift and new awareness of truth will occur very fast. It has been in the process of change for the last decade, and we are now experiencing and owning the finality of that change. We must express who we are in all we do.

Men, who are true and comfortable with their identity, will know that their strength of masculine self is the pure power, and it is breathtakingly beautiful. It is solid, loving, and protective (not dominating or controlling). Men will gratefully support and celebrate this change to fully embrace the freedom and exploration of their female counterparts in all their magnificence. He will feel the balance within himself and enjoy the full expression of his masculinity through her. The two will lovingly unite—perfection as it should be.

We can ask for no greater union in spirit and flesh.

In the union of Jesus and Mary Magdalene:

Mary Magdalene: My body was Mother Earth, my spirit was keeper of the flame, and my mind the expansion of the universe in all of its existence condensed into a single flower. I saw God in everything, and therefore I was God.

Jesus: And likewise, I came forth as representative for all male humanity to show that we are capable of creating and achieving infinite possibilities. All potential is clasped within our hands, as long as we make choices that encourage great respect for the strength we harness and the responsibility we hold for our children, their mothers, our great earth, and the of love of one another. We surrender blinded of ego, and we open to the vision of a path of heart.

Our strength, our perseverance, our inspiration, ideas, and theories can and will be used for creativity, growth, education, and guidance. It is our connection to God—no less.

With both male and female children living and embracing this new reality, their growth, expansion, learning, and expression of one another is rebirthing a world of tolerance, appreciation, respect, and great love.

Amen

Winds of Change   7/5/2012

We are standing in a desert. The wind is howling. It is a challenge to stand without being pushed by the force.

Perhaps they are the winds of change.

We are standing together. Suddenly you look into the distance and point your finger towards the horizon. I can see what looks like a city far in the distance. It's brightly lit and appears to be buzzing with movement. It's alive with a population that produces all you could want and more: food, shelter, fabrics, refuge.

A voice tells us, "Go quickly! Walk now without delay, as a storm approaches that will be intense." I look up, and the clouds seem extremely full and heavy, almost bursting. They appear deep purple in colour. The rumbling sound of a storm about to hit is loud and holds an air of anticipation. The wind is blowing even stronger now, and we can predict that once the rain begins its fall, it's going to be like a floodgate opening, washing over everything.

You appear excited and full of strength as you plough through the wind in these harsh conditions. It is difficult to walk in sand, with this headwind obstructing normal breathing. I walk a few steps behind, battling my pain. To give up now means what? I would sit here and be pelted with a million grains of sand and a million litres of water about to fall from the sky. "Some choice!" I cry in frustration, but I cover my mouth with a cupped hand, trying to shield my mouth and eyes from the abrasive sand.

"Come on!" you yell. "We are nearly there!"

I'm a few feet behind, but I'm coming. I'm numb inside and out. I wonder what's next? All sorts of thoughts enter my mind. *Why is this happening? Why is it so hard? Why don't these forces leave us alone? I'm tired, just so tired.*

*   *   *

Jesus appears in an underground jail cell, which is similar to a dungeon. He is being retained there for disturbing the peace, which is quite ironic. He *is* peace. He teaches exactly how to create peace, live peace, be peace.

The revolt is of a political nature, to deny an educated man's freedom to a worthy and valid opinion. Feathers have been ruffled. Egos have been threatened.

Jesus looks up and says, "I may free myself from my cell, but that wouldn't give you the right to speculate, to assess, to collect all the data you need to define and differentiate, dissect and decide what you choose to believe about me. I am captured, a non-threat. I will not disappear, so search your heart.

"You may choose to rally against my captors and those who accuse me. You may do so, and in that very act, you choose a position that defines you. You are free to make any choice, and in doing so, gain strength and courage, resilience and definition of your beliefs. Our desire for freedom eventually surpasses all control and inbred fears. You may be asked to prove your belief, to stand before judge and jury and swear on the very energy you communicate with now.

"But know this: as you choose, follow your heart. Always. Truth is the one universal heart of God, where we unite together. As we unite as children of the cosmos fused by the eternal flame that burns warmly within you, you will know true comfort and will always feel love and safety."

The cell door of the dungeon opens and beyond is a beautiful garden like Eden.

We are safe and very free.

God with Jesus

Amen

Perfection   15/5/2012

Jesus holds both hands to his heart and then points to a large image of a human eye.

Upon closely viewing this eye, I see that it reveals a small window within it, and in this window there appears to be the energy of *lull*.

Do not engage with fear. As intent you are on pushing forward quickly, there are natural rest periods, whether you accept this or not. Your body and your system tell you when it requires rest, but you believe otherwise. I say rest and prepare.

We don't need to specifically point to the aspects that appear to be depleting your energy, as you well know it's identity. These periods of inner reflection initiating the release of old programs and patterns allow you to reconnect to your heart and true self, who is already free, successful, abundant, and joyful.

There is no such thing as time as you know it, but there exists an energy band of activity and rest, shifting and working through particular ground-level energies, such as other people's fears. Then a process begins of clearing this, reenergising and refocusing to reach a clear view once again.

To trust in a God who loves and supports you also means to trust yourself.

Disengage from thoughts that are trying to include you in a viewpoint of dread.

You know this is not reality and not your truth, but is created through the lens of another. This is just as illusionary for them as it is for you; however, as they choose to keep connecting with illusion, that is their choice and free will at this time. Move forward and allow yourself and others the freedom to choose.

One can argue, "But I feel the impact of their dread. It affects me!"

And I say to you, "Stop! The only block in your path is your inability to recognise that there are none."

When you draw from your true Source, who knows no drama or game to evade thee, when you fully accept that the world you create is truly your own to be responsible for, it is then you will realise that you already have the key to the kingdom you seek refuge in.

The density is fear, the heaviness of "lack" that weighs like a ten-tonne boulder on your shoulders because we choose to allow the beliefs of our partners, friends, politicians, and nations to influence us. Drop the boulder and live your life.

Whilst we live in relationship with all on our planet, and our relationships are of utmost importance, we cannot allow another to control. Together, with freedom and respect, we enjoy building, creating, manifesting, dreaming, sharing passion, and sharing realities.

Let no priest, partner, practitioner, or politician tell you otherwise. I am here to tell you that there is only one P-word you need focus on and use as an affirmation whenever you feel overwhelmed, and that word is *perfection*.

You are perfection.
All life is perfection.
Your choices are perfection.

Believe without a shadow of a doubt that your goals are forming and manifesting, just as you see them, as your feelings and thoughts are centred in a state of perfection.

Be free. Walk away from what no longer serves you and your direction. I will not stand in judgement of you, not now or ever.

Jesus

It is true: never before upon earth have we experienced this shift in energy where personal journeys inspire the significant global changes. And as we are creative vehicles of the planet, it will be felt on every level, all together. We are a major part of the living energy upon earth.

Time has become a utilised, irreplaceable function that drives humanity to their daily tasks, their education, their health, and playtime. God functions in the omnipresent and with eternity providing an ever-flowing love frequency that supports you during sleep and awake time, whilst humans cannot conceive it. Divinity says, "I see your lives can be in the present and well lived when dedicated around certain time slots, provided balance is the manager. Give equal time and commitment to creative growth and development, service and self nurture, giving and receiving, sharing and expression."

The gifts you share, the healing you provide through the time element of your day is worthy and is delivered with love, as is your intention. Your service to people is not fully understood. For some people are still see it as a hobby. They consider their spirit selves and attention to it much like a fad diet. It is humorous on some levels, but it is not so at the same time. Like a parent who adores and looks out for all her children, she hopes for perfect health, clarity, vitality, happiness, creativity, and joy for all of them. So to does God hope for awareness and conscious inner shifts within his children, who release unhealthy patterns and inspire creative strengths, passion, love, and joy.

When I walked upon the earth with the sand firmly compacted beneath my feet, my skin bled too, as if it were brazed. My head hurt during moments of frustration, like anyone else, but I knew I had to focus on grounding myself and reconnecting my inner self and my heart with that of my true Mother and Father Divine. Once I did this, all of my true abilities had an opportunity to flourish like a garden of flowers on a warm spring day. I would do all I could to not allow the negative emotion to support the obstacle. You and I are no different. We are made of the same cosmic star dust, and our souls are united to beat as one. The human experience is no doubt a great challenge, but well worth the effort and experience.

Whenever you claim, "But I cannot do it! It's all too hard, I have no power!" or "I don't believe it can happen for me," you are disconnecting from your true self and abilities, which are able to create and achieve whatever you wish.

You will manifest whatever it is you believe, even if it's failure. It is not in your current stage of evolvement, and certainly not to your advantage, to replay all of those old programmes in thoughts and actions. You and I are one. You are able to surpass all levels of suffering, personal sabotage, and poverty by connecting to the your authentic self, your cosmic DNA, your connection for an ever-loving being who only knows your perfection and success. You and I are one, and your belief in that will move mountains.

More and more are awakening to their inner truth, and with this new dawn, they are honouring themselves, each other, and their bodies, minds, and decisions in a way that serves the level of evolvement they are at, at this moment. So whoever receives also honours the assistance they are receiving, whether that be from obtaining healings or buying books. They honour the truth in realising, without inner balance, "My whole life is in disarray."

The shifts in people are happening very fast. The speed at which the accelerator pedal has now been pushed will cause some instability and emotional phases. Many people know this and are listening to their own rhythms, whilst others need gentle acknowledgement and guidance.

Call upon me whenever you feel you need extra strength and support.

Your work is that of God. You extend from me, in an earthly, direct manner. You are very loved and nurtured. For that is God's truth.

Feel the sand beneath your feet and pray from your heart.

With love,

Jesus

When one walks the path of the Lord, the path is golden.

There is no such thing as disappointment, really. Disappointment is an altered state of reality created by a negative perception and emotion. What is your reality, and what do you perceive to happen in the future? Today? In one week? It is your belief in an outcome that gives fuel to the momentum behind the creative energy.

Releasing your intent to God, whatever your wish or desire, is a powerful action, as it reinstates trust and relinquishes all control. Trust that God is taking care of all the finer details, enabling the plan to come to fruition, and aligning all of the exterior elements to bring about the balance.

Humans have extraordinary power, and when that power is not harnessed or is used negatively, it can also affect change. It can alter and destroy. The key issue for your spirit and your evolvement is to use that power to nurture and support your goals, increasing your happiness and joy and receiving guidance to how best serve your greatest need: to fulfil your life plan.

I love you, there's no doubt in that. I will harness, nurture, and project that love unto you like the sun shines upon you on a warm summer's day. You stand underneath the warm rays with your eyes closed, looking up towards the brightness, but you dare not peek. It's just too bright to see with your eyes. So you smile gently and your face absorbs the warmth, the glow, the radiant energy of my love. So it is and always will be.

This loving golden glow will be present wherever there is love and will be fully embraced by whomever realises this great gift. You will be blessed forever more as you embrace your relationship with the divine being who is always with you. It truly is the path to freedom, true love, prosperity, hope, and joy in all your earthly cares. When you share and deliver the awareness of such gifts, offering assistance to your brothers and sisters, you open their eyes to it. They may squint from the brightness as you did, but they will feel the love in its immeasurable magnitude, be showered, and feel grateful. This is what you are made of. You live and trust by my word.

As above so below.
The road ahead is golden.
Come walk with me?

Hand in hand.

Amen

Humble Beginnings 18/6/2012

Opalescent rain falls from a perfectly blue, cloudless sky.

Jesus stands with me, and I can clearly see the water drops on his face. We are getting quite wet, but the water is nourishing and hydrating. It is also a significant sign that the drought is over.

There are desert sands all around, and the city's buildings and temples are some miles ahead, so we walk. As we get closer, I see the magnificent pyramids. I'm told they are light transmitters receiving energy through the top, then the light filters through its perfectly measured physical vessel to administer the energy at ground level.

I too have returned many times in my life. It is no mark of failure to revisit your roots or humble beginnings, as it is for many. Every time we visit, it is different and never the same. There will be a new perception, a new learning or reflection, and so familiar territory can have a completely new energy and feel. It is no doubt a beautiful realisation to consider, that nothing remains the same.

As people, we practise something called *intuition*. It is what feels like a magnetic attraction to something that feels right. It is very good indeed. Because you listen to the calling, you are ready to receive.

I tell you this: never fear what appears to be an unwelcome visitor. All occurrences allow an education of personal growth. It is never otherwise.

This is a message to the people of all nations:

Be it that you embrace the untimely visitor, as he delivers you a message about yourself. We would not allow misfortune to come to you unless you recognise it is your soul's requirement to release unhealthy patterns and beliefs. Much is created from the human perception of life—some of it negatively so, some of it positively so.

When one learns to recognise that one's exterior world is the result of all one has created within, one will become far more selective and self-aware indeed. These are the teachings for humanity. Your perception that random events push and pull and orchestrate your lives has no truth whatsoever. It is time you awakened to your inner creativity and the power of choice. The people of earth are ready to remember.

Deliver the teachings and encourage people to reconnect to their hearts. They may return to home base or their inner temple, as will you whenever you need to reflect on your path yet to travel.

The rainbow comes always after the rain.

With love,

Jesus

The Great Celebration Is Here   21/6/2012

Jesus steps forward.

Today we mark the day of great celebration, and my heart glows with love and gratitude. We are on the edge of a phenomenon. It is of worldwide proportions, as it was meant to be.

We refer to a vision of the golden tree: This beautiful golden tree you see behind me contains all of the wisdom, courage, strength, and truth you could ever require. You have fed well from this tree, and likewise, you have nurtured and supported its growth. Now it glows with loving health and vitality, bearing fruit for you to consume and hand out once more. As healers and educators, you are assigned (you have assigned yourselves) to earth for your space in humanity as light workers.

You are about to reveal the healings and teachings to people who are ready to receive. What a great day indeed. Never before has such empowerment, soul nurture, and connection been offered to the people to realise their own lives as being completely in their own hands. This will send a shockwave of divine realisation. But again, they are ready, and so are you. Educating and lecturing, workshops and meditations are going to support their change and their healing. Once the people understand the fundamental concepts of what is actually happening as a decoding and releasing, an unravelling of imbedded fears and illusions, the process will quicken. But it has already well and truly begun. This marks an end to a two-thousand-year-old delusion of passing on the responsibility or blaming each other, or even God. It's time that we all own what we have and will create. It is surfacing on many levels. People are ready to rise above and live their purpose.

This is inevitable, and it is happening now, spreading across the minds and hearts of millions. Keep the energy and momentum up with the release of *The Chosen One*. Remember, like yourselves, healing has a journey unto itself and the proceeding layers, issues, and growth will follow quite quickly. The beauty with these educational texts is that even children can read and heal from them.

Can you see the enormous golden beam? This level of energy is pure love energy. It anchors the book and yourselves to its methods and teachings.

There is much work to do, many people to reach and educate, but you will understand and embrace it as it all presents.

At this point, I ask about another publisher and opportunities to expand to reach more people.

You are attracting a great deal of attention. If the people are noticing, feeling, and responding to you, so are the people who run these organisations. Focus not on how; rather allow the joy of the miracle to touch you.

Trust in what I say. For this present moment, reap the joy and absorb the rewards and remain open to all of the contacts and feedback you receive. Connect your heart to your ultimate desires, then get out of the way of yourself to allow the contenders, the messengers, and the assistance to present.

I will be with you.

With much love,

Jesus

Bridge Over Troubled Water   22/6/2012

"Like a bridge over troubled water, I will lay me down."

Call upon me in your hour of need. It doesn't matter what is the essence of your woes, I am but a heartbeat away. We will build the bridge together and walk arm in arm onto new lands, towards your new consciousness and a new awareness.

It is only fearful because you believed you had to swim, but that is not necessary. We build, we strengthen, and we move beyond your previous boundaries and thoughts.

As we walk one step at a time across the bridge, the water appears very rough and choppy, and the wind blows quite cold against our faces. The inclination is to focus on the external discomfort of the water spray and freezing wind. Is it not? Suddenly we stop halfway along the bridge.

You say to me, "Now, focus. Focus on me. Look at me, and look into my eyes, my dear friend. You know in your heart that you are going to make it. You may not know what to expect or how to fathom your new reality as yet, but you can trust in this feeling in your heart and trust in my supporting arm around you."

I begin to focus on the warmth of your words and the united goal of making it across the bridge. We are now just over halfway. The waters are beginning to calm, and the wind is softening. I can now to look upward instead of guarding my eyes from the previous high winds. The second half of the bridge is easier. Each step is stronger and there is a flow in our stride.

You loosen your embrace as you feel my confidence beginning to rise, and yet I hesitate and lean towards you so as not to release our connection just yet. You assure me, "I'm here."

As the end of the bridge approaches, the horizon produces the most extraordinarily beautiful sunset. The oranges, reds, and yellows mark a celebration—a celebration of life, of succeeding against our biggest obstacle, ourselves.

The words *I love you* echo warmly through my mind and heart, just as the first step is placed upon the new land. It is new, fresh, unique and alive with opportunity. I look for any sign of familiarity, but visually it is all entirely new.

Somehow, my heart knows this place. It responds with acknowledgement, gratitude, and self- love for having the courage and determination to continue on, no matter how rough the seas or powerful the opposing winds.

A loving, familiar voice echoes once again through my heart and mind.

"You have arrived."

With love,

God

Come my child, rest within the safe, loving energy stream of God. Be it that you feel like it is your home. As it is, in truth.

This temple represents your haven, your home. Your place to rest, to be, to create.

It is the house of God, but he does not want to see you live within his home discontent. He loves you and wants to see you nestled, safe, warm, and happy.

When we rest within this house, all of the earthly cares are placed into a true reality. How much of the current state of affairs is legitimately threatening or worrisome? You have nothing to fear. Your relationship with family is a co-creation of past and present opposing forces. Stay true in your intent and unwavering in your beliefs and goals, and it will be so. Your siblings are living and evolving at a very different place and time from you. Your care and attention to your mother's and father's hard work benefits the entire family, unlike their perspective and intent to benefit only themselves. But it has no binding strength nor basis. Do not entertain a moment of worry or doubt.

*   *   *

We are standing on the beautiful white marble entrance of God's house. A path illuminates before us, and I'm beckoned to descend the stairs and begin to follow the golden path. After a little winding way, a corner is turned and an enormous diamond-light palace is standing. It is breathtakingly beautiful;

it is a representation of the foundations, the stability, the creative force in form, which is about to manifest.

This palace represents the end result, the fruition of desires to create and secure so much more to help the masses of people. Each sparkle, every light beam, is a collective creation of the hard work, dedication, and commitment to humanity.

There is a body of water around the palace that is calm and fertile. It glistens and mirrors even more beauty.

The full moon shines above, casting more light upon this palace of peace. We are in total silence and in total calm.

This is bliss.

Rest and release your need to answer to others; remain with love and awareness and complete comfort in the refuge of my home. Your place here is eternal.

I love you.

God

Through the power and might of Almighty God, I plead with you for your assistance. Dear God! Help me! What does it take?

Rise from your aching knees, dear one. There is no need to beg. I am here, and I offer my help all ways.

"Do you hear that static noise? It is the sound of a thousand entities powerfully vibrating, violently, through a god-body. It cannot and does not reason. It only knows the destruction of light to deny creation."

This man is very open. He opens himself, along with the response of "being in" life with you. His mental body never rests and suffers from exhaustion, as such.

Anything and everything can penetrate him through his third eye. His natural instinct to defend or to go into battle matches the circumstances he needs to knock him into a state of reflection. It is of human experience to continue along a path, receiving many knocks along the way, to which we have the option to reflect and respond. If we continue down a given path and it is not for the betterment of our souls' evolvement, the knocks will get harder and the intensity of grief and regret will increase, until we reach surrender.

"Have you had enough yet? No? Okay, perhaps this will bring you to inner reflection you need." Each one of us is presented with options, and as time is of no essence, no matter how fast or slow we respond, there is always a consequence and an answer for any given action.

There is no avoiding the responsibility. It is what comes in the wake of a passing ship. We all must acknowledge at least half of the responsibility for what we create in any given circumstance. No one is exempt.

When we react in self-defence, it indicates the "need to defend self," in other words, the need to deflect a strong attack or force. What could have been attracted with such an incident? There are many potential reasons, but we closely look towards what a person emanates out into the world and therefore attracts as the lesson, karma, or result. Does he depict peace and creativity, openness and allowing? Or is he forceful, judgemental, cynical, and controlling? We also all must realize that we live within a world of laws and acceptable human behaviours, and there's usually another choice. We must reap what we sow, and so forth.

Potentially, this is a time of change, reflection, and transformation, and if fully realised as such, it could be a profound awakening.

What will he choose? We cannot directly interfere; however, we can and will offer the love and support in alignment with his non-ego self, his higher being.

How much of this should burden the partner of a person experiencing this deeper learning and relating challenges? Where does your part begin and end?

You are to reach out within the most open point of your heart and ask for the strength to retain your freedom in the choices for your life, now and always. In doing so, you lovingly utilise the law of allowing and create an example of leadership and strength. This is a great gift of guidance that one is free to learn from.

You can never be held responsible for another's actions, no matter who they are to you.

Remember sometimes the answers are in the unexpected and sometimes are shown in something we don't wish to consider. Open your heart completely in the most accepting, humble way, and you will discover all of the answers you seek.

I love you and support you always.

God

Many generations of popes flash before the screen, waving from the papal chariot to adoring crowds.

Why do people connect in this way? What level of perfection do they feel or see? What creates a yearning to be acknowledged by a holy man in flesh?

I see you all the time, and so much more, I feel you.

We still live with so many human conditions and misconceptions. Man still questions his image and likeness to God. Thankfully, some of you are opening to a greater truth. Ultimately, your acknowledgement of my short earthly existence and much longer spiritual existence has allowed you a greater understanding of my intention as earthly guide to all of humanity.

Let's look at this in a real sense. My life on earth was one of tests and irrepressible faith. Along with my quest to teach and expose as many people to their God self as possible, I was met with much opposition, in anger and threats. This eventually led to my detainment and persecution. This process, whilst not favourable to any human being, was a necessary historical event for evolvement. It is a wider perspective of such magnitude and forethought.

Would you now imagine that your actions and life affects thousands of decades and many generations to come? Would you now imagine that your words, your reflections, your suffering and your grief, your happiness and achievements, alter the perspective and affect many generations to come?

It seems so illusive, but it is one of the great truths of mankind. You are given an opportunity to heal, connect, and affect many others lives with your love or lack thereof. You can concurrently pre-pave the environment and subsequent lifetimes ahead you will create. The beautiful notion and truth of current incarnations is that most of the heavier and burdensome, ego-driven, power-possessive lifetimes of history are over. People are choosing to look past their current circumstances to spark a point of change. The infiltrating influences are many, and they must draw on great strengths to harness a position of healing and break free from previous societal, genetic, and karmic thought forms.

When you have an entity as influential and as powerful as the church, there will be many speculative and non-speculative views. We acknowledge speculation, which was not even permitted more than fifty years ago, and in some areas is still not to this day. The documentation and theology laced with dogma has not allowed free-thinkers to exist. One was beheaded or hung for blasphemy, and there were millions of souls who died in this way, including you—likely many times over. This is an imprint that most of us share in experience. We therefore acknowledge this and work with it as a mass consciousness to shift it.

Unless we do so, and free ourselves from within the binds of fear for free speech, evolvement will be limited by a range of fear ideals run by church leaders and theologians. Excel and explode beyond the limitations of past generations, beyond the veil of fear. In the threats of holy men (as they call themselves), we realise that their intent was to instil fear and expel the truth of God and our existence. History only plays a part in deciding where we need to learn and where we no longer wish to go.

The path ahead is a path to freedom and ultimately to God herself. The human ascension process is enticing you forward to reach the state of nirvana you know is attainable within your soul. To reach this state is to do so on earth, not in heaven.

This has always been the intention: "on earth as it is in heaven."

Remember, time has no relevance. Five minutes or five thousand years is just the expansion of energy moving your experience and then bouncing off your exterior world to reflect back a result or an awareness. Focus your intent in expressing truth and reigniting the love and awareness in others as you speak. It matters not whether they question you. Do not take it personally. They merely seek their path and do so by exploring, not questioning your authenticity.

Be not alarmed by ego; it merely presents as a defence against a responsibility for a higher perspective. Bless them, bless them all. Acknowledge, defer, and dispel. You are strengthening against the repercussions of this and through that process teaching others to do so as well.

Eventually, the masses grow in unity and all will feel a relief. The earth is changing, and the shifts are occurring at a stronger and faster rate. The work is supported through this, allowing people to clear their illusions and misconceptions profoundly and efficiently.

We keep walking onward with passion and free will, and with God lovingly guiding the way.

Amen

An Angel's Message   12/7/2012

Complete and total surrender, dear one. You know in your heart the path that lies before you. You have waited a long time to experience all that is presenting to you now. You are to embrace these moments like an athlete accepting her medal. This path has never been known as an easy one. Much training, much learning, and acceptance have been the key concepts allowing your evolvement to continue. You chose to continue and took the steps forward where there were no guarantees. Courage and persistence are the magic ingredients of this course.

You are now wearing the *bride's dress*. You are no longer preparing or making the gown; the gown is fitted on you. You will now detail and bead it, and when the time is right, accessorize it to be ready for the ceremony, the marriage, the commitment in soul and all of self, to this. There's such change going on around you now; and whilst it may seem subtle, it certainly is not. This is an exciting time of growth and opportunity, and you will have doors open before you that have not been available to you previously. It's all in perfect order, so pace yourself, work towards your goals, and be very happy with the results.

When you have faith, persistence, and an unquestionable channel of energy utilized by you, it means God and your entire support team is present and you are listening. Pieces of the puzzle will fall into place, and life's delicious menu will be on offer, showing you your options. Going forth, which way to create? Be present in the moment! Love the miracles bestowed upon you, and ask God which way to go from here. We are all supporting you and showering you, both with love and tender encouragement.

As the path unfolds, we light the way. Warmly, tenderly,

Angel Seraphina

Jesus speaks:

Do you see it? Isn't it a beautiful sight up here? Here is God all around you. The clean, crisp vision of sunrays upon clouds, the air so oxygenated, it carries a life force so enormous, the universe breathes one rhythmic breath together. You're so loved, everyone of you. So what do you desire from your opportunities? Time to take an inventory of your expectations based on whatever you now design.

Let's touch down now.

We walk upon luscious, cool, green grass, the wind blows softly, and you can smell nature. All life is communicating so powerfully, however silent. You don't need words to fertilize a forest. This is the power of life and the energy of God. The entire universe works within this stream, creating upon creations, moving, growing, and shifting evermore. Where do you wish to get on? As you assess your options and work through many challenges relating to the material world—money, time, support—these thoughts can create a large bump in the road and certainly can appear to slow your creative process.

But we know the human experience is perfectly supported by the desire to evolve; therefore, any dramas or considerations that cause a momentary lapse of reason or non-reason are just part of the process of realising our full abilities to have full choice and power, without any apparent restraints. Money, time, and other people are of no true affect. It is just a belief about ability and self-questioning that initiates doubt.

These things are enough to interrupt the bliss of the creative process.

I would now point out how perfect that is. If you were to remain up in the clouds on a plane of existence of sheer beauty and miraculous manifestations, and by just the mere thought to create you would do so, then you wouldn't be having the human experience of creating through the physical plane with all of its luscious and powerful energy of the material world blended with energy, love, and light, right here, right now. What does God want? He/She wants what you want. So what do you want?

Create a letter that lists the exact items. What to you wish to create? Do you require monetary assistance? What's the ultimate reward for you when creating this solid expression? What do you hope to achieve in the short term and long term?

Personal fulfilment that develops into a unity of love for a desired quest inspires healing. To feel love, safety, to be expressive in various ways, to allow vulnerability, in its purest form.

When this is expressed and felt, when one achieves this in flesh, you are embarking on the creation of heaven on earth.

Be specific with what you want to create. Allow the gates to open and admit the messengers, assistants, and coworkers to be sent to you.

Focus and enjoy your current tasks at hand and stay grounded in them. Jesus waves his hand over my heart.

With love.

The more light we infuse and consciously use upon earth, the more it creates. The Eden that will exist upon earth and in all dimensions it mirrors will fertilise the birth of nirvana.

Negative energy in its current form on our planet attempts to control and manipulate as a way of survival, to invoke mankind to act unlovingly and dishonour one another. Our shifts in consciousness and energy will not sustain such acts in the near future. You are at the forefront, part of the ones leading the way. Spread these words of awareness. Allow your example to teach others and inform them that they have a choice, as the time is at hand. The more you remove yourself from darkness, the more you acknowledge and render it powerless. Fill your life with light and love, and you will dissolve the darkness entirely, until one day it will be no more and we will attain heaven on earth. As it is written,

Amen.

Note: Like a river which is polluted and begins to cleanse and regenerate, the water, the animal life, and the plant life collectively support one another in this process and proliferate all together. And it begins with one action. When the light and clarity are infused to support life, it regenerates and recuperates quickly. Choose health and happiness now. Support and create your positive visions now, without delay. Everything you choose to connect with will present as you powerfully create your reality in every moment. When you feel the pull of modern life, retreat to nature—a forest, the ocean, a riverbank—and look, feel, and connect. This will help to bring you clarity and positivity always.

Thank you.

Amen

Chapter 5

Business Healings

Like water sucking fast down a drain, so was the energy of money flow for the original owner of this business. His business dealings, and the ill feelings they caused, related to dishonest business dealings and business investments where misconceptions were heavily involved.

The location in question is where the Ascension Centre will be built. Our intention is to free the location of any karmic, past, present, or future negative energies that create an unhealthy environment. The result has been faulty and failing amenities causing unnecessary draining of funds. Our intention today severs all past ill feelings, thought forms, and karmic connections to the previous owner, so that the future project has a clean, pure slate to build on. From the foundations up, it will be clear with no obstructions.

Suddenly, there is a vision of an old-fashioned amphitheatre full of people. They are all throwing fruit in anger at the previous owner. He is in the centre, dodging and ducking from the missiles of fruit. After a while, the people stop and leave, having realised they too were playing a part in the equation, which alters and affects their evolvement as well. They realise that this man, whom they greatly dislike, has helped them experience and learn from a particular aspect in earth life.

The area suddenly fills with light, and a loud, deep humming sound accompanies the infusion of light. It is so powerful and all encompassing, it completely disintegrates and transmutes the karmic debt. It is gone. There is no longer a need to carry it once all parties are aware of its reason and required release.

What was once a drain pipe down has now reversed to become a huge beam of golden-white light shining up towards the sky. Another golden-white energy beam roots downward to anchor the Ascension Centre.

Instantly, I am standing in front of the completed building. I push through the beautiful glass and gold front entry doors. "Good morning," I say, smiling.

The decor so is beautiful, distinguished, pure, and magnificent. The environment is a hive of activity. The Ascension Centre's owner, Trish Trani, comes from her healing room to check the computerized diary. The appointments are fully booked six months in advance.

Coffee time—with gratitude! Drinks come from the café downstairs by a good friend and business associate, who personally delivers them so she can say hello to us. Her daughter plays happily in the crèche downstairs. There is a telephone call regarding a media interview, and our receptionist is asking questions to ascertain when and where. All is smooth and working in flow.

On the fifth and sixth level above are residential apartments. Some of these apartments have not been fully completed as yet, and there is a bit of an urgency regarding this so they can be leased or sold. I pass a gold-framed picture in the corridor upstairs. It is a replica of a painting, slightly faded, of the beautiful Mary Magdalene.

The carpet in most rooms is red. The runner up the hallway has a lighter border in a cream colour. It's very beautiful. The plaster work on the walls is complete with ornate decorative cornices. The appearance throughout is like a fine hotel.

Jesus suddenly appears, walking up ahead in the corridor. There is a blue, purple, and gold energy around him. He is observing, looking, and enjoying the fruits. The tree has borne fruit, and he is so pleased. "You had many challenging times, but you never gave up. It is here and now, as real as your hands, the rewards you see manifested. Now your work continues on a large scale, and together we unite. The best is yet to come.

"I also protect your home and clear any resistance or unhealthy energies from it, so that you reside always within a temple of God. This, here, is now where you belong. The unhealthy feelings at home are unloving thoughts, which we now clear."

Published books are also being featured in the front windows of The Ascension Centre on a small table and on bookstands. They are paperback.

The path is now clear, the light shines above, showering love to you and your dedicated angels.

Thank you, Jesus, guiding angels and archangels, Mary Magdalene, and God for providing us with the opportunity to heal.

God bless.

Healing has taken place, and all blocks have been removed.

Amen.

In the name of the Father, the Son, and the Holy Spirit. Amen.

A small, thin man speaks. He presents himself standing on the sand of a hot, dry desert. His head is wrapped in light cloth. He appears to be in his early sixties with sun-parched skin. He is a shepherd. He is speaking very quickly in an ancient Egyptian language, and he is purposefully pointing to a distant pyramid, which is also a burial site. Thoth ensures all is well, and Jesus steps forward.

It is so easy to engage in fear when we are unsure of an outcome, but trust that what has taken you this far will ensure you see the result. Your book, *The Healer's Journey*, has been encoded in frequency with fifth-dimensional healing. It can be felt when one holds it. Be it that your faith extends further. Speak, think, and act in full confidence, for we do not guide our beloved's aimlessly.

Keep your intentions clear, the outcome of which is to build a temple of light. How the universe will deliver this reality is left to God's unlimited devices.

I realise your factual and earthly life requires a pattern of events to acknowledge and evidence to ponder. The surprises and scope of manifesting such a desire have no great effort. Accept your ability to know that the only obstacles are our own selves in fear. The temple stands right now in a parallel universe, and as this is the soul self or blueprint of the material creation, so it will eventually stand in your physical world. The book will sell many copies.

Speak to me with loving intent and have the intention of flow magnified. Local bookstores will respond well; however, they will have little understanding of its power healing abilities and messages. It is therefore a worthy consideration to have education sessions, book signings, and information nights, all advertised in advance and put in place.

Be in control of your marketing and media. As with your ability to entice energy flow to all things, so you will in the sales of your book. November release. Christmas is a perfect time to acknowledge and embrace every heart with the presence and healings of the lineage of Christ. If you focus only on restrictions of time, money, or scarcity of any kind, you will obstruct the creative flow the universe. The universe has an infinite connection to wanting only to help you. Trust and let go. That way any avenue, any and all miraculous avenues from many different sources, may present to you.

Allow all flow and all possibilities seen and unseen to open to you. Having trust and faith means exactly that. Allow all possibilities to support and provide, not just the ones you expect to receive.

There are the infinite resources available to the universe, but what needs to be acknowledged is divine timing, your purpose and resilience. Let go and let God.

This text has creative energy vibration and will heal within the hands of those who hold it. A frequency of my love will be residing within each copy.

As it is written. Amen.

Don't jump too far ahead. There is so much more to enjoy in this moment. At this time you can continue to create more—

don't stop! Be excited, live happily, see beauty, multiply it, and then multiply it again.

You are strong, and your support is strong.

You ask, "If I am to walk the path of light, will I be rewarded, dear God?"

"My beloved, if a golden sea brings forth joy, I bathe before you and ask you to join me in the waters of eternal love, for this is where you've washed my hands and my feet. Here the reward is everlasting. It is bliss."

There is a vision of a chapel. It is the temple of light, and it has beautiful stained glass windows. This is great reward.

*   *   *

Many angels are shown playing musical instruments.

We are protected, loved, and guided. Trust, be clear, and let go of expectation.

Allow flow of universal consciousness, and creativity is here and now.

That is all.

A large mushroom cloud appears. Its origin is a representation of what has ended.

This anxiety-based energy surfaces because of an ending of a union, bond, or relationship between two people. During the union of two, there are attachments on various levels that are solid and most definitely fused. Just because two people part ways in a physical sense doesn't mean they have parted in other ways. Energetically, the attachment, or what we refer to as "cords," may continue to exist for up to seven years. Serious relationships, or relationships that have a physical and emotional bonding, join in energy and as such are likened to a field that connects so similarly, it can be identified almost as one. Connections such as these can remain long after a physical separation, causing emotional and mental dysfunction, often leading to unexplained feelings of powerlessness, depending greatly on the circumstances and afterthoughts and feelings from the separation. People can often feel as though their ex-partner is still connected in thought, as well as physically. You may frequently run into your ex, no matter how hard you try to avoid it.

These continued attachments hinder future relationships and must be completely but compassionately severed. The areas of the physical body relating to the connections and required healing are mainly in the lower half of the body.

The stomach, liver, intestines, kidneys (solar plexus chakra), sexual internal organs, bowel and bladder, and pancreas (sacral chakra) are the most common areas affected. Additionally, experiences of sore legs, hips, knees, or lower back are also common symptoms. Which mirrors are presenting will be exactly where the individual needs to pay attention and acknowledge whether it is a healing, a personal development issue, or a release being required as an ending is taken place, or all of the above. There is never a crossing of two people for no reason. Every single person and relationship offers growth and development, whether it ends or not.

It is also very common that with committed self-development work, an ex-partner may resurface by making contact with you. This is usually because your energy field is changing and strengthening, and they try to attach to that. They have a high sense of your energy field, particularly if it hasn't been adequately severed. They may feel that you are now permanently unobtainable. This makes it extremely appealing for some, especially for those ex-partners who have lived off your energy in the past.

We know that chronological age has very little to do with relationships experienced; and more to do with your personal evolvement. It may be a partial family and genetic pattern/program mixed with soul purpose, but nevertheless we certainly orchestrate our connections with our beloved(s) before incarnating to this lifetime. Ultimately and on every level, and no matter where the origin is in your case, the important thing to remember is that every person and your relationship with them was attracted by you both mutually for the lessons, karma, or soulmateship to be experienced. Therefore, never regret a beginning nor an ending. Embrace the wisdom gained and view the crossing as purposeful.

Once a person has retrieved their only true source of power through the practise of self-love, then the attraction of those who support and appreciate that within your relationships will become clearly apparent. Only healthy and mutually satisfying connections will result. The attraction will fuel the magnetism of the love one feels for themselves, rather than the love they require from you. If it is less than mutually balanced in equal giving and receiving, acknowledge and reassess what it is you're looking for and why. Otherwise your relationships may be repetitively draining and needy.

Love oneself so much more! Let go of anything that doesn't serve you and all you deserve to experience. See only love in all you do. It is a fine indication that you are moving into a far better cycle of attracting a partner who resonates with your love and light. When you experience a relationship like that, you will never again need to experience painful relationship lessons and empowerment issues.

Remember always, as challenging as relationships have presented to be for people, we are always shown what needs to be addressed within ourselves. Perhaps you may ask, "What is within me that requires so much attention through my partner?"

Be aware of the common trap of trying to heal your lovers. No one is able to change their lives unless they wish to do so, no matter what you do or say or provide for them. This is *always* part of their own learning and growth. If you choose to accept another in your life, with all their perfect imperfections, do so and acknowledge your great strength in allowing them the freedom to be all that they are without trying to change them.

This courage and unconditional love will inspire your own healing, with flow and remarkable release, particularly if the favour is returned.

Commit fully, love one another without abandon, accept and grow, create and support. Do so for each other, but most importantly sign and honour this contract to yourself.

With much gratitude for this guidance from Spirit.

Amen.

Academy of Light

We sit at a long dinner table as many people gather in celebration. Along with people who are closely connected, a type of governing panel called the Light Workers Council joins us as special guests. We are celebrating another successful anchoring. The heavens rejoice, and light workers from all over the world are grateful as the light infuses and penetrates, spreads and glows, with Mother Earth and her offspring. This commitment to God, the decision to be in service to every soul you encounter, provides an immense sense that I am working within and through you.

"Come the day we will have nothing more to heal, we'll revel in the joy of the living and in service to others."

Each anchor that occurs worldwide creates a concentrated point of healing love and light. This aspect joins with another, linking energetically to become more and more, until all people will reawaken to their divine aspects and quest to heal any human obstacle or frailty.

Some information is not permitted to be disclosed, as faith, intent, and personal growth are in relationship with the mysteries of the intrinsic logic of God. In truth, divine intervention has no human logic, as miracles present no formula. Trust that as you are co-creator in the house of God, in service to salvation and providing a light unto the darkness, you will be provided for, so that timing of your plans and the centre's construction will fall into place.

It will be wholesome and important to have a place of prayer. It is quite imperative that teachers of light are guided into the academy to learn, reveal, and share in wisdom and service to all those asking. There will be the teachers of all levels from all modalities, including advanced practitioners who will be exceptional in skill and ability. The corridors are very light, and there are different-coloured mandalas on the walls, energetically gridding and stabilising the passageways and healing rooms.

The academy will be recognised worldwide and certainly have Australian accreditation. Many certificates will be issued and teaching qualifications sought from practitioners wishing to expand and excel in this area.

The academy stands longer than our working life.

There may be donations received to assist in the running of the academy, and large companies and corporations offer sponsorship and funding.

Students are required to wear white with gold piping.

We will connect with many brothers and sisters of light from all over the globe. Conventions and educational forums will be conducted as well.

There is absolutely no obstruction; she stands beautiful in her etheric self, which is the blueprint or spirit self of the physical.

Many blessings, love, and light.

God.

Thank you for assisting me with this revelation today.

Unending gratitude.

Amen

Rats scuttle across a dimly lit warehouse floor. It's cold, and the energy is dense. There were men who had gathered here to wheel and deal large sums of cash laced with dishonesty, misused power, and fear. They gathered many times in the past, but no more.

The vision is of a dense energy in the lower chakras of the body, and the business creates a great imbalance and drain in fear of loss. In the past (and present), people may have killed as a result of this fear. We will not entertain those actions as our current focal point; here in words, however, we focus on the healing that is about to be done.

The business, its associations, friendships, buying and selling, and all future endeavours, holds a much lighter vibration than its past. The owner of the business was having difficulty recovering funds and having fair and just business dealings because his personal energy and frequency had lightened and no longer matched the business associates he had. They are feeling this too and make up any excuse not to pay him for his services. His vibration emanates a wealth energy that they are envious of. These people do not articulate or are not fully conscious of the energy they feel. On some level, those who are purchasing items from him also feel a particular uneasiness that they rationalise as a gut feeling, and at the last minute, they change their minds and withdraw from the purchase. Additionally, the business owner's personal friendships are consistent with the same low frequency and vibration, but loyalty ties them to him, as many years have bound them.

The Healing

With pure intent, passion, fire, and a joyous high frequency, an extremely high-pitched sound unheard by the human ear is placed like a force field around the yard.

The owner is to continue upon his path in his business; however, he has certainly felt the strain upon his body, the frustrations of delays and money not rewarded to him. He will now experience that the past frequency of the former business associates, friendships, and wheeling and dealing will no longer be attracted to him. All future prospects and endeavours are of an honest nature, issuing respect and payments for services rendered without unhealthy delays. The work he produces, or anything sold by him, will be viewed as valuable, and his efforts will be well rewarded.

Like-minded like-frequency will be attracted in all workers, contracts, jobs, supervisors, buyers, sellers, and friendships.

The business premises is protected with the very white-blue light field.

Archangel Michael and Archangel Uriel.

Regardless of personal reasons, or that of your business or careers, when you all make a conscious decision to evolve to the existence of your royal crown and realise your self in ascension, your God self will function so effortlessly and with such joy and bliss that the apparent dramas of this plane will be insignificant and but a flicker of the past.

Ask for assistance and speak my name, and I will be there. Every prayer is always answered.

In love and eternal light, dear ones.

God

Sheets of kyanite energy thunder down onto the earth. It is a shield—a shield that is able to protect and filter out unhealthy energies.

The Tarot card "The Chariot" presents.

The anger displayed is a sign of dysfunction. It simply means a forceful and fearful energy exists within the perimeter that does not match another or wishes to penetrate another. It is a little bit like an energetic push and shove—two steps forward, three steps back. But do not be concerned. The clearing of this aspect will ease and eliminate this dysfunction.

Two thousand copies are ordered and sold. We are celebrating and laughing with happiness. Growth is evident. Following from this is a sheath of energy that acts like a wall. It is transparent but very strong. This wall represents disbelief, fear, and jealousy. Again, there is nothing more valuable in this life than love expressed, as well as lessons learned and being able to deliver, teach, serve, and express love even further as it flows onto another. Everything you experience is aligned to this dynamic.

Yes, it can be frustrating at times as we pursue the goal and have to deal with the apparent objection, but it is merely part of the experience. If we remove the intensity of the disapproval, the impact on you will be less and you will be able to distinguish between unravelling drama and the need to practice resilience and quiet persistence. The thinning, transparent layer of fear has opened to our kyanite shield. We can use this kyanite shield whenever and wherever relevant to ensure the protection of ourselves and our purpose. It will also provide calm and clarity.

The publishing company's building has three seagulls flying overhead, circling energy and vacuuming debris and negativity from the building and its environment. The shift in energy since some earlier clearings has resulted in a few reactions and restructuring in work flow, but overall this next healing provides the extra vacuum required to align everyone's clarity and function.

The book is on a conveyor belt—white cover, gold writing, as yet no photo has been imprinted, but this will come at the final stage.

The Ascension Centre stands in its template form. It is existing in this energy form, but it is thickening and getting heavier, shifting towards the physical world.

A golden lion statue sits waist-high near the entrance.

He reminds you of the love, faith, and strength it took to get to this point.

We pat him every day as we remember and enter.

All blocks have been removed and healing has taken place.

Amen.

A magnificent white horse gallops towards us as we stand ready to receive her.

She's pure white, powerful, perfect, and passionate, and she delivers strength and continuity. She represents an energetic and physical force of nature and its ability to work with you.

You stand outside the Ascension Centre on the street, consulting with a colleague. The energy has now altered and will continue to alter during this process of physical preparation, construction, and finally occupation of the building. Your colleague is showing you energy grid lines being created and supported for the building. In its template, it is in place, and the raising of your vibration and consciousness is allowing an enormous stream of energy and light to stream down to all associated with its manifestation. Be not concerned or upset about people who choose not to connect to you or be near you any longer. Acknowledge and know this is part of the process. Perfectly aware yet unattached, you are conscious of this new dynamic.

Suddenly the scenery changes: I see you walking through an Eden-like landscape. It appears like a forest, lush and abundant with plant, animal, and insect life. You wander through, appreciating and acknowledging all the natural beauty around you. The message is to continue to be at one with your beautiful surroundings, receiving all the guidance and love you need to live, inspire, love, and heal.

You're aware of a voice relaying a quiet message: *You may notice the difference in people around you. August will be a big month.*

Out of the trees, the white horse appears and beckons you to jump on. Happily you do! The fusion of energies is quite profound. Diamond-white light streams shine out from you and the horse, and as two beings, you become one. Her love, beauty, vibrancy, strength, vitality, and perseverance is fused within you, and together you are a mighty force. Onwards through the forest you charge! The union is so exciting and magnetic, its force creates a speed unknown upon earth.

She suddenly takes flight, and you're both soaring above the trees. The breeze, the air so clean and crisp, sparks a clarity in your visions. They are of your reality and clearer than clear. Below you notice the forest growing seemingly distant. Whilst you loved this home, you have outgrown it. The beach below still beckons a call, and there's a brief contemplation that at some point, you will need to reconnect and heal in these waters. For now, however, this flight is euphoric. It's a lovely reward and progress at last.

Your beautiful white horse lands directly in front of the Ascension Centre. You give thanks and gratitude. The horse will remain within you. Energy/vibration are now at a level and intensity that is being directed from Source. It matches and blends, dancing in full union with the centre and all connecting souls.

Amen.

A mushroom cloud of very light pink calcite cluster appears. It is really so very soft and beautiful, but yet so powerful. It surpasses the density that had presented and is now eliminated. Jesus appears to validate the healing today, indicating for us to continue and clear. The mushroom cloud pops within the centre. Baby white-pink energy filters throughout every room, every corner, under tables, around and in any crevice. The lovely pink cloud eliminates grey energy that was present, almost like a type of spiritual fumigation. It is now done.

The energy subsides, and Jesus begins his walk. He carries out an inspection of the premises. I see him walk from the retail space, up the corridor to a spot that is in need of extra attention, between two practitioner's rooms. He eliminates any residue with the wave of his hand. He then proceeds to the bathroom area and repeats the same. He turns and walks to the kitchen and blesses the place in which we prepare and nourish our bodies. "Spend more time honouring this process in a quiet time to eat—together, if possible." All people should do this.

He walks to the meditation room and feels great joy here; he blesses the space, and into the shop he progresses. He circles around the giftware, incense, and crystals, blessing each and every section, the front reception desk, the register.

He steps outside and is now working with a powerful love of pure God energy (pure white in colour) to link and anchor the Ascension Centre. He suddenly becomes fifty feet in height! He is with Archangel Michael, and an electric blue pure radiant energy surrounds them both. They place their hands upon our building and stream the energy over to the Ascension Centre. An imagery of very fine brick sand falls from the sky.

Construction will begin with these masters of light as our project managers! You are to focus and pray to them at any time regarding the construction process. The most beautiful white horse playfully and powerfully beckons you to join her. She represents the strength and power of longevity. What is not in alignment and does not resonate simply falls away. You do not need to keep creating any dysfunction or block as you have surpassed any karmic, genetic, or soul lesson. You connect to the higher vibration to ascend and learn, guide and heal.

Be steadfast with your values and your intent. Allow the flood gates to open to pour in more of the same.

Once the manifestation begins, let no person or energy distract. People will connect to the healing energy of your books, and upon holding one may feel the healing energy emanating from it.

Ridicule comes from arrogance. Educate well and clients and practitioners alike will speak from pure experience and an open heart. No question will be left unanswered. All will be revealed and understood.

Many books will be written. Your journey in writing, healing, and educating people is just beginning.

Jesus stands in front of you. He prompts you to place your right hand on your heart. He then kisses your forehead.

All blocks have been removed, and healing has taken place.

Thank you.

The Healers Journey: Current Status 12/8/2011

I see a well-known spiritual author pick up a copy of *The Healers Journey,* appearing curious. She flicks through some pages then stops to read. She calls out to her assistant, "Get their publisher on the phone, please."

The current publisher perfectly manages, accumulates sales, and distributes net profit with efficiency. With the number of copies in production, this system works well. But at some point, when it becomes too much to manage, another larger body can take over.

Hold your rights and monitor your own sales. This will give you the flexibility to make choices and perhaps reach more countries and people worldwide. Archangel Michael is ensuring your strength and stability in this area, washing away any dividedness with blue water, balancing the emotions.

The beauty of the Internet and cyberspace is that there is no limit to where a product can be exposed. Source energy is ready and waiting to be utilized once the book is released.

The release of the book sparks intense interest in your healing work, and in Ascension healings. So many people want to know how to use the book for themselves.

There is a wealthy entrepreneur, a businessman, who is inspired and wants to learn more about the book and your work.

*   *   *

There is an overseas spiritual magazine in the United States that becomes interested in writing a story.

*   *   *

There is a solid image of the Ascension Centre with the book featured in the window.

In a bookstore, in New York, the book is featured in the window. It is a warm sunny day.

*   *   *

How beautiful it is, as *The Healer's Journey* now appears with the photo and binding in place.

Arrangements of bookstores libraries, publishers, celebrities, and media to inform and/or send a complimentary copy of the book to will be next on the agenda.

Every part of the journey is protected, guided, and loved.

Thank you God, Archangel Michael.

Amen.

Healing Without Words   19/8/2011

With a gust of wind, millions and millions of leaves, purple in colour, lift and create a tube shape, a swirling vortex of purple beauty. It turns and swirls, showing the detail and separation of each leaf, then dissipates and creates one great mass of purple once again, turning and swirling, growing in size and mass until it covers the countryside, the oceans, the cities. This imagery represents a unity of souls and their connection to God. Negative thought forms no longer control their feelings and actions. Collectively, it is the engagement of the heart as their intellectual guide that encourages one and all to accept what is evident in their lives and allows them to fully embrace healing. No longer do they reflect and fear. No longer do they obstruct their souls' yearning for freedom, light, and love.

The purple energy begins to integrate with red swirled within it. The people are ready to embrace their healing in the love light and faith of God as they anchor into earth.

People are changing; no longer do the traditional methods work or resonate. People will begin to trust their instinctual voices within.

This is happening now to people of earth; the purple and red energy is present, helping all to release old programs that are no longer wanted. The vacuum is ruffling up all those leaves to allow free flow.

"Rest the book, open paged on your body, sleep, covers over (it will heal as you sleep)."

We are approaching a time where lengthy practices of reading are primitive to healing (smiling—with the exception of beautiful poetry). One will be touched by the word of God and be healed.

Amen

"No, I'm not leaving just yet. I need to work back a bit and get this project to the next phase."

Courtney is speaking to colleagues, saying goodnight. As she stays, she reflects on her own thoughts. *I am quite determined to give a little more to this project.* She smiles pleasingly to herself. *After all, these girls are special.*

Energy of Spirit, energy of intent and desire. Energy of manifestation and one's goals to see them blossom. Spring is blossoming and on our horizons. So many people are dedicated and intimately involved in this cause, and whilst it may seem lengthy, we are working at full capacity considering and combating all interceptions of humankind. Again, to live it is to learn it, and you are quite correct: there isn't anything that cannot be achieved with faith. It is important that with each and every acknowledgement, you are also learning, and this will be part of your teachings.

Jesus presents:

I walk amongst you. Do you see me? Yes, you do. I spread fuchsia-pink love energy from my palms, and I wash you with it. Do you feel that lovely rush of warmth and excitement in your heart? It is me. I am near, never far, and we prepare for a great time. You are dedicated and very strong.

Archangel Gabriel presents:

Keep united, keep love as your focus. People will flock as the word spreads. Look at the streams of light connecting the healing from America to Europe, Asia and Middle East, worldwide, because the healing is required worldwide.

We have begun and we will continue. The Eden, the euphoria, awaits our quest to relieve you all of your vices, misconceptions, or doubt. We help the people, all those beautiful souls, towards nirvana, to emerge collectively as one in a heavenly pool of light.

Earth-anchored, heaven-bound, dear ones.

Love you.

Archangel Gabriel and Jesus

The tremendous beams of light shine through the clouds. The light is directly over the Ascension Centre and the location of the chapel. Jesus shows you the template of the chapel as it already exists. With this vision, there is an undeniable knowledge that the chapel will be there as well and be available upon the timing of the new ministry for the people to access, worship, and heal with open doors.

Correctly acknowledged, the news of the sale has been for this very reason: so that you have the opportunity to clear any obstacle and align our intention, belief, and faith in the existence of the template.

Like anything that exists, you must acknowledge it is a current reality and release the need to control the "hows" and "what ifs." Do not involve yourself in this energy-wasting exercise, as the truth of the matter is that anything can change in twenty-four hours, if not in a blink of an eye. Why question a deeper meaning and purpose when faith is the most powerful engine to drive your destination? We create our own obstructions and blocks with concern and worry. It is a frequent human choice and pattern, one that we all battle with sometime or another. But this is also part of your evolvement and learning to trust in the light body and it's wise existence guiding and creating within you. If you fully trust the unfolding path and embrace your call, then you will attract countless resources to support it.

One day money will no longer exist, but for now the world and its economies function around this currency of exchange. This dynamic and exchange has been undergoing much change, both in function/usage and the re-evaluation of its physical need in our lives and consciousness. Both personally and in business, these exchanges are undergoing a dramatic makeover. We are using so much more bartering for services and items, and we are using credit cards and Internet purchases as a normal part of our daily retail practices. We are more conscious of the needs of people, and we are actively making a difference. We band together as a local and global community the moment something happens in the world. We see the borders melt away as we reach out with our hearts, minds, and donations to assist another in their time of need. It reiterates that overall, we band together as a community of humanity, and it's our belief in the overall goodness of each other that keeps our hearts engaged and our faith in a better world. And it is so.

The entrepreneur is human, with a soul and higher consciousness, like anyone else. No one is exempt from the challenging course of life on the planet, though theirs will be from a different perspective. Wealth is only one aspect of human existence. Many are re-evaluating their mission and responsibility, personally and professionally. Many are viewing their larger ability to make a difference and create a positive identity as ambassadors for the betterment of their world or their society and affected population. The possibilities are extraordinary when the entrepreneur has found his/her connection to Spirit and desires to assist and expand consciousness. In committing to a financial and operational dynamic to those less fortunate, the entrepreneur balances giving and receiving in the naturally abundant cycle of life and continues to receive more, allowing them to continue to give to society as a whole. The possibilities are endless and infinite and certainly not limited to money. The giving may be needed in the form of time, people, health professionals, resources, education, or training.

Likewise, for the assistance and support of your environment, the people of Melbourne and Australia, the chapel stands. The way in which it is signed to you is of no concern. Draw it, paint it, label it in your hearts. It is acquired already. Remember, the earth requires more and more anchored and light-filled premises, and this will definitely be one of them.

There will be business people, entrepreneurs, and corporations who will want to support it.

With gratitude,

God bless.

The water is dark and murky, like there's oil in the water. One cannot see through the density. The water is an element of emotion and lack of free flow. When so contaminated, it is feared.

Opening the heart to allow the free flow of a trusted light within you will clear the water. To open your heart, fear must be eliminated. This takes courage and intent for a journey with aligned goals.

Take note of the dynamics of today. The turn in the road is significant, and the awareness of an adjustment of your energy fields, as sensitive as they are, will be a focus as well. Fear of commitment, fear of the unknown, can feel and appear like solid wall. The lower chakra energies will be affected, with blocks relating to survival of the self. This dynamic will divide the room with respect to yourself and others around you. The higher the energy frequency, the finer the intricacies, the more definitive the roles and quests of the individual and the collective consciousness will be. The power of a group tht is functioning with love, defined goals, firm focus, self-belief, and strong passion will be unlimited in creativity. When one realises the beauty and connectedness of this dynamic, it is an overnight success. There are no leaky taps and no wishy-washy thought forms. Without judgement, we bless and release those who are not meant to be present. Like a bus travelling along a road, we do not question the stops that people choose to get off at, and certainly we feel the same thing with individuals who wish to get on.

In a larger sense, we are all connected through our energy; however, for the individuals who have soul quests and karmic clearings to attend to, the overall the consciousness will be on the same page. As we know, the energy and consciousness of the planet is shifting to a higher vibration. So in the shift and flow, like the tides going in and out in a rhythmic cycle, certain people will present for particular teachings, commitment, and contribution to the group, and others will exit.

It is perfect. Bless and release them with love. When we allow love to enter each act we do, there is room for so much more healing light to enter. We do not need to feel anxious or worried, or justify everything we do. We need to practice more being rather than doing.

Bless and release the transition.
Bless and release all those participating.
Bless and release the part of you which fears or feels disappointed.

It is in the hands of creation. No issue or dynamic is too complex. In fact, it is an autonomous reaction to create balance and goodwill, longevity and love, virtue and compassion. If it is imbalance you feel, allow the response of equilibrium, as this is the awaiting destination from your choice to heal, learn, and move on.

There is the perfect opportunity to expand to the next level in this wondrous journey. As this issue is close to the heavier forms of control, we choose to acknowledge that all things fall into place and find a corrective balance of natural design.

Bless all.

Healing has taken place.

Amen

A giant earthmover presents with the power of a thousand elephants!

The earthmover is scraping, shifting, and digging where necessary to remove toxicity, debris, rubbish, and related unhealthy attachments. The definition of what belongs to a positive outcome and what doesn't is now in focus. As a hive active with the sweetness of light and vitality, all bees wish to be here in the abundant and beautiful energy of this hub.

All are welcome to visit, but do not leave anything behind. Take your belongings with you. Empathy is a beautiful human trait; however, one must know the difference between empathy and codependence. The latter always turns to a web of ongoing dysfunctional responses in relationships. It defers responsibility in people and in their life decisions. Worse, you can be left with the heaviness of the energy dumped on you, and you'll be consumed by another's woes and destructive patterns, which do not belong to you.

We use this almighty energy earthmover today to move unwanted debris and clear the consciousness of carrying others' burdens. The eighth (an infinite number, 8) of this month invited many of these needed changes. We now practise and stabilise these changes.

We want to exit this site with no dirt left behind. In other words, completely clear the old and mirror the exact desire you wish to create in the physical. It is beginning with a clean slate. Empower your decision by insisting all monies owing be paid up-to-date, with no further work to be performed until this is done. This firm standpoint allows one the opportunity to break free from any work-related bullying. If any level of desperation regarding money and sourcing more income is emanating from you, then the firm standpoint will be weakened and compromised. Let go of the old, and embrace and give all your energy to a trusted, sustaining income source, which is ongoing and presenting now.

We understand that all of life is continuously moving. We are creating continuous changes through energy, affecting all areas of life, including work. We are working with an energy that is demanding results, and with that expectation we will always be moving it forward to obtain them. You can try to obstruct, control, manipulate, and force situations; however, if something is in a position opposite to your ideas and you refuse to see this, then the result will be as it's meant to be, regardless of your persistence of resistance.

View everything with an enquiring, seeking mind, and listen well for your answers. Let go and trust you will be shown how to achieve the easiest, most harmonious way to experience your dreams. Progress may seem to be slow or stagnant, but really one must look at all the changes, dynamics, and presenting clues to realise if your thoughts and actions are aligned with your intent. It is a tremendous choice, power and creativity, with logic and responsibility intact as well. It is important for us to remain focused and present and anchored to earth, with steps in the direction you're facing.

It is interesting to view what happens when we engage in doubt and fear. We allow the heaviness of fear to penetrate us, even at a minor level. We experience blocks in progress, stress, and ill health. The higher the vibration and perspective, the more doors open and the more we receive unexpected assistance from people, and opportunities can present. If you expect all levels of your creativity to be light-filled and ever-developing, it has a momentum and power that attracts like energy to it. What energy is that when converted to matter on earth? Or what energy is *like attracts like*? It is one we might call prosperity or abundance, wealth, health, and joy. It's comfortable, warm, and generous, self-sustaining and flowing in reserve.

This is the key. Want to change your life? Consider it already changed. The universe is already supporting your every choice and at this moment, whether you choose creativity and growth, or doubt and fear. The lesson here is awareness of self as a powerful creator open to the infinite possibilities of life providing via the easiest route possible.

Your path is clear, concise, passionate, and ready to be accepted with full success and happiness now.

Thank you.

Amen

Gabriel: I heed your call, and your healing today is required to allow the next phase of your business to excel beyond its current boundaries.

An open and giving heart sometimes has no differentiation of whom and what to give to; therefore, this aspect or dynamic needs attention for many people today. It is particularly mentally and emotionally taxing if the giving is somewhat conditional or if we have an investment or an attachment to the outcome. There is great wisdom in the expression, "You can lead a horse to water, but you cannot make him drink."

Thirst for water, nourishment, self-fulfilment, personal vision, and goals is a strong indication of one's desire for achievement and growth. This is a willingness of our wanting to exist happily. Each one of you needs to ask the questions, "How much do I want it? How much am I willing to let go of ego, control, and anothers' visions of who they think I should be?" Allow your own power to decide and create your dreams to manifest in your life. There is a symbolic fountain to drink from. It is the infinite fountain of plenitude. Hydrate your body and your soul, and trust in the infinite wisdom within you. As you own the process of change, reinvention, or rebirthing, your vibration will only attract those who resonate at the level that supports mutual growth. In alignment with that, you will not feel the need to convince anyone of the need to heal; rather, you will offer the reasons for your choices and express the journey thus far, leaving the freedom of choice entirely up to the person you're sharing with.

Archangel Michael, Raphael, Archangel Gabriel, and Uriel will work lovingly and compassionately with these individuals to assist with their energy clearing and detoxification until which time they seek, on a conscious level, the energy work.

Leading by example has always been and will always be a very powerful tool. Mentoring, guiding, and teaching resonates very well with you and your life-purpose goals. If you're passionate and successful, others will feel inspired to be that too.

To connect to the empowered, the strong, and the souls who wish to join us in the creation of health, peace, and individuality on earth is a cocreative and joyful expanded growth and a secure foundation for those who seek guidance and love. Educate every living being with an understanding that they have an infinite connection to Source. Their own divinity and purpose has led them to be attracted and joined to us in furthering their soul's passion alongside one another.

We acknowledge the improvements and adjustments you've made in your business's plans and projections, technology information and updates, and in your professionalism and service. The calling forth of all those who have been attracted to assist you are surfacing, along with the timely release of your first book, *The Healers Journey* and your new website.

All is well.

Amen

Oh Michael, how fitting it is for you to be in this blessèd position! What a way to have your awakening.

Stunningly white sheets of energy mixed with gold dust; bathing in the light is us all. We soak in God's loving shower. It helps to cleanse the toxicity, the dense encodings of the genetic fortress. Michael, it is time to reveal the immense popularity (as you will see it), and then a realisation that within your grasp is a phenomena you don't quite understand. The book's creation in its form is carried forth by a trinity. The two women, Alexandra and Courtney, are fairly open, Courtney more so than Alexandra; however, Michael is a renowned sceptic and scientific analyser of all things.

But, Michael, ironically you are now faced with one of the most profound and desirable tasks of all time. How little you know at this stage. That is okay, as it is part of your personal soul journey as well.

We have all crossed paths before. Your soul was incarnate at the time of Jesus's crucifixion. There was reference to deliverance of a letter to the church leaders with respect to a mercy plea from many pilgrims to save his life. Michael, you delivered that letter but did not believe in its contents until you saw the face of the Lord. You fell to your knees in tears. His eyes burned into your memory as you asked and begged God for forgiveness. You cried and cried, your heart knowing he was the son of God.

Thousands of years later reveal the karmic and genetic clearing to this aspect. Michael, it is time for you to acknowledge your role in believing in the return to earth of the Christ lineage, which has resurfaced to embrace the earth with her healings, teachings, and messages of hope. You have the role of promoting *The Healers Journey*. You remember your awakened heart right there at the cross. As painful as it seemed, your heart's awakening solemnly promised to never forget. The genetic encoding from your father enforces with male dominance that there is nothing in existence apart from matter related to science and the most superior of beings is mankind.

Your father instilled a belief system that supported study, education, and reading as tools to advance, but very little engaged from the heart. Happiness was made out of achievements, score cards, and money. "Be the most informed person at the dinner table, and you will be admired always!"

Michael, you are about to remember. A sensation will befall you once the book begins selling, but you feel something "weird" within you every time you view it.

Think less, feel more, and ask your heart to remember.

Blessèd are you.

Within God's ultimate, divine plan, we trust.

Amen

Ah, how perfect you are! Beloved angels, listening so intently.

We are using modern-day resources in the form of the web to promote, advertise, and sell our products and services. Formerly, the information and technology had not matched the energy and vibration of the business; therefore, past employees, website creators, and designers still had an imprint infused (energetically) that imposed a different, outdated feel.

I am shown the company and website designer that you should choose.

It is important that the website creation and release of *The Healers Journey* work well together. Much like an explosion of interest, the website and book release spark an attention to the business and escalate it to the next level.

A beautiful star-filled night sky presents with the astrological sign of Scorpio. Perhaps this symbolises November. The energy is very passionate and creative.

Continue with the design process, and trust all is in place to bring your business to the next level with the correct people, products, and web support you need.

It's a conscious web, after all.

The Final Healing for The Healers Journey's Production 20/10/2011

A beautiful white dove flies and lands inside an open windowsill.

There is a sprig of an olive branch in its beak. The vision then moves back farther, farther, and then farther again to reveal that the window belongs to the stone wall of a cottage. The cottage is attached to a lovely chapel. We are in the south of France, and it's a beautiful sunny day. The grass is green, and the trees and the buildings look like a painted landscape of this beautiful patch of countryside.

There is an added emotion: an air of humble relief that the time grows near. Some locals predict the coming of a feminine power, one whose lineage reconnects this region with its extraordinarily rich history.

Holy and rich is this land. There are living oracles, frozen in time, who will remember her.

*   *   *

"Oh, sir, how challenged you are! Your health, your vitality, and your blocks (all coming forward for you to acknowledge and heal now) bring about circumstances that you misinterpret as not working.

"Rest your over-analysing mind, which is making you weary and unfocused, and allow this power of love and healing to permeate every part of your being so you may benefit. You are putting up a fight against your own nourishment and desire to heal, which will only cause you added intensity, as you misinterpret it. This is a healing tool, dear one. Do not feel embarrassed to admit that you feel a connection and energy coming from it. This is exactly its purpose. You are feeling the power of it gently brushing your cheek. You must permit the healing to touch you. Allow the new, unchartered waters to drift you from the old into the new shoreline."

She's attractive, you think.

Remember the face, you hear in your thoughts.

The road is now clear. This man's healing blocks have now been cleared to allow the completion to take place.

Above the buildings, our large white dove descends, ensuring the final stage commences.

Much love eternally.

This is a desperate bid for survival. A low frequency in many small streams (entities) attaches to high frequency of light. It does this as it is aware the light will ensure its survival.

Rodents are successful in maintaining their species. Seen scuttling over the rubbish that humans have left behind, they seek out and find plenty of life-sustaining food. However, in their droppings, the toxicity can be so great severe health imbalances and suffering towards other life forms can eventuate. The droppings are quite symbolic here. They represent fear, desperation, and anger—all the basis of low-frequency energy.

When a reattachment appears (what was formerly present clears then returns), it means something hadn't completely left its primary place. This may not mean exclusively a physical presence; it could still be present within an energetic, thought, or emotional sense. The energy/entity/attachment itself has a vibration that is attracted to its survival and continuance. It is not necessarily intelligent, but it is certainly resistant to dissipation.

Once a shift in your awareness has occurred and you decide to release it, you may experience a rise in your emotional state, given that the energy begins to resist and hold on. The energy is no longer balanced in the internal environment, which you are changing. Frustration develops, as it can no longer feed off your life force. Lack of self-love, ego-driven thought forms of self, victimhood, righteousness, desperation, loss, anxiety, and depression are all symptoms of this type of unhealthy attachment. You may experience all or some of these reactions or emotions as it begins to break down and release. This is where people can become disorientated and upset. Know that the feeling of these emotions is a sign you are releasing effectively, and as long as you are aware and willing to work through it, just keep going. These low-vibration emotions are *not* your natural state of being and are not yours at all. You must understand—it is this energy's ferocity that integrates all levels of your emotional, mental, and physical bodies. It will feel like yours, but it certainly is not.

Once that environment (your body) is lightened and cleared, the energy that had established itself can no longer hold on and will dissipate and evaporate like water upon the hot sand. Your strongest assets whilst going through this experience are your mind and your heart. Take very deep breaths, breathing in green and pink energy light through your heart, and ask your healing angels/guides to assist and support you through the clearing. Practise affirmations on an hourly basis if necessary: "All is well, I am safe and releasing, I am loved and supported, all is in divine order right now." Continue to breathe deeply. Meditation, exercise, plenty of sleep, and good nutrition are all very good support elements.

The body can feel such disarray on a physical, emotional, or mental level. Whilst it feels very real, it is an energy that you have the power to release. This may take some time and commitment. You may need to practise a bit of patience and perseverance whilst experiencing your clearing process, so remember this: every day, every hour, every minute, you are a little closer to your desired version of yourself. He/she is truly courageous and magnificent, and you need to be even more loving and compassionate towards the beautiful being that you are. You are doing a great job. You are taking the steps to a healthier, happier you. Hang in there, and commit to your greatest investment: you.

You may experience physical symptoms or sensations in the head area (headaches, dizziness, disorientation), neck and throat areas (throat chakra), at the base of spine (base chakra) particularly near or at the coccyx bone, lower back pain, pain or discomfort in the stomach area (the solar plexus), and sometimes in the legs and feet. Whilst experiencing these symptoms, if you are concerned about any pain or discomfort, please seek the advice and assessment of your doctor and/or healthcare professional.

From a metaphysical perspective, the coccyx is an integral location of the anatomy, being the southernmost tip of the torso. It is a conductor of incoming energy from earth and energy infiltration and balancing. It is highly influential to the auric bodies and responsible for a healthy connection of the physical body to the earth.

Lower frequencies generally cannot attach at the upper regions of the body and its chakras, as the frequency and light velocity is too high to coexist and will not survive.

The low frequency can be likened to a virus which enters the body, attacking the most vulnerable area and then spreading if not treated. Recognition of this frequency is imperative to a healthy life in all ways, whether it be within your body, your business, your family life, or if you are planning to travel or have children. Whatever the desire for growth, movement, or change, humans will always have the irresistible urge to release and recover from anything that doesn't match the happiest, most aligned and peaceful version of yourself for your life.

It has been noted that when a person or his business has overcome great challenges and is well on the way to an expanded future of growth and advancement of any kind that he may suddenly experience a negative response or situation.

This prompts one to ask, "Well, what does this mean now?" We acknowledge and advise taking another deep breath. Do not be concerned; it is merely validation of what has been cleared and healed and what's been left behind. In fact, it is a time of celebration of strength, persistence and evolvement, and proof of what no longer exists.

The more dysfunction, ill health, or manifestation of an emotional, mental, or physical kind, the more the need to acknowledge and commit to self-development and energy work to clear it and move onto the life you were designed to live.

Thank you. Inspiration, motivation, and education! Amazing forethought so we are prepared and can assist all people at this level.

That is all.

The Healers Journey: Release Date!   26/9/2011

A postage van bearing U.S. mail stops outside a building. The post delivery man gets out a brown paper package to deliver inside. Within the brown paper packaging is a completed copy of *The Healers Journey* to be presented to an executive in the new releases department of the publishing company. The creative path is almost completed. Nineteenth October 2011 marks a significant date for proofing what has been put together so far. Release date is scheduled for mid-November 2011, but we acknowledge a small delay with the official release date, which will include the release to the web on 1 December 2011.

We now invite the scope of its healing ability and the truth of its love to resonate in your heart so that you may experience the first of these "healing tool" texts in a trilogy of books to be released. This book will ignite your curiosity to begin with, and then once the spark within Self recognises the energy or vibration the book provides, you will have already received one of the many wonderful benefits.

Many of you will understand instantly and offer little resistance. Others may require more time or a slower process. All individuals are completely within their freedom to choose what resonates with them and in turn consider and allow a possibility of something unique and illogical by scientific methods. Feel the freedom to explore an alternative path towards healing, education, and expansion in all ways of life that is dramatically changing on our planet.

There is a flame which is alive in your heart. It releases ego, conditional love, and control. We are not defined by external needs and wants any longer. Our existence has expanded to a fifth-dimensional vibration and reality. The flame within allows every dream you have to manifest as it warms and inspires the glow of your soul. Your acknowledgement of your flame ignites awareness of the law of attraction, working in and around you constantly and therefore magnifying and positioning all you require in your life.

Amen

Sands of time funnel through an hourglass. It never stops. At each moment the grains are moving and flowing. They nestle into a new location until the weight of the movement creates a shift once again.

When a group and its consciousness no longer share a unified vision, it lacks strength. It leaks and creates a frequency with holes, allowing other vibrations and thought forms (doubt, fear) to penetrate and intercept it. This is time wasting and holds no benefit for anyone involved.

If someone feels they no longer suit their environment, peacefully make plans to relocate. There is no need for a big dramatic exit. Such displays are unnecessary and unacceptable. Rather, go in peace, dear ones, if this no longer feeds your life and soul. Do not look for someone to blame, as that unproductive and depleting. View it as a time of shifting sands that is completely acceptable and a natural cycle of life. It is a gift to have the support, guidance, and love you experience from your divine guides and angels along your journey. Any projections and fear you experience in your creative environment are manifested from you and your vision of what you think is reality. If your vision sustains lack of freedom and choice, then this will be your experience. If your self-worth predicts dissatisfaction and disharmony, then you will limit yourself to this. You can be whomever you wish, and you may create this most effortlessly. It is your apparent limits in your abilities and the blocks that cause this, which creates resistance instead of creation.

When the team no longer embraces the same vision, it is fruitless to believe that the original vision of success in its original form can be fulfilled. It is a colliding force of opposing energies creating pressure and little productivity. It may coexist for a short while, with a number of incidences occurring to further reveal and confirm the inevitable. This is a non-creative environment, and a separation must occur to allow each to find their new, natural place to grow. And yes, as the branching off occurs, there is much relief as the pressure valve is loosened and all the negative energies of fault, blame, and fear can disperse. Ultimately, this is the resolution and freedom all should rightfully have.

Shifting grains of sand, moving and not resisting the movement, flow effortlessly to a new resting place until the next shift. It is natural, it is movement, and it is life.

We live, work, and love with an open heart and mind, offering freedom and growth to all. May we only attract the same in others.

Thank you and amen.

Meditation: Prerequisite
Healing Modality   29/8/2011

Shower me with your love. Your energy beckons me, but there is some sort of resistance. On the edge of the highest vibration of bliss, we consciously and actively shed the energy that no longer serves us. Having learned and realised the fifth-dimensional existence, you now sever and remove, clear and vacuum any debris still existing within your business on all its levels. This means in all areas, including physical, mental, emotional and etherical on earth. Amen.

Former practitioners had a successful outcome in mind, naturally, as it was to sustain and nurture themselves and their practise as well. However, this business always has carried a strong healing vibration, and no individual would be exempt from the opportunity to consider and heal their own presentations. They would be shown their triggers, just like anyone else. Working within a fairly intimate environment would allow obvious mirrors to present in each person as well as the owner of the business, creating a great opportunity for all to address and heal their collective and independent issues.

Each previous practitioner who contributed to the business certainly healed while working there and then, for a variety of reasons, left. Upon each and every class or workshop held, there was an aspect or energy that was left behind by the practitioner and their personality, as this is a natural occurrence that happens. It is a bit like a relationship when it ends. The memory, energy, and impression of that person remain until they are compassionately but actively severed. Furthermore, other employees and clients alike may further enhance this energy by referring to them (either fondly or otherwise); therefore, there is an ongoing existence in thought and energy long after the practitioners have gone. This is unhealthy for the further development and growth of the business and her current practitioners' popularity and progress.

The clue was evident with a recent clearing for a client and her new business venture. The question was asked, "What was that space occupied by or used for previously?"

"A healing centre," was the reply. What we knew instantly was that any past and uncleared residue would remain and connect to the new business, impacting it positively or negatively until it was cleared.

We are being shown a tremendous energetic fact, and with empowered awareness, we are shown the practise and the educational perspective to help ourselves as well as offer our assistance, wisdom, and clearing/healing to other businesses.

With respect to your business and the modality of meditation (as a weekly workshop offered), our viewpoint and education on this is that it allows the client to begin to open to their inner wisdom and healing journey. It is also beneficial for clients who are in between healings to maintain and assist a healthy body and mind, particularly if they are in an environment that is unsupportive of their healing. It is also very beneficial for those who experience a lot of mind chatter and uncontrolled thoughts. Everyone can benefit from this all-important modality, providing peace and overall calm and well-being. When practised consistently and with commitment, many areas of life improve, including clear thinking and concentration, restful sleep patterns, appetite and digestion, and the ability to respond well in stressful situations.

A new educational flyer is suggested to pinpoint the benefits of meditation and the wonderful opportunity to all to enhance and improve their lives and overall well-being. This will obviously educate people and help to abolish misconceptions about this valuable practice. Title it "Meditation at Enchanting Angels: Commonly Asked Questions."

What are the benefits of regular meditation?
Why is meditation at our centre different from some other traditional forms?
Why will I benefit?
Will I receive messages/guidance?
What level of experience will I need?

This is a solid, educational modality that is valued, respected, and understood by clients and practitioners alike. It is an essential and integrating modality to current healing and mediumship clients.

Within this business, we work for the betterment and ascension of earth.

Blessed are we.

Amen

As his heart thumps in his chest, there is an adrenalin overload in his body. This man constantly questions the existence of any law or balance in the universe—and in his own life.

Do not mistake that his negativity regarding your vocation is about you personally. It is not. It is about himself. Where balance exists in his world, it is a strong give-and-take agreement. It is a simple black-and-white obligation. "You do this for me, and I'll do that for you." It is a fair trade, and it is even.

He has existed for a very long time with this perspective. At the same time, he continues to have an expectation of failure, either his own or someone else's. He expects to receive from an agreement of fair trade; however, he expects equally to be disappointed by others! As he signs up for a new job, contract, or opportunity, he pre-empts a negative outcome with respect to receiving. He has a belief system that expects disappointment for his efforts.

How can one opt for such a negative and destructive habitual process? This is the case for many humans who have only chosen unhealthily in businesses, in relationships, and in health. They actually self-sabotage their personal power so they will not be disappointed in case they are right about their negative viewpoints. Additionally, success actually becomes feared. "What if I actually succeed? I'm afraid to succeed! Why? Because success is for those who allow vulnerability and risk. They don't have fear of exposure or failure, and I do."

This generally leads back to control issues in allowing a certain amount of risk and faith to pave the way. When you have a need to control on all levels, you cannot allow faith to enter. Disappointment is something you can guarantee and control, which is a self-fulfilling philosophy of pain. And you can be right!

Many people live like this. They do not trust themselves enough to use their personal power and manifestation abilities. They self-sabotage all attempts of success so they don't have to have the exposure, fear of failure, and responsibility that comes with it. They would rather be a victim and blame the rest of the world and have the greatest excuse not to grow. Exhausting.

It has nothing to do with anyone else or another's success, as this is simply his mirror of self.

Do not allow his current emotional and mental state to affect your vision and creative power for yourself. We acknowledge that your environment and partnership is challenging as it coexists with you. Keep your focus strong and unwavering, and allow your example to lead with grace.

You do not follow the same belief system or philosophy as your partner. Unlike what marriage and partnerships have taught you, that it was your duty to drop your own beliefs and follow only those of your man, we clearly confirm it is not necessary or true.

You are what you believe and will become. No man or woman is excluded from this truth. You must not allow the choices that others make to alter your belief or vision and what lies ahead for your reality. This is a great lesson for all.

Negative and positive events are occurrences that follow from a belief of your power. Use this power wisely and lovingly.

As habitual creatures, we often set in stone a belief after experiencing it. How can one ever change an aspect when the expectation has been prepared?

Two words, simple powerful words:

open
and
allow

When near him in prayer, in work, and in rest, say the above words as an affirmation on his behalf. Repeat these words and allow God's love to influence.

Amen

What is intended will be so, as it is intended to be a text of healing to anyone who holds and reads it. A large white copy of the book spins above the building in a dance of light and energy.

It carries a very joyful, light frequency as it effortlessly spins in the air. This is of course symbolic, and it is very good. The creative process has touched many people and influences along the way. Your positive expectations, your energy, and your faith in knowing that your book marks the beginning of a long career in teaching and healing holds your primary perspective and pending reality. People will believe as they wish to experience at this time, and you will be unaffected by opinions. Your primary focus is to guide and offer a taste of one's ability to succeed in all areas of life, to heal any apparent challenge whether it be physical, emotional, or mental. These challenges may be connected to your business or your family dynamic.

Through the acknowledgement of our past experiences, we assess and connect the dots, embracing and accepting the power we hold. This confirms there is an unending Source from which we can all access every desire and creation possible.

The Healers Journey now begins its own journey. Her birth and presentation spark a new possibility of intrigue and perception. Media may be confused and reviews may be mixed; however, place no importance on "factual" evidence and opinion. The energy encodement and loving vibration within her pages will reach forth and touch the hearts of many.

We call forth all soul-connected writers and journalists, magazine editors, and short summary writers to review with an understanding of a higher Source. Working through this text and with an intrigue of wondrous possibilities, we encourage all those who wish to engage and look with love, clarity, healing, and grace. All are beautiful and empowered beings who choose to connect with a Source that will lead them to true self discovery of Self.

You have a great opportunity, as you stand on the edge of a huge change. Teachers and healers alike, you will experientially and faithfully lead by example, and as you do, you will eliminate much past and present emotional karmic and fear-based aspects, as well as mental past and present aspects, alongside those you guide and heal. You will be able to create so much in your lives and those you guide.

Amen

New York, where dreams are made . . . welcome to New York.

What a huge energy in this place. And of course, as expected, all is possible here.

Creativity is abundant and exposure very possible in the United States. The media was created in the United States! It is no doubt a place upon the planet to experience all that is possible to connect you to producers, writers, agents, and all levels of media. They are the display board of the world, as well as London and all of Europe.

The first thing that is quite striking is that street pavement is so very wide! It is a warmish, sunny day.

Suddenly, the scene changes. You are standing at the top of a beautiful mountain overlooking the vast landscape stretching over many thousands of kilometres in every direction. Jesus approaches you and stands beside you. He is pointing out to the vastness and making reference to the unlimited distance you are now able to cover.

In its physical sense, the creation of a book is somewhat heavy in matter, and those expecting logic and formula will find it difficult to understand in the beginning. It is still so necessary for the people to read and ingest, ponder and evaluate. It will certainly help during these times of change upon our planet, when we are challenged by the dramatic energy patterns touching us all. In your future, mere intent will deliver the desired information, healing and wisdom. There are those who already practise this, but they are few.

At no point are you alone and unsupported, and you know this. Your quest is also mine, as we share the joy and excitement of our goal for healing towards peace.

Questions in the public arena are no different from those in your business each day, and realistically, people from Australia or the United States, the United Kingdom or France have the same life challenges, regardless of their location. We are one world, and humanity displays little difference in her desires for life: love, happiness, peace, security, direction, connection, and abundance.

Accept a refreshing and exciting openness and acceptance from a large population overseas as they are exposed to more, and consider a great deal more than some sheltered or traditional populations.

Come what may, and accept and allow every opportunity to present.

Each new day reveals the next creative opportunity.

Enjoy and savour the waiting.

Amen

It Is as You See It   11/10/2011

If we were to be viewing our environment energetically rather than physically, we would see a very different picture from what our physical eyes can see.

As you know, you are powerful co-creators of all you intend. Now with your intention for further growth and prosperity, you would heal to disperse, remove, and eliminate entirely any karmic blocks, fears, any unhealthy and contradictory emotion in this clearing today.

A grey mist with many strings, almost appearing like very thin wire cords, was viewed in the environment. We now set forth with healing intent that the mist is lifting and the cords are fading and disintegrating. When certain circumstances occur, particularly if there is a significant change in your business environment, i.e., an employee leaves or begins, a business associate offers a product or incentive and you accept, a new contract is signed, or even if you change banks, the energy and frequency in the environment begins to change. It is always advisable to initiate a business clearing, so that your renewed perspective, new energy, and refreshed plans can be streamlined into your new reality. Putting forth an intent of releasing all that was past that no longer serves allows for the specific clearing to take place. This specific request clears any residue, fear, and thought form from past circumstances that may still be present.

The new day is unfolding right now, and all that we desire is the matching practitioners, clients, suppliers, sales, bookings, and enquiries from people who will be in alignment with the new and clear perspective of a light-and-love-filled business, ever growing and ever changing.

Our prosperity and abundance will match the what we attract; therefore, be as we desire.

What an important role we all have on this planet. Never has there been a time more accepting of the innate power each of you hold within yourselves. Yet you may cry, "But the economies all around the world, the markets are crashing! We are losing our businesses and our homes!"

What an opportunity that presents to you. As a physical example, you are now shown the power and co-creative ability to make manifest your poverty very well indeed, as you pay so much attention to it. The very thing you give so much fear to (money, wealth) is the very thing you lack, because you hand over all of your personal power. If the human race were to wake up tomorrow morning and realise that all their emotions, perspectives, thoughts, and actions actually enforce and empower their fears of losing wealth, they may stop for a moment and consider changing their channelled power towards prosperity rather than poverty. When you all fear constantly (with great powerful emotion) the loss of jobs, industry collapses, economies crashing, tax increases, interest rates rising, and everything else we consume and bury ourselves under on a hourly basis, we are in fact, feeding an oversized loss/drain co-creation and consciousness.

You are convinced it is so, as it is everywhere. Feeding unto itself as you invest more power, more dread, more fear, more suffering. You confirm your fears by turning on your televisions and reading your newspapers. I am not suggesting that you put your head in the sand. Being informed is personal power and being ready for change. Do you feel that in your body as you read those words? *Being informed is personal power ready for change.* And it begins with you. Each and every individual holds power to make a difference. You may exclaim, "But how can I change the world? Eliminate poverty? Overthrow selfish government decisions?"

Stop reverberating what isn't working and begin with yourself. Trust that your change, your new direction, your position of positivity, your leadership in your small way within your small world will expose a frequency of change and spark an awareness in those around you. Those who view your altered, trusting, and peaceful perspective and the positive changes in your life will feel inspired and will naturally begin to question their own lives, their routines, their decisions. On and on and on it goes. It begins like a gentle wave lapping onto the shore and eventually the tides of consciousness begin to turn.

You have a great opportunity, as you stand on the edge of a huge change. Lightworkers and teachers, you will faithfully lead by example and by doing so will eliminate all karmic, fear, thoughts, emotional past, and present distractions. This is true power and true change. You will create a very different picture and a physical existence that matches one's soul, exposing and utilising the infinite wisdom and knowledge that is within Self.

Amen

Humans can be so capable of such deceptive actions, and sadly it is energetically costly and certainly taxing on the Soul.

What karmic debt one accrues with one's ego's choices and actions (with or without money or items exchange) eventually will be corrected into balance. It is the unseen, an irrepressible force, that governs the cycle of the entire universe. It is just so. There is no judgement, no fire and no fury.

Karma is a correction of balance in the justice of soul.

We, as Soul, desire nothing more than to have this balance and are driven by it within a huge, unending energy wheel of existence. There is no avoiding it, and no desire to avoid it either. It is accepted and honoured.

People and their egos are temporarily out of soul-consciousness and in an unhealthy ego illusion during times of manipulative, hurtful, controlling, and dishonest actions, including co-creating criminal activity. The power they believe they have sourced is false, extremely negative, and low in frequency. It will eventually attract more of what it is likened to itself, causing self-destruction. There is no supremacy and no longevity. Karma will always correct the balance.

Do not seek revenge. Release the circumstances by opening your arms to the universal frequency that is always supporting your karmic balance.

Trust and believe. Let us seek a better way. Your true inner being, the one connected to all life, understands this plainly and simply. There is no desire that cannot be obtained or fulfilled. Whether it be the job, house, car, relationship, business, or course of study, it is all available to you through your connection to your highest energy Source, and will bring forth all of your wishes in this life.

Do not get in the way of your creative process by holding ill feelings towards self or another. This will block flow. Many of you have strong negative emotions and thoughts about your abilities and opportunities, or you think life is scarce or unavailable to you. There is an infinite flow of endless abundance, opportunities, people, and even money that will be attracted to you in flow and in the creative process of what you wish to achieve and receive.

I could reiterate over and over about negative attraction and creation of situations and circumstances (and appropriate karma), over obtaining items of pleasure, money, and false power in exchange for the misfortune of another. It is not possible that one can turn a blind eye or pretend it didn't happen. Every action and intent is accounted for, always. You will know very clearly, via your own inner guidance of strong feeling, that an action you are considering is not for your or anyone's highest good. If you pursue a negative action, consequences will always result on various levels. We must now look towards intent, which supports conscious choice of what you really wish to create.

Finally, if you have made choices and decisions based on good intent but you were not consciously aware that the outcome would not be positive, karma will be always and foremost related to your intention and secondly the outcome. There are many scenarios; however, we ask you to have awareness, openness, compassion, and kindness in all you do and acknowledge every valuable lesson. We are all connected, so consider yourself in all you do. Would you harm yourself intentionally? Or your sister? We are all affected by each other's actions.

Allow your inner guidance to resolve all business and money concerns and exchange matters and you will create more abundance and flow. Trust in the infinite flow of the universe to deliver the prosperity in whatever form or method required and accept and allow it to present to you. Your positive emotion and expectation of your desires is a very powerful magnet. You have unlimited treasure available to you.

We call forth light- and soul-aware clients and business connections to educate, give, and receive. We are growing to unlimited heights to allow further nurture and prosper together in our quest and our purpose.

Amen

With love

Moving Forward   13/10/2011

Fog. Anger and frustration. These are fear-rooted, false, or unbalanced emotions appearing to be real. It is a frequency, one that feels uncomfortable and volatile. As sensitive and open vessels, we are considered light workers. It is a wonderful and appropriate gift of intuitiveness; however, it can also feel quite uncomfortable when experienced in a negative way. We are currently experiencing symptoms of an energy infiltration that is connected to all here, particularly in the head (fogginess and confusion) and through emotion.

There cannot exist a persuasive power of any sort that has not been invited in on some level and therefore have a host to adhere to. Where energy has no matching vibration or karmic connection, it cannot reside, or more appropriately, affect the receiver.

This is extremely intricate and relates to many separate associations and connections, all of which should not and cannot be fully identified. In doing so, you connect further to it, fear it, form it, and give it power. We simply step back, acknowledge it with an identification of its general root or source, and intend on clearing it energetically, physically, genetically, emotionally, mentally, on all levels, now.

We stand firm in our heavenly guidance and feel the love of our divine hosts descending down in a golden-white glow to assist us in this clearing. As you transmit the releasing frequency, the clearing of energy clutter or hooks is evident, the body is relaxing and the return to the God Self state is evident.

Empowered and calm
Love of self and others
Believing and receiving
Giving and teaching and living on Path with a passion of awakening all and ourselves. Humble in our knowing and learning every day. We give thanks for gaining wisdom, as we will be able to offer guidance to others.

Allow your compassion and forgiveness to forward your movement. It will be smoother and steady. Understand that the energy has no personal vendetta, only an attachment in energy.

Amen

Reap All You Sow

A wise decision indeed. It is necessary for you to conduct this clearing today to co-create flow and the manifestation of The Ascension Centre.

It is much like removing weeds from the soil before your new planting of fresh vegetables and fruit can grow.

It is most important to step away from the dense and desperate energy and completely detach from it. It is desperation and self-serving and it does not concern itself with who is suffocating.

If you allow the drama and density consume you, it will. A an amount of personal strength and focus is required. Do not make or believe it to be a personal quest. Your parents will be confused and upset in the confusion.

Each person is communicating their case convincingly, authentically, that their own reasons are of the greatest importance. We see cash flow prosperity, ensuring funds are present. It is all about how this entire process is handled. Begin your quest with your planned vision and firm goal. Envision the sole owner of The Ascension Centre be you. The expansion of your debt is relative to the business advancements and growth you intend to venture upon. The others are not committed in the same way nor have they the scope to invest in the time and energy. Some require a great lifestyle, so do not be mistaken. Only purest and like intention need be part of the partnership here.

Plan to settle by way of buying them. This is the most fair and most viable. This also gives you scope to sell a property to lessen debt, if needed. A number of clearings to assist with projected fears will be recommended.

There may be some curveballs thrown; however, keep calm and focused. Keep your eye on the goal. Multimillion dollar businesses have surpassed much more and have reached countless of agreements worldwide, worth a great deal of money, with peace ending. You are no different.

One step at a time with appropriate clearings at each level will be required.

The seed is laid.

This is all for now.

Amen

Oh, look! So many cherries on the tree. They are plump, juicy, ripe cherries!

Apparent wounds of self, we are truly humbled by its presence, and in our tearful, surrendering recognition, we are accepting of the gift of awareness, allowing much to be learned. Wounds are not medals to be displayed after war. They signify such confusion and dismay, usually brought about by the need to be validated and loved, via the position of victimhood.

Victimisation comes from a disconnection from Self and God. The result of the lack of recognition of self-value and grace in your life. It is not from a judgemental God, his hand slapping downward upon you without mercy.

What is that belief anyway? She is the creator of all experience. If you create lack, victimisation, poverty, and confusion, your life will reflect that. God allows you to experience whatever you wish. You have choice and free will. However, He will always urge you, guide you, give you the many signs and support around you to be kinder, more loving, and conscious in all She knows you're capable of being but have forgotten.

Ego wants to control with masks, roles, and identities. This is not reality at all. There is only one true you. But our various identities help to save the rest of ourselves from the pain we may be experiencing. So we divide it up and want to understand what occurred with that portion of you. When the ego has suffered a blow, it needs self-justification and sometimes revenge. We may want to justify the injuries and question the righteousness in the eyes of God. An emotional spiralling will almost certainly occur from this perspective. We will try to contemplate and understand the deservedness of an outcome and injury: "Why did God do this to me? What did I ever do to deserve this?"

It is with tremendous courage, absolute healing, and internal/ego revolution that we accept with complete responsibility the education and healing you are about to receive from a choice you made. And yes, you may need to heal and self-nurture for a time. One must recover well and when ready go forth with great strength before embarking on the next leg of the journey.

Many still walk this planet in an illusionary state of separateness. None of you are separate, alone, or deserted. Ever. But only you can decide your road, the direction you wish to go travel towards your growth, self-leadership, and creativity unlimited.

Assess and reassess again. Question your motives and align your goals with your greatest creative potential. If you are unsure the direction to go, ask! Ask and you will be shown. The signs will appear in your life in a variety of unlimited ways: the next song on the radio, a signpost by the side of the road, or a passing truck. Ask, trust, and enjoy the experience. It is one you had yearned for, to fully embrace in all of its perfect and imperfect ways.

Amen

Pending the Release   24/10/2011

The miracle angel card, which displays Jesus Christ on the front, is shown.

I see him in conference with other light beings. The words *Light Council* can be heard, and with this vision the acknowledgement of help and pending miracles is imminent.

A very large golden slide, sparkling and lush, indicates a free-flow experience is now. Holding your faith and belief in your goals can be challenging when the physical evidence is to the contrary. During these times, your co-creative flow may feel like it dips. Don't allow any negative thoughts to spiral into an illusion, which creates blocks. Even if the energy you feel belonged to another, someone who doubted their path and experienced that outcome, it is not yours, and it has no hold on your reality. This too is cleared now with a diamond-white quintessence stream. Allow it all to begin now. There will be a proofread coming shortly, then it will be printed immediately.

Three hundred copies will be ordered for the centre. We are now actively preparing for the book launch. How busy it will be.

With thanks.

It is now a request that we ask for a person to join us in a sales capacity and general administrative role. I see a lovely blonde woman with big blue eyes. She's delightful, quietly passionate, and she holds gratitude in her heart. She wants to open her journey to healing slowly. She trusts in her path and the force that's leading her. She feels entirely new, not a person who is currently connected to the business.

It is understood that as powerful energy and light workers, we are creating in every moment. As this is so, we acknowledge the need to dissolve and disassociate from any negativity or attachment of lower frequencies. We need to know how to do this fluently, as this skill will be shared and taught.

Keep your intentions clear about what and who you wish to attract to the business and her projects. There is nothing of concern.

Amen

Fear Is an Illusion   27/10/2011

Fear is an illusion; we know this. It's our response to it that gives it power.

To avoid disruption from presentations of fear (and therefore illusionary concepts), we reinforce focus of your vision and ideals. Do not leave any loose ends. Do not allow someone else to decide for you. When your intentions are set with detail and you feel great powerful passion towards them, this is impenetrable. Anything else will bounce off like a force field. When there are questionable areas or indecision—unfinished business, so to speak—it allows for other energies to infiltrate and affect you. This doesn't mean you should become paranoid over every unturned rock; it simply means to listen to your intuition and messages. They have served you well in all your ventures.

You will be given the opportunity to regroup, organise, clear, and focus. No more will you be met with unmanageable surprise. Get your paperwork in order and keep your mind cool. Too much chatter creates fatigue. Talk less, plan more. Expect some objections. But as you intend will be, so do not worry.

A scene presents: In the midst of this sunset, you are walking up the hill. It is silhouetted. You are moving forward, one step in front of the other, firm and determined. You will succeed. Keep the focus on your goals. Do all that is necessary to achieve this with no ill feelings, anger, or bad intent. Compassion and forgiveness are the keys here.

Unforgiveness keeps those bound to you whom you wish to release. Your energy is very strong; turn it to love—the love of God, love of Self, love of your children, love of your mission. See it stream forward from your hands, your body, your heart, like a huge force of healing energy, allowing all of those involved to heal and to see only the quest of existence in harmony and bliss.

This consciousness releases all and everything that is not in harmony with your path and enhances your vision to attract only things, people and circumstances that do.

Amen

In closing,

For those who misunderstand,
Offer them understanding;

For those who are lost,
Offer them some direction;

For those who disagree,
Allow them their freedom, their voice, and set them free.

It is in these very things that we learn to let go and let God. God bless.

The Healers Journey is presented, open halfway, with pages exposed under a beam of light. It is infused strongly with an energetic encodement, allowing one to use it as their healing tool, dispersing heavy or toxic energy and reinstating a healthy vibration, aligning chakras and energy bodies once more.

We are all one with a life force existing and pulsating a rhythm that flows within and around all in creation. Within our individuality (as part of/many different parts of one), we are to experience Rise. It is a misconception that one battles to avoid experiencing a fall.

Falling is simply a result of not recognising where you lost balance. There may be a problem in your foundations, compromising a secure footing to carry you forward. As spirit beings in the physical state, we are always ever evolving, and on earth (as a mass consciousness) are taking some strong leaps forward at this time. To stumble and perhaps fall means growth. One never got anywhere by standing still (metaphorically). There isn't anyone who is not feeling the rumbling of their inner being, on whatever level that may be. All people are experiencing something. This is inevitable. Even the rich and powerful, the government figures, the movie stars, the economists, the doctors, the artists, and the scientists. Your media will show you television reports and news indicating certain personal and global stories and the responses of people. We are becoming more connected to our higher consciousness, more in tune with humanitarian and global issues, and we are prepared as a whole to make a positive difference. Yes, there are still areas that seem hopelessly enmeshed in battle, war, and famine. However, it is with great shifts like those of our current time that the confusion, deprivation, or inhumane incident gives us the opportunity to act.

A mass consciousness can and will make a difference, and we are making that difference. We already know that our creative power is delivered by the law of attraction. People are beginning to realise how an empowered individual can move against adversity, fight for freedom and win, and protect and provide for the unfortunate. We have seen many great people display courage, determination, and passion in fulfilling a need to serve in humanitarian causes. Many joined them in response to their inspiration. In many different ways, we can all do this, and we can choose this today. The people of earth want development, and they want positive change. They are growing quickly from infancy to maturity in consciousness, and this is needed.

The Healers Journey encompasses the story of our journey through infancy to teenage years. Into this next text, we continue to evolve into the maturity of adulthood, which the earth requires right now.

Can you honestly say you feel more pain from grief, betrayal or loss than your neighbour feels? No, of course not. Pain cannot be compared or measured in this way. No one feels more or less than anyone else. We are all here together, equally deserving and with equal opportunity. As we love ourselves and appreciate our gifts, we naturally accept and appreciate all that is to share with each other.

Delivered through this text is a gift of awareness. People have over-analysed and intellectualized everything to the point of imbalance. One can no longer feel and trust what's right for them. It is time to feel. Through this process, an understanding will come that will not be exclusively science or data, but one of inspiration, passion, and progression.

As an individual chooses and embarks, it will begin, slowly integrating to become a collective, a consciousness of all.

Amen

The slower and heavier vibrations around you and the business are lifting and lightening. The personal journeys of all of you, including your clients, have progressed forward. It may seem not so, but it is much lighter and clearer than before. Each one of these beautiful souls is connecting to their personal journeys, and that in itself is perfect.

Only a few at this time are taking such spiritual teachings to the globe. You are choosing to be ready for this task. It is with great joy and excitement that we incarnate with such a fantastic quest; however, it is not an easy road to reach such heights of awareness. It requires great strength and determination to see it through. All of what you experience is a journal of learning. Provided that within these challenging incidences you are also recognising and inspired by your great achievements and are fuelled further to continue with positive energy, then your progression is growth filled and educational for all.

Respect is not something you earn. This is a false statement and an illusion of man.

Respect is a form of self-love. It means the love and care and gratitude one has for oneself. Do not seek respect outside of yourself. This indicates you do not believe respect to be within you and emanating within self, for self.

If someone displays an action of disrespect, it is really how that person feels about themselves. Therefore, the low frequency of little or no self worth actually projects the feelings of inadequacy towards someone else. It is not about a lack of respect towards the person experiencing this energy from another.

When a person or situation leaves you feeling disrespected, look at how you may have experienced an emotional response to being mistreated in the past, how it left you feeling, and why. The big one: what is it about the message that makes it believable to you? There will be some level of an unloving belief towards yourself.

A great shift is taking place. Certainly new beginnings of a higher level of consciousness among people will excite and ignite a new stream of people ready to connect to their God self through you, your healing, and teachings.

Rest knowing of this with calm. Engage in the highest of actions and thoughts, and sustain and maintain your light body with great health.

For all those who are not ready, bless them and allow them their freedom and choice.

For all those who are ready, embrace and educate. Advance for evolvement with love and the highest consciousness, that is God.

That is all.

Two men in the editing team are seen working with your book. One of them is feeling quite depressed; the other carries a low and dense vibration. Both are currently easily distracted from their work. Whether it is fellow colleagues or their own thought patterns, they are feeling unwell and lack productivity.

The younger of the two begins to read. He begins to feel a shift within, and unbeknownst to him, it is beginning the subtle breakdown of energies that currently engulf him, greying his world. He is depressed and is looking for help. He hasn't experienced anything outside of traditional methods before.

Salvation, he thinks to himself. *Ha! Nah!* His higher being knows, but the density of his energy keeps him in a hopeless place. This is the entire point. The healing vibration contained within the book helps to breakdown this hopelessness, and the healing can begin. Our book offers hope, and he can feel it. Keep reading, boy! The older man is not aware of any love or light flowing within and around him, as he is shut down. They both present as current blocks in your progression, as the current inability to see a higher perspective and trust in something outside of their current circumstances. There is hope and there is love.

Dear God, we ask that you help us to surpass this delay and allow the healing of these two individual people, with love and compassion, to bring about all editing up to date and the finalisation of all corrections to bring forth *The Healers Journey* now for release and distribution to all who need her.

An energetic stream, which appears like clear water, builds and explodes into the corridor, gushing into the offices, cleansing all within its wake.

Observe the next three days.

Amen

Pre-Stage to Ascension   *23/11/2011*

Indeed, it is a light-filled time. *The Healer's Journey* has embarked on a long, evolving journey, and it has been the journey of self. The pending birth, the release, and the presentation will be in a few short months. The horizon is crisp and clear. The air is beautiful, and the palace, crystalline in appearance, stands shining. What an image! It is of course symbolic, but it is here to show you that all you create does manifest. It is a matter of your recognising of the evidence of that creation.

Having gone through this time and the experience, and having learned the lessons, it will never return again. Your change in perception, attitude, thoughts, and feelings will support the new in your life. We are in the process of ascension. Your current temple of light will grow and develop to encompass the larger one. It is the prior step, if you like. Your business is growing and developing into this new existence as you also experience much personal growth and development.

Further writing and books are coming. Create the sanctuary; take the action to support your vision. This is your greatest time. You will see the miracles, as they truly support the changes you require.

Outwardly, the dynamics produce an entirely new, plentiful clientele, additional workshops, teachings, preparation for lengthy verbal workshops, and stage works.

January 2012 represents the sun, a beautiful gold disc shining so brightly and beginning a new era.

Approximately December 2012 ends this pre-stage, and you begin to plan the Ascension Centre.

Dedicate sufficient daily time in stillness, prayer, and self-appreciation. This is very valuable to you now.

Many angels surround you.

Congratulations.

Amen

You are protected, dear one. Know this is your sanctuary. The temple at which you offer your gifts and guidance of God's love is light filled and conducive of a very high frequency, hence its powerful healing capability.

It is true that with such high vibration and light so highly energised at a sustained level, the shedding of "cloaks" will take place. In some cases, an instant disintegration of some energies will occur just upon entering the front door. It may be shown through a shaking up of one's emotions. This occurs because a frequency that cannot remain within the body whilst present within the temple must leave. It is the nature of the temple. It is the intent for healing that we leave our baggage outside, to take off your coat and your shoes and enter in complete surrender and prayer.

Be it that you ask within your prayers. Ask to be shown as you seek guidance. Surrender that which no longer serves you, as your higher being has the wisdom. The healers and teachers who work within the temple call it their home. Respect this home with the love that is offered, and give gratitude for their gifts. It is a sanctuary for all, as we are all children of God. With love and commitment, the healers and the teachers are ready to guide you to your ultimate creation.

Be it that all people of the highest intention are willing to disrobe at the door entering with surrender and reverence. Be ready to receive joy, to accept your bliss. Love resides within this temple, and many angels wander throughout these rooms. We give thanks to their presence, for they are our holy helpers indeed.

We are the temple of light and deliverers of the new reality.

It is within our vision and divine mission to experience the rising and expansion of our Spirit, to integrate and give forth the teachings as we guide humanity along the path of ascension. As we all experience planetary shifts, energy expansion, and energetic changes on earth, we are aware of humanity's awakening concurrently. It is inevitable.

We are ready, and so are you.

Decrease your noise and increase silence and prayer. Listen to your inner being, as the soul has led you here.

Welcome to the base of the mountain. The mountain is the temple, and the temple is you.

I love you so very much,

God

Abundance. Prosperity. Growth. You want it? You've got it!

It is very clear that you are following through on the messages, or more appropriately, the guidance that is given to you. You are taking appropriate action as a result of this guidance. You are listening, and therefore you are working in flow. Your ideas and dreams are presented to you, and then you are shown what to do next. As you are sensitive and feel the energy around you. You now complete the picture. Your business has a formal plan, as it should. You have acknowledged this in a practical sense, and it will create the support you need to create the vision you desire. International recognition and success comes via the media and is supported and used via your website. Your website and information pages allow people to request and book energy healings and readings, which can be paid for by credit card. This will allow an international and national streamline of clientele. There will be language translating services too (via the internet to automatically translate foreign language) so that the recipient can understand their reading and/or healing script.

There are many changes and new ideas being put into place to accommodate future growth. This is positive and necessary. Flow and flex with those changes. See yourself as growth in motion, still allowing the surprises or unforeseen to make their wonderful entrance. Each of you are encouraged to keep your vibration high and your vision clear. Don't pay too much attention to the small things. Acknowledge and learn for future reference and move on. There's a whole wide world out there waiting to be contacted, so be mindful where you place your energies and attention. Passion and belief are the magic ingredients of a miracle pie.

There is structure and balanced ingredients, correct amounts and preparation of the mixture. But once it's all combined and a final touch of love and faith are added to come out of that oven so delicious and fulfilling, nourishing and warm, you will realise you have made it all come true.

One slice is never enough. And that's great, as it should not end with one slice. As we evolve and grow, so does our appetite. Feed the hunger until you're full. Plan your next meal and then eat again. Nourish and grow and receive.

Amen

Four pillars of light present in the star-filled sky. An ascended being comes forth as a messenger and guide. He is light, a being whose outline is blue and white. He holds a councillor's position; his role is to assist businesses, groups, and associations who are working for the betterment, health, and well-being of humanity. He was incarnated as human during Grecian times but is now in service from this dimension to assist the individual and the group consciousness to pursue their life purpose, health, and prosperity.

Dear ones, I see you concern yourself with what is unnecessary. Your commitment to your quest is acknowledged and your requests (prayers) have been heard and answered. The old or past is gone. You are creators, and the undesirable circumstances of the past (which was an expression for particular life lessons, karmic attachments, or negative creating through your learning) has evolved, as have you. At this level, you are not to fear or be concerned.

Reaffirm your joyful and abundant position as an absolutely untouchable, powerfully resonating God force of love. Nothing can or will penetrate or affect or diminish your light, ever.

Those who are in alignment with your vision and the future you are now creating are coming to you now. God will not give you anything other than what you ask for. You can now see the light beings approaching the middle of the area between the four pillars of light. They are souls who are moving towards you now. There are four people. They are light workers, and they share the same passion.

The ebb and flow of energies, the calling forth and exiting of certain vibrations and energies, are moving and shifting continuously to allow your growth. As you call forth new people and set forth new experiences, ideas, and required actions, the correct or matching vibration or person will present as a result of what's been connected. Multifunctional and co-learning comes into play for various teachings, and when the teaching, lesson, or activity is complete, it will then move on, sometimes disappearing or disconnecting in some way. It is all part of the journey of life. As you are creating with intent, you are already very much in tune with the co-creative process.

Move forward swiftly and joyfully, blessing all the souls of those who contributed along the way, and look towards the unfolding miracles of each new day. The more you receive with gratitude and wonder, the more will come your way.

Honour the journey as much as you celebrate your destination with joy and glory.

Amen.

Your business is ready for transition. It is with the greatest respect and practitioner expertise that your business be raised to the next level. This level is the prior step to the Ascension Centre.

You are experiencing the formation of your new reality. The expansion, energetically and physically, will be felt by you first. This has allowed the thought to allow the action that is now necessary to take. The closing of the front door and the creation of professional consulting rooms has shown the world where you are about to go. The necessary pre-paving and the shifts allow the birthing of this strong team of God's angels to continue on their co-creative journey towards the Ascension Centre. More books are on the agenda, and a strong clientele will be growing, with bookings exceeding one month in advance. The clientele and the public are aware of the required planning. Like with all professionals, a pre-booking is necessary and will be valued.

Consultations and education are prerequisites that will aid people to understand the way in which you guide and recommend the step-by-step personalised journey of the individual. They will quickly understand that they are valued and cared for and in return value the service we provide, step by step, from booking to pre-consultation to healing and/or reading to re-booking within a four-to-six-week time span. When the client is seated and comfortable with a relaxing tea, the service and care focus will be part of the new environment, providing a tranquil and safe space for them to reflect and prepare within. Returning to the healing sanctuary will be strongly desired, and people may book three to six months in advance to ensure their position. With the release of your first book, *The Healers Journey,* and the new website, current clients and new clientele will lovingly and easily flow, feeling blessed to be part of this wonderful opportunity.

Get ready. As you downscale the strong retail influence and reopen your doors as a professional practitioner's suite of God healing/educational services, the popularity will be immense.

Post a notice on your website. With great love and excitement, we are celebrating with you!

Your loving angels and beings of light.

Amen

As our book (my sweet) makes its last journey from ethereal into physical, I touch my heart, and with so much joy and love I have for you, I place my hand on the front cover. Light, immense light, extends out from sides of the cover, and a very clear image of an eye is shown.

Doubt surfaces if we spiral into another's doubt of themselves. Do not waste one precious moment. Science has no place where angels walk. What is evident is that man wants to label everything beyond all reasonable doubt like in a court of law based on theory and evidence. We cannot pre-empt, predict, and analyse a miracle or a touch of grace. It is the very thing humans cannot control and intellectualise, and that's the very thing that unnerves them. They are forced to acknowledge and trust the heart, which is so hard for so many.

My beautiful one, we emanate from the temple of heaven, where there are no judges or jury. We encourage you to eliminate from this moment any need to prove your authenticity to anyone. It doesn't matter, it truly doesn't, as time will allow many to embrace their unwavering faith. The hungry are many, and you are offering them bread. Earth has entered a phase in time where the heavens rejoice as a long-awaited time grows near. The spontaneous awakening of many people is in alignment with shifts in consciousness. Many souls have wanted to incarnate during this time to have karmic alignment for future lifetimes.

The power of the business dynamic of the church is at a tremendous low.

Socially, culturally, and economically, the business is losing to a new force, one that encourages freedom, one that inspires growth, one that illuminates a path of self-discovery, and a true relationship with me and with God.

This is a divine objective.

Your work, your healings, and your books reconnect my life force, my heart, and the love of God back to people, reigniting the flame within the heart of humanity. The aim is to bring back the unity, awareness, wisdom, compassion, and love for everything we see, for everyone we touch.

God resides in all of us and we are all one.

I love you and give thanks to you, my divine child of immense will, faith, and love.

Jesus

There will be three in the United States, one in London, one in France (Lourdes), and of course Australia, with an office in Sydney. Later Canada, Italy, and Germany will follow.

The Ascension Centre in France will be smaller in size, but will be extremely beautiful, as it honours and strongly features your Mother, Mary Magdalene. The centre in Lourdes is your favourite and the one you like to visit most often, as it connects you to her energy strongly.

The scope of this franchise is far beyond your expectation as it is a multimillion-dollar creation running to capacity.

Agents and accounting firms with international links to local companies are hired to coordinate and balance the finances. There are marketing teams, advertising people, book sales, workshop scheduling and seminars, and educational programs to facilitate. Each co-owner manager is hand-selected by you and trained by you. They invest money into their centre to enhance growth and provide a service and wellness opportunity which is unique. Profit margins and rewards are theirs to reinvest and enhance further business growth. These managers/co-owners are all highly dedicated, passionate representatives who work in service to God for all of humanity.

It is expanding. It will be fast.

You will find that extended amounts of time may be spent abroad during the selection processes of winning contenders, who have applied to open franchises. You may also wish to be physically present when specific locations open to educate, guide, and mentor.

With gratitude,

Amen

The Creation and Birth
of The Chosen One   5/1/2012

The scene opens with Jesus standing on the shoreline. It is a beautiful beach, and he's looking out to sea. He is waiting for something.

Forward in time, I see you waiting in the reception area of a publishing company. It's approximately twelve months from now. You are smiling, radiant, and excited. You are there to have a meeting with some representatives over the next book, and it is a very exciting time. The most notable feature is a wall with an emblem, and other interior decorations in black and white. It's a large area with comfortable couches and a large reception desk.

We are in the United States of America. We have been approached by this company. People who know people have talked, and news is spreading. You have sent partial manuscripts to get the recognition. There's a name on the door. In cobalt blue, it says "Graham McKenzie."

He's a numbers man: figures, business, and world sales and data.

Dear God, allow the process to flow and doors to open to release *The Chosen One*.

He had difficulty in understanding *The Healer's Journey* and personally doesn't connect with it; however, he states, "It is not about what I like. It's what sells that I care about."

You are in a position to decide ultimately, and you feel that it is not quite right. You decide this company is not the right publisher for your book. He doesn't respect or understand what he holds in his hand; he is disconnected from his heart. You thank him for his time and graciously leave. Sometimes it is better to wait for quality and connection to present rather than be in a position of desperation, which will lack the results you desire.

Jesus presents and takes your hand, and along the beach you stroll. You will not need to go searching, for I will bring it to you. You will know. Prepare the writings, prepare the structure of the book, and have it ready. It deserves its loving, gracious creative process. Passion and faith will keep energy high, but don't make it a chore. The more love and gratitude that is infused into the pages, the more the reader will connect, and that's your intent.

Don't worry about missing the boat. This is not possible. We haven't set sail yet. I ask that you trust the correct timing and connected people will present to you as need.

In God's loving embrace,

Amen

The Healer's Journey

A cave of celestite crystal, beautiful, powerful and inviting, is seen. The energy emanating from it is one of communication in flow, understanding without being analytical, healing and soothing, comforting. It is angelic by nature.

Jesus approaches from deep within the cave. He holds a book in his left hand. It is a copy of *The Healer's Journey*. There is a light behind him as bright as the sun, and he exudes bliss, peace, and comfort.

I hand to you a copy of this book, the one we created together, you and I in a connection of soul over many years and physical lifetimes in the quest to continue as destined. I am here, as you call to me. I cannot and would not ever leave you. We are one and the same. I am you and you are me.

Let us not be distracted by that which is designed to distract you. Earth life, as magnificent and opportunistic it is, has the elements in place to create apparent obstacles on various levels. You choose this, no more. Be it that lover, friend, or foe presents to distract you. Choose wisdom, love, and learned lessons. There is nothing more to do other than reaffirm your intent and unwavering desire to fulfil your dreams.

With your energy and intent, I support you to remain. For if you look into the world as I do, you will see truth. You see the pretty child who smiles but has no home, or the aged man who is disrespected with no place to rest, world poverty, senseless wars, all negative creations of man, and you may feel overwhelmed by this image. But as I view them, I send them love. I send them an alternative: a hopeful reality. They must choose, as must you. I pray that my desire for them inspires hope that they may change.

One can change their experience and their lives in less than three seconds. Decide what you want and choose what is your true heart's desire. If you don't know, ask to be shown. Ask the question, "How can I live to inspire myself to grow beyond my current limitations and then take one small step towards change right now?" The dynamics of your world will change upon that instant. Others will feel inspired by your example, and through this, you may help alter one's perspective of their own self-limiting beliefs. I hand you our book, and we begin.

This book will make its way unto whoever is meant to have them hold it. We have or hold no limitation, no preference, no judgement. We open the gates to allow all to heal. With that comes the response of love (smiles). Enjoy this moment and hold onto me.

I am with you. Promotions, education of staff, clients, and enquiries will be necessary until such time as an outside team may be needed to handle such enquiries. These are the physical implementations to allow further teaching and writing of more books.

Mary Magdalene joins Jesus at his left side and smiles lovingly. She says, "I will connect with you when needed."

Just before release, so ground zero healings on the streets of New York; Los Angeles; Melbourne, Australia; London, England; Provence, France; India, Eygpt, Rome, Italy.

This healing has taken place.

Amen

The Ascension Centre Healing 2012   23/1/2012

A neon-blue energy presents and disperses. I am shown taps and pipelines—the basic view of plumbing, as well as unexposed areas in the walls, the ceiling, and under the floor.

I see the electrical systems; again, the energy is shown as neon blue. There are also some black patches, and with that a bright-white energy is injected to balance and transmute the area. The white light is in itself intelligent. It is able to follow the dark patches even as they move and seek corners to hide. The entire premises (all three premises next to each other) filter through this neon-blue and white light as cleansing energy. It is clean, crisp, and receptive. It allows flow, ease, creativity, and movement. It doesn't object or delay. It is the energy pipe cleaner of the universe. This is necessary to do frequently to clear and clean the space to maintain an environmental and an energetic health of the business's body and reproductive organs.

Consider for a moment where the physical flow of water comes from and the point at which electricity enters the building. They both appear, due to mechanics and engineering, to be externally sourced. They flow literally via a pipeline into the property. We therefore recommend that what is brought in, circulated, and dispersed be fully maintained periodically. It is a wise investment indeed, much like a clean and pure diet including fruit, protein, vegetables, and adequate water, is beneficial for your physical body.

Blessed and clean is this holy temple of light.

With love and gratitude.

Amen

The Healer's Journey:
Wash Your Hands   24/1/2012

Jesus speaks:

Do not worry; acknowledgement is all you need. Your action in response to this situation is perfect. Dearest one, there is nothing upon this earth or elsewhere that can stop the plans you have. Your sensitivity can sense infiltrating energies. It is designed this way so that a clean slate is created before you. Have no judgement or concern. When you wash your hands, you wash them to clean and refresh your skin, to smell the lovely fragrance, and to know in your mind your hands are clean. You have no mental or emotional attachment to the dirt or oils on the skin; you just know they are present, and so you wash them. I want you to view all infiltrating energies in this way. Then immediately upon washing your hands, open your heart and connect with me, with God, with your Mother, and with the joy communicating from your own heart. This is reality. This is truth. It's beaming forth in a stream more powerful than the tides of the oceans. When you feel this connection, you are more powerful, more creative, successful, and impenetrable, and nothing can intercept this. It is your response to infiltrating energies which create the ripples or an opening. So remember: simplify and wash your hands.

All the pieces of the puzzle are coming together for the fruit to bear. The renewed appearance and structure of the business is vibrant and matching your renewed perspective. The new website and your book surface together to reveal a new force in your business's reality. Do not doubt, as you are undoubtedly creating.

Suddenly, a supermarket appears with brand-new, shiny trolleys. You are shopping there. All of the purchase items are very high up on the shelves, but you are tall enough to reach for them. It's the supermarket of the universe asking you to trust that there is plenty to go around for everyone.

Then the Ascension Centre is shown. Walking within her corridors, you walk behind Jesus; he is wearing a light blue robe. Along the corridor on an upper level, the carpet appears to have a burgundy runner. Jesus points to various rooms off the corridor and says, "This is perfection, and you are yet to fill these rooms. They will come. It is joyous and wonderful. Keep your focus; remain united, happy, passionate, and strong." Smiling, he turns with arms extended out to the side, open palms facing towards you.

He fades backwards, an intensely bright light behind him. Pure love.

An image presents of the Holy Spirit and water flowing over God's hands.

Amen

An energy waterfall showers down through the roof in a divine imager of God's hands. It showers down as a clean, vibrant flow gushing throughout every room and into every crevice. Through the pipelines and electrical conduits, throughout all electronic and telephone lines, like a river strongly flowing and cleansing the entire building, the water energy filters and perfectly cleanses her internal organs as well.

Be it that when you cleanse, wash with God's hands, so that all is pure and healthy, washing away what no longer serves you. Your creative energy requires a clean surface.

Effective communication is an aural and visual understanding. It is delivered via a frequency of sound like a radio wave of and sight with pictures or imagery. When the frequency has a clear channel, there is no distortion or confusion. The ideal understanding is simple and available. The website, your staff, and your telephone lines are all undergoing a wash of complete clarity. Four or five incoming telephone lines will be adequate for all enquiries. Phone stations positioned in selected rooms allow a call to be taken in various locations, provided verbal communication does not affect practitioner sessions in progress.

You will be overjoyed with the how the new communication system has increased business flow, productivity, and bookings. The new consultations, client education, and formal information brochures are implemented and well received by clients.

With love and gratitude.

Amen

Magdalene Healing   8/2/2012

A flash of red fabric is seen in an open door. It is a doorway leading to an office. The red fabric is the shoulder cape of Mary Magdalene. This is her healing today. I see her enter, and she scans the room. She is fully aware of every intricate detail, physical and nonphysical. She raises her right hand and places energy symbols in the corners and above doorways and windows.

She places energy pillars around this person's desk. Her passion and presentation is very strong, and she works fast. There is a pile of books on the desk in a messy manner; they overlap and tilt. They are this person's marketing projects. He requires more solid attention and appreciation of his creative campaigns. Currently none of his projects get the recognition they deserve, as he is not energetically or physically healthy. This man presents as unhealthy. His finances are unhealthy, and his energy has a depressive leak. His genetic lineage and also a relevant past life link him to a religious/freedom based battle in Scotland. He suffered a traumatic death for faith and freedom. He now lives in a self-imposed prison and denies faith and miraculous rescue.

His grandmother in this life lived a contradictory life. She was extremely verbal about her belief in God and faith, but she lived her life in victimhood. She was miserable and uncreative, overweight, unhealthy, and depressed. His sister shares the same energy.

Indirectly, this is a divine call, a multifaceted choice of various actions. Mary Magdalene, the feminine power and healer of God, re-establishes his energy from fear-based imprint of a belief that females carry feminine martyrdom and weakness.

The sword presents. She cuts the cords of a battlefield where he died a young man, leaving life in his prime for the sake of his country, God, and freedom.

She waves the sword around almost like she's dancing, or performing a series of martial arts movements.

She suddenly lets the sword go. Pointing upward it hovers perfectly straight in the air. The blade illuminates and raises up to the heavens in a white-light explosion. The healing is done.

Magdalene walks to the desk and places your book from the bottom of the pile to the top. A young junior office girl passes by and senses something. She enters the room. "This one's next," she says quietly, with a smile.

Her energy is light, new, and warm.

Healing has taken place.

Amen

On a cliff top, I am standing. I view the area, and it is not of the physical earth; it is a representation of a symbolic nature. Kilometres below is the ground. The cliff edge is so high that there are clouds at eye level. I look down, and there are more clouds blocking my view of the ground.

I am given the message that this is an internal world of self, where all we imagine and desire begin the creative process to manifest. It is truly an internal landscape. As above, so below? Yes. The area in which you begin creating is entirely your choice, and your ideas about what you envision in your manifestation are also all your own design. Whether it be a large creation, such as a multimillion-dollar business, or a smaller creation, such as a glass of water, there is no difference in the actual creative process. It is your believability in the universe's (God's) ability to bring this forth with you that is the key. God as an entity granting wishes from a high seat in heaven above is not a reality; however, the energy force in which God's power Source works through you is immeasurable. The co-creation is the divine dichotomy, because God cannot solely (soul-ly) create without you, nor you without God. The irony is this.

It is not a separate circuit board feeding power to the house—the house is the power. On it goes. As people are grasping at straws, they're awakening to understand their true being as an expansive co-creator enabling them to master manifestation to identify self.

What do you believe yourself to be? Who do you think you are today? Tomorrow? Why wouldn't you want to aim to soar at great heights when you have the power of all creation at your fingertips? It is utilising wisdom and sense of self. This encompasses the concluding pages to the book you have used as your life's manual. Were they your words? Your beliefs? Or someone else's general assessment? How can you base your life and direction on this? Do you fear rejection, failure, being cut at the legs? Only you create the reality you repeatedly confirm by creating it in advance with your powerful thoughts, which cement your beliefs. Begin to look upward! Begin to view yourself and your visions as being part of a high altitude world where the ether is so fine, so light, that creation is achieved in an instant.

The lower your creative power is aimed, the denser and slower the manifestation and rewards. Raise your expectations and your sights to the rewards and achievements you would offer your most beloved son, the happiness you would want for your own child. With that desire, with that love-fuelled intention, you offer what all children of this vast and dynamic universe is entitled to: fulfilment.

Amen

The book begins its spiralling down from the sky, falling from the heavens onto earth and into the hands and hearts of all who need her.

The intent of love and healing is strong. Your intent is to heal the world. Those in receptivity will be magnetised and together intertwined, a co-creative experience of discovery. Being a creator, you are the innovator of your own experience. However, God will always hand you a surprise or two. Whilst experiencing life on this planet, we have an extraordinary amount of information and physical experiences to act out for evolution. This is a time and experience like no other, as we understand very clearly that we're all connected.

Abundance is the free-flowing belief that there is plenty to go around. Abundance is joy manifest and the expression of healthy self-worth. One who has healthy self-worth usually has material wealth. But wealth can be identified in many ways.

I may have an abundance of energy. I have an abundance of creative ideas. I am abundant in everything I attract, including money, love, health, and opportunity. If there is any doubt of my belief that I am worthy of all of these things, it will affect me emotionally and will interrupt flow. If I believe I am not as good, as wealthy, or as lucky as others, I create that energy and attract more of that belief. The body will vibrate a fear whenever the word or question of wealth is raised. The intent then alters to one of desperation and survival, not of free-flowing abundance and prosperity. Desperation and fear block the process to create.

To be persistent and to be desperate are two very different positions. Persistence is necessary for longevity and belief in your goals; the latter is non-creative.

It is important to eliminate doubt. Work with your thoughts and their ability to connect directly to ego. Believe in yourself and your goals, and most of all, feel them! When becoming overwhelmed by what appears to be lack of flow and your thoughts spiral into fear, retreat into prayer, meditation, or some simple deep breathing exercises. Focus on your in breath and out breath, feel, see and experience your chest expanding and your body being nourished by the fresh oxygen. After a few moments or minutes, come back to your mind with a clearer objective. And you will. Practise again and again.

Remember to stay in the reality and the power of now. Every moment is a creative possibility. Everything is changeable through your intent and action. Bring it back. Contain your energy when the expansion integrates at each new level on a daily basis. The personality and human self needs to acknowledge, reflect, and understand. She is learning, growing, adjusting, and changing, and that is perfection.

Meditate, imagine, and gaze upon the Tree of Life. Powerful.

The Volcano   21/2/2012

The volcano erupts! It is spurting, exploding orange-red lava from the top, flowing all over the surface of the mountain, spilling, gushing, burning away the current foliage. It is not destructive in that sense; it is creating a clean state and a new beginning of new life to birth.

From the sky, a diamond-white beam shines down and connects to the volcano at its peak. This energy is assisting in the purging, if you will, healing and cooling to allow the introduction of new energy of light and creation, which is already beckoning forth. The light disperses the heat and quickly cools the temperature, particularly at ground level. In an instant, lush, green foliage is miraculously replaced where the once fiery landscape smouldered. The air is cool and fresh, and water can be heard trickling nearby. The area has completely regenerated, and new life in various forms—animal, plant, and insect—coexist again. A few lizards can be seen at the water's edge, and there are fish in the water.

As you walk up an embankment, there is something golden in the distance. A tree stands, beautifully laden with golden puffs on its branches. These gold puffs are almost like the appearance of soft, golden fairy-floss. This tree is symbolic and is associated with your growth and expansion. There is also a coloured energy of red and blue swirling around the environment.

Suddenly, Archangel Michael descends from the sky with his flaming white-blue sword. "You have begun to walk along your newly created path. It is paramount that you recognise and act immediately, as you have done. You have successfully allowed the doors of your positive creation to swing open. You have acknowledged past relationships, and events only indicate the level you've grown to now. Let go, exceed, and excel. The wind blows strong, fresh winds of change and flow. Your chosen tools, whether they be the telephone, computer, outside signage, books, or word of mouth, will carry the frequency of you and the matching vibration of grace. There will be no dispute that will cause you to falter, as we will know this to be ego. And ego has no place where angels trek. Those who are willing to accept the guidance of their hearts will connect with humbleness and gratitude, as we all must do."

My cup floweth over with enough for all.

The great Archangel Michael stands over the business in his grandest and largest version, an estimated sixty feet in height!

With love,

Archangel Michael

The Snowy Gathering   28/2/2012

Thundering down a snow-covered mountain, you are riding a sleigh and holding tightly onto the reigns. The beautiful huskies pulling the sleigh are very focused and know exactly the direction they need to go. You are enjoying the speed and the chill in the air, which is streaming across your face. There is a gentle shower of snowflakes in this area.

You are going faster and faster, but you are relaxed and happy. The sleigh suddenly stops at the bottom of the hill, and you stand up and get off the sleigh. A short walk through snow leads you to a quaint cottage. It is made entirely of a wooden logs, and a peek inside reveals a cosy, warm atmosphere. You briefly knock at the door before entering. The huskies settle down to rest.

Inside, the cottage is warm, a temperature and glow gratefully supplied by the open fireplace in the centre of the room. A man is seated on a wooden chair with his back turned to you. He's wearing a polo jumper, and he's warming his hands towards the flames of the fire. On the other chair is a Tibetan monk in the full attire of orange robes. He gently smiles at you. You approach the man in the polo jumper and touch his shoulder. He rises from his chair and turns to greet you. At first you believed it to be your father, but it is not. The beautiful, gentle man greeting you is Mr. Neale Donald Walshe. "So lovely that you made it, Trish. Thank you for coming."

This is a prearranged meeting, as such, a connection required to discuss and formulate a possible partnership, and a discussion about the current education, teachings, and healings for all people. The sharing and bringing together of great wisdom, united faith, and energy allows for a powerful, loving, and positive partnership. The Tibetan monk is a tremendous peacemaker, an enlightened and loving being. He brings forth elements of meditation and expansion of being to influence personality and deny unhealthy ego ideals and thoughts, to initiate spirit in all human dealings and processes of life. He is to teach us to be rather than do.

Ascended masters gather etherically in the cottage to offer their loving support and energy. Quan Yin, Jesus, Mother Mary, Saint Germaine, Hilarion, Mary Magdalene, and also Lady Nada and Meldezdeck.

A gathering of love, a love gathering indeed.

You stand and face Neale, palms facing each other, your left on his right and your right palm on his left. A great white light shines in and around the palms that are joined, beaming out around and behind you.

This is the joining of forces, an agreement of spiritual partnership to God. The attendees clap and express joy at this infusion. Lady Nada grows and expands in her glorious pink light. She is joyfully overlooking the gathering. This wondrous blessing and contract is made.

We move forth and give thanks, calling upon each individual and deity/master to assist when required upon you life's mission. You excitedly and openly move forward, being open to receive messages and inspiring thoughts to create in all your endeavours.

Thank you, with much gratitude.

Amen

The energy of this emotion could be described as disappointment, which when combined with sadness creates a loss of power within. We are aware of the emotion and energy of disappointment as we understand it eventuates from an individual (or group) who did not receive what they intended or expected to receive.

The contract or agreement may be between two entities, whether that be two individuals, or a company and an individual, or two companies, who make an agreement to exchange money for a service or product(s). When one party dishonours that agreement, disappointment results, which equates to loss of power for one or both parties. When one feels disappointment, they may respond in anger, perhaps even become threatening.

The co-matching energy here is the element of disappointment. However, with respect to your own agreement, this came to be because the contract was associated with a desperate energy. Initially, you were so elated and happy to have your book published after experiencing quite a few rejections, but the disappointment came later, once the contractors did not take their responsibility or your product seriously.

At that time, you did not consider whether the publishing company's energy was matching yours. A great lesson learned once more that as an entity (half of the contract or agreement party) brings forth their part of the intention to merge with yours (the other half of the contract or agreement party), the pending energies unite to fuel the purpose of what you are creating together and your intentions about it. This is a tremendous energy and consideration to investigate. Choose very wisely in all partnerships and agreements of all kinds. To bring about the eventual birth of a product, service, or creation of any kind, there must be an honourable and aligned perspective and a matching agreement.

All unhealthy projections, emotions, and certainly the energy of disappointment is released today, which allows our message to be freed and shared.

This aspect has an interesting and relevant cliché with respect to the level of secrecy some scriptures, books, and texts have carried in the past. It is unnecessary to hide truth, healing, freedom, and wisdom. The people no longer want secrecy and fear. The changes within people mirror a time of evolvement inspiring fearless exposure, faith, openness, wisdom, acceptance. Any fears releasing are an inevitable side effect for healing; however, overall, humanity is progressive, courageous, and strong.

Formerly, people thought God was inaccessible, living somewhere up in the sky, or maybe even not. Who really knows for sure? He would be depicted as an angry, wise, old being casting harsh judgements over his people and their mistakes. Thankfully, these fallacies and fantasies are as outdated as their history. Thank fully we live and create in a time that embraces a relationship with God/the universe/divine energy. In addition, great ascended masters, angels, and light beings guide and support our way evermore. The veil is thinning that separated our worlds. We are awakening, expanding, understanding. The blocks were on the mental body, but they are disintegrating and allowing a penetration of the higher vibration of love, which is truth, into your lives.

There is no need to concern. Honour your agreements with love to all.

The earthly mission is powered by a force of love light, and so many of you are feeling it: the teachers, the healers, the writers, the musicians, the light workers, and assistants of all kinds. We thank you.

With love and gratitude.

A worker is pictured with a posthole digger.

"Why am I killing myself?" he asks. "Why do I have to prove my worth? Others make so much more money than me, but I work twice as hard! The only thing I have is my pride, my dignity, and my tough skin. If people are scared of me, I prefer it, so they don't 'f' me over. If you're too nice, you'll get screwed over your whole life."

For this man, his intense thoughts are like prayer and affirmations of his existence, as he repeats the same thing every day.

Do you enjoy your work? No? So what do you want? It is a daily mantra you set forth when you iterate the experience of hardship, extreme effort, unforseen errors, and the icing on the cake—no pay.

You are receiving exactly what your creative force is passionately expressing.

You expect negative, unhappy, unfulfilled, and unpaid experiences, and that's exactly what you receive. Stop! Stop miscreating!

The larger company that keeps offering you consistent work is your point of change and opportunity for a new path. Your security and regularity of work and payment is guaranteed; but for every reward, there is effort and cooperation. The rules of the game must be understood. You will need to work under structured rules and regulations, so having the flexibility and cooperation to work under direction is imperative. Less talk and more action means they will see your efforts, loyalty, and performance. You will be well regarded and will have opportunity for growth. There is scope for advancement and moving up in the ranks to higher positions and matching remuneration. Get involved and get interested, as there are many uncharted waters where you can discover some larger fish.

Create some calm, some quiet in your inner world.

Creation blossoms in a quiet space.

Amen

The landscape shows the desert sands and the dunes at sunset, with the most magnificent oranges and deep blues, black and gold surrounding them. The imagery is quite beautiful, but it also represents a viewpoint, an internal perspective, involving stillness of the mind, body, and spirit.

In the creative process, the desired environment and progression are uninterrupted and ongoing. This allows birth and growth to flourish within their own intricate program. The information stored inside the energy pattern will be allowed to form and create with other relevant dynamics to form the whole of the intent.

Often we see progression as slow, and this brings frustration. When results are not appearing fast enough, we begin to doubt. As we acknowledge this, we feel tension. We begin to hold tighter as we look at the presenting evidence of movement and progression. We begin to measure and ponder and panic. Once your mind opens to this doubting level, you may even begin to notice and validate outside influences as apparent blocks in your progress. No one can block your progress unless you believe they have the power to do so. Your belief in their power creates a perfect environment for the outside world to disrupt your flow.

You are a creator! Nobody can create or destroy for you. By your entertaining the thought of fear that the other has power creates the very interception you are wanting to avoid. But in truth, you created it! Let go of the reins you hold so tightly. Let go of the ideas of another affecting your life. Let go of the need to know how and why. With the worry chains removed and without expectation, creativity and open doors will present.

*   *   *

Your world can sometime appear as if it's made of a large population of people travelling all together on a cruise ship. We are all headed for the same destination on this voyage, but each one of us will encounter different experiences upon the ship. We are all different in that some like dancing, some like polo, and some like chess, but we appreciate those differences in one another. You don't have to dance or force another to dance, and their opinion of dancing does not alter your enjoyment or desire to do it every day. Your desires and your goals are yours to create, but loosen your grip and allow the universe and God to weave your web with all the aligned dynamics. Expressions of joy and gratitude fuel creativity tenfold. Your fatigue shows you are working against flow, attempting to guide the ship single-handedly, not allowing the natural course of life to sail to shore.

Forget your calendar and your clocks. Adjust linear to inner and outer to dimensional in a timeless realm where all is possible instantaneously. Release your arms, hands out wide, then open and relax your heart. Go back to your desires and intent and refocus your belief in your creation. Resistances are fuelled by fear. As powerful beings and with your sensitivity very heightened, you will know when it's time to sit back a moment, reflect on thoughts and feelings, and sometimes allow yourself to take a break from it all.

Whether you are running a shop, a clinic, a family, or an empire, no one is excluded from self/soul care and love.

You have been missing this.

Love,

God

"We begin by weeding the garden, turning over the soil and adding the plant food and nutrients to allow our new plants to thrive. The added topsoil is lush and mixes well with the existing soil. Turning the soil over and mixing the nutrients in is so lovely! The seeds are laid. Now add a sprinkle of water and stand back and watch it grow. One more thing to add: a prayer of intention and don't forget to offer gratitude." - *God*

Dear God, I have prepared this beautiful patch of earth I am 'renting' so gratefully from you. I intend to utilise this soil well, as I have prepared it for such abundance and shared growth. Anything planted within or any seed left to germinate will thrive! The growth will be fast and very strong. It will also enhance further fertility, producing much more of the same and more of a new species of my choice. The greenery— lush shining leaves, beautiful coloured—and sweet-smelling flowers are prolific. It is very good and will be self-sustaining. I tend to the garden to ensure love, intention, and food are given, and my garden responds so well! She offers me the fruit of her cycle with pleasure and gratitude.

In this growth and expansion, we support and attract bird life as well, which adds to the natural cycle of the garden. The birds shelter but also drop seeds and droppings, which enhance new growth. It is a sort of offering and a gratitude for the shelter and insect life to feed on, also abundant in this garden. All life benefits from my garden. From the worms in the soil, the germinating seeds, and young plants, to the stronger, more mature plants and trees, to the birds and insect life within and above, the entire cycle is expression, creation, fertility, and abundance.

A great one, a being of light and love, presents. With his arms outstretched, he turns in a clockwise direction, waving his healing energy over the garden. He blesses its lifecycle and progress. The garden responds with a wave of gratitude and love.

The cycle begins. Create your garden today.

Peace, love, prosperity,

Amen

The office worker sits at her desk. She is quite stressed and deep in thought.

She rubs her forehead, thinking about how to respond to the large influx of enquiries about a blacklist her company has been placed on. She is fearful: fearful of commenting, fearful of the backlash, fearful for her job and her position. She seeks clarity from the directors, but everyone is tight-lipped and evasive. The company is under investigation for breach of contract in advertising services, which are misleading and misinforming clients. There are claims against them, and they will have to attend a court hearing on a number of claims. As a result, there is a lot of bad press and public shouting of "Scam!" Worldwide, the response has been most unfavourable. This company has shown negligent and unethical behaviours and practices.

The team below her realise that if the company survives the public backlash, the company will still exist; however, whether all staff will be secure is another question. Fear surrounds the company, which has functioned for over eighty years but has now fallen prey to bad press through disgruntled clients.

Whilst we acknowledge the karmic connection and the universal need for correction in all directions, we ask that this pending blacklist be balanced and fairness be delivered for all involved. We ask that no innocent parties be scrutinised unfairly or bullied. We ask that all innocent parties, including all clients, be given the contractual agreements they have paid for and the company see to their obligations efficiently.

This is their opportunity for grace in all directions.

Thank you, God.

Amen

Jesus is sitting on a small hilltop. He has a hood over his head, and he's looking towards a beautiful horizon. He's truly absorbing the beauty of the sunset with all her incredible colours. He stands with the assistance of his shepherd's staff. There are a few sheep grazing around him.

He turns towards you and smiles. "I say to you *allow*. I say this to you with all of this word's accompanying energy. View the process as simply another cog in the wheel. It is part of the wheel, and the wheel is in motion. Every new acknowledgement of this process is movement forward. Allow and move forward. Clear and free any fears, doubts, worries, or concerns. That is the true meaning of *allow*. The tighter we hold onto something in a particular way, the further it alludes you."

The RRP value of the book is $28.95. A dollar or two would benefit as donation to the Ascension Centre. All people are very happy to pay this amount for this hardcover book as a healing tool. The amount also helps you recover your costs in producing the book. In alignment with your intent of delivering love and awareness, *The Healer's Journey* shouldn't cost you. *The Healer's Journey* is a gift to all those who read and absorb the energy in healing, as it's designed to deliver.

With love and compassion, it was created, and so those who purchase will understand this message and philosophy. Teach them and they will know.

The books present in a wooden container, protected and tightly bound and headed for Australian shores. There is a great air of excitement around the arrival in June. The publishing company wants payment prior to shipping naturally. Your shipping and freight arrangements are well and secure. With respect to insurance, your freight manager will discuss this with you.

Your price raises merge together well with increased popularity. The high-end business and corporate clientele will not be concerned by the price raise and will see it as an investment. Remember that with the previous price raises there was an adjustment period? This will be the same.

Jesus wants you to know the crate is travelling here now, and he is accompanying it all the way here.

There is a magnificent orange energy like a veil, or more like a massive energy cloud, all around it.

You are wearing a gorgeous orange top at the VIP book event here, accessorized with gold jewellery. It looks very beautiful.

All is well.

Ferocious, spitting, and snarling energy is angry and resistant to leave. Its host perfectly emanates a body and frequency that allows its existence and growth.

Having been passed through genetically and karmically, it now understands its force is losing an anchor. What infuriates it even further is the light bodies around it. The volume of high frequency disrupts it like a high-pitched noise. The creative force of joy and love is its end. For some time you were supportive of its life, as it kept fear of money losses alive. The more it would scream "Poor," the slow, seeping, doubting energy would appear in you, causing a lot of fear, doubt, and wanting to give up.

One of the highest vibrations, and an effective tool in healing, is sound; therefore your children healed and expressed through music. You have supported their work and growth. This sent forth a wave of absolute rage, as the energy was completely outnumbered and powerless. It no longer has power on the mental, either, as no one chooses to listen to the rant any longer and no one cares to be threatened.

Archangel Michael stands, completely exuding an electric-blue aura around his body. He holds a shield and sword and has come to eliminate this destructive frequency from this plain of existence. He will ensure its complete disintegration. You choose not to be held back by such density.

Mother Mary appears: "Sweet child, look at me. I am the example of mother feminine. I am healer, nurturer, listener, and I surrender. It is with these great gifts I walked the earth, brought forth my son, and surrendered to my process. I was challenged and afraid at times, particularly as I watched my child's fate unfold, so I prayed harder, listened closer, and surrendered even more.

"I am here to help you surrender, dear one."

Jesus stands over your heart with two assisting angels. He places both hands over your heart and is healing you. There is an encodement occurring. Your chest appears to be lit up like a sun. The area is a large, bright light of Christ healing. No more will the low frequencies of another, whether friend or foe, influence you. Archangel Raphael descends and creates an emerald-green aura of energy to all in the room.

We give thanks, dear Lord, and acknowledge this healing today.

With love and gratitude,

Amen

The Entrepreneur   12/4//2012

The entrepreneur is a person who works with an unlimited creative expression and manifests it. He produces an exchange of currency that is so expansive that when dispersed, it filters back into its own growth and creates further opportunity to keep productivity alive. Once the momentum is going and flowing, it virtually self-serves. Like a giant, turning wheel, it just keeps rolling.

Wealth creates this type of energy. This is not to say wealthy people don't have problems; quite the contrary. Their issues are just different. Often their challenges and issues relate to a personal level or health; however, their ability to create flow energy is firmly established, as there would be no signs of weakness or vulnerability in the base and sacral chakras. They don't entertain or own fears of loss, poverty consciousness, or creative restriction. Their fertile force can grow very rapidly and almost effortlessly.

When an entrepreneur aligns themselves to be fully engaged from the heart, as well as their ability to manifest on a large level on earth, this unity of bliss with God and earth life choice is an exquisite and highly responsible position. This is the ultimate. Oprah Winfrey is a classic example of such a person. She is a healer/teacher who has achieved great material wealth so that she could serve so much more.

One must believe they already house the energy of entrepreneurship to attract its likeness. If we are feeling poverty, speaking lack, and projecting need, we will invoke more of that as our mirror. Lift yourself from the worry of your life and feeling as though you are just barely sustaining or surviving. These beliefs can often be associated with a genetic predisposition or an ancestral encodement, if you like, which is imbedded into a human for survival. This can be particularly significant and challenging for someone where there was a genetic lineage that experienced slavery in work to survive. This can be so ingrained, they will expect hardship and loss.

Entrepreneurs are attracted to the like frequency of creation. For the most part, money speaks their language, and they seem to create more of it, often and quite effortlessly. They are keen, clever, and balanced business people who have a knack for choosing the most abundant of investments, agreements, and contracts.

The heart/light worker is coming from a different starting point in their creative expression as they aim to create an abundance of healing, wisdom, great health, and opportunity for the purity of being, and from that point, inspire and motivate entrepreneurship in themselves and others. This then utilises the "Oprah Winfrey dynamic."

When one engages the heart, faith, and belief within their creative flow, it magnifies and multiplies very quickly. In the core of your being lies a knowledge, a peace, a quiet voice who will tell you, *All is well and you are on track.*

Listen to that voice.

When something is needed and in demand, it becomes attractive and desired by people. The connected entrepreneur wants to tap into what's attractive to people, successfully supply an abundance of that desire, self-fertilise and grow, and give back to those who supported his creation and growth to begin with. It is a cycle of the universal flow of giving and receiving. When desire meets solution, it matches to create resolution.

We wish to create a world that features your healing business on the front cover of *Business Review Weekly* with the caption:

Have you factored in your business clearings in your business plan for 2013?

The world of business is shifting and becoming conscious. We know that where the belly is full, it may not mean the heart is. This balance of both is truly the formula of creating entrepreneurship.

Trust that you are in the right place, right now, to learn the next step.

Some level of an advertising campaign would be recommended, and certainly your website's "Corporate" tab requires invention. Give a factual account of how this energy work will benefit the entrepreneur.

That is all.

A Shared Path?   18/4/2012

The resistance that has surfaced of unhealthy energies is disallowing the continued journey and growth of the Mother Ship. One who nurtures, honours, and grows alongside the mother, grows, honours and nurtures the self. When a place in the road is met, where some are fearful or divided about the next leg of the journey, it is time to allow the road and journey to divide. Allow them the freedom, allow yourself the freedom, to decide. Ideally this would be done with peace and blessings for safe and happy travels.

When people do not respect and honour one another for their own choices and beliefs but rather allow a draining to occur from another for strength, the dynamics completely change. It then means you choose to carry them, heal them, and stifle your own growth. This is part of an old consciousness, an imbedded belief that encodes through hundreds of lifetimes, that the healer, nun, witch, medicine woman, sage, oracle must rescue the weary and forlorn.

The individuals we speak of may have had past life connections with you resulting in a similar karmic holding pattern, a non-creative environment with old injuries of self. There was a particular incident involving a violent axe attack to the back and left shoulder. Another displayed a volatile mother-daughter lifetime. There are many, and without bringing to life the individual stories, we are collating them in an energy ball from which we acknowledge their existence and an attachment on a karmic level—one we resolve to heal and release completely.

We also acknowledge that the growth and expansion of this business's energy and future opportunities will create a wave of attention of this same nature, unless you resolve and heal the past attachments and the former relationship dynamic. It is unreliable, inconclusive energy, which is only red while the temperature is hot and otherwise non-creative. We eliminate the effects of such energies today. Your work, your passion, and your focus is not of a temporary nature. It is a vocation of a lifetime.

We acknowledge each individual, with their own makeup, genetics, experiences, connectedness, and beliefs, will have their own journey and progression, and you will have yours. Those who are in alignment with your growth and theirs concurrently will show themselves and will walk along a similar or complimentary creative direction. It will appear with ease and balance. You bear no attachment to anything otherwise. Trust you will be shown each moment of inspiration and be guided to pinnacle points.

Movement or progression appears to present in waves. Things can appear stagnant at times, but in truth growth appears this way. Momentum builds for a growth spurt, with a slower or rest period to follow. This is a natural cycle of all things. Trust, release, and let go.

In peace, love, and joy, the highest vibration surrounds you.

Amen

A spinning vortex, like a super-fast spinning top, is creating an energy of light-headedness. The light sparks and clears as it turns. This wheel encourages time and movement, eliminating all in its path to ensure uninterrupted flow. It reminds me of an energy drill.

Your book presents, opened halfway with a glowing white light from the middle pages. It's so bright, you can only absorb the information, but no words can be read. It is a download.

There is a little shortness of breath, but that is part of this clearing and as such represents taking your breath away. A conscious-meets-unconscious unifying of one heart and mind directs you powerfully towards your soul's purpose whilst concurrently inspiring more balance, more growth, more evolvement. Another wave of inspiration drives creativity to activate and achieve once again. The process is ongoing. There is nothing more destructive on a soul than the presence of stagnation.

The language of soul love is purely growth. It is the essence of her existence and her food and fuel for life. So when you acknowledge that your circle of accompanying souls have changed or are changing, do not sadden. It is unquestionably a sign of growth and subsequent exterior changes to attract its match.

Continually reaffirm the release of anyone or thing that no longer matches your level. Release and let go, allowing your progression to fruit to the next level. Negative mental dialogues can create a holding pattern you do not need.

All processes and machines are well functioning and flowing systematically. We ask God to ensure a productive, fast schedule.

With such gratitude and love, we give thanks.

Amen

A white FedEx van is seen driving down a tree-lined street. The driver stops outside a beautiful, typically American-style, double-storey home.

This scene represents a delivery of *The Healers Journey* to homes, particularly of people associated with teaching, publishing, and people in the mind/body/spirit industry, in America.

In the United States, Great Britain, and Europe, there is interest as well. Australia follows a fair way behind, which is not unusual.

A well-known American author sits on a couch. The room is cosy and warm. He picks up the book, flicks through its pages, and he reads it in part. He stops and contemplates then reaches for the phone.

You are asking now, implementing every spark of faith, to please assist this process. In light of this favour, we ask that every step be made forward easily and effortlessly, and doors be open wide to allow flow, prosperity, interest, and immense attraction. Your intent is clear in releasing a series of books to assist humanity with her healings of body, mind, and spirit, and to awaken to a surfacing reality of power in love and faith. You are testament to this. Please free any binds or obstacles, on any level, to allow free flight.

In trust. Thank you.

Amen

Standing one in front of the other, in a direct line, are Ascended Masters Quan Yin, Lady Nada, and Jesus. They radiate an energy of pure love. They are a love trilogy of heaven.

The building's appearance and design is one of a chain of the Ascension Centre's as a company. There are buildings that are leased out, under the Ascension Centre logo, allowing companies and corporations to lease and utilise the business space. The energy in these buildings is abundant and prosperous in flow. There are the Ascension Centres functioning as healing centres as well.

The Ascension Centre's signature look is one that appears like a hotel. The entrance or lobby is always luxurious and designed to make one feel pampered upon entering. There is always the presence of stonemasonry, carvings, statues, polished floors, and luxurious carpet and furnishings.

Where did all the money come from to build so many of these and additionally sub-lease and lease entire buildings? You are not only receiving from the sales of books. If that were the case, it would take many hundreds of years. We look upon the area of the stock market, with investors in a company with worldwide links, particularly in commercial properties.

You have only scratched the surface. Open your scope to learn about all types of investments, including corporate project management and development. Education and awareness is the sister word for trust. Trust in what you believe in and what you are creating.

Most of it doesn't connect to Australia, so look offshore. Trust you will know when all the pieces come together.

MIRVAC and other such chains have a similar creative formula.

Thank you.

Amen

The scene opens with a truck driver. He is wearing a cap and has a match sticking out of the side of his mouth. He calls on the radio saying he's left the OHL warehouse and is driving to the airport. It is lovely to see. This man is experiencing a really great day, and he's verbalising this. "Yeah, I woke up this morning not feeling so hot, but since coming to work, I feel a weight lifted! Go figure! Ha! Must be the weather!"

He hums along to the radio. The cargo on board is *The Healer's Journey,* and from an energetic perspective, the entire load glows in a gold. The flow is effortless, the loading dock is running to schedule, all the workers are in good spirits and feeling motivated.

A lot of them are listening to their favourite music, and they all feel high spirited.

The cargo is co-ordinated and well positioned into the aircraft. The flight is due to depart at one o'clock and running to schedule. Once landed in Australia, the cargo is transported with ease.

There's a little stagnant energy around the freight manager in Australia. It is a blanket of stress, a static air around him. It does not affect the transport; it is just his energy. He misses the vibration consciously but feels something in his chest. He's dedicated and concerned about his role in the transportation and wants all to go well. He follows up and ensures the freight is loaded efficiently. Transport to your business address is efficient and with delay. Estimated arrival is 19 June 2012, and all is well.

Thank you

Amen

The challenges you are experiencing take great strengths to overcome, and you display this each and every day. Attention to things that require awareness and some level of action is wise, as we wish for no further spiralling out of control. We live upon the earth, and materialism and financial commitment have methods we need to abide by. Life in flow has structure as well as faith. When we live with balance, we reap the rewards. We cannot exclude ourselves from the world at large because we are part of it. If we exclude our physical existence, we then experience a lack of flow in a material world. Awareness of all the laws and regulations around us is wise; to react to them is not. Use a budget pyramid or similar system to chip away at your debt. This will balance and control your expenditures versus earnings.

Start by creating a list of utilities. Take all bills, including insurance, electricity, phones, rates, gas, internet, water, etc., and add these together for a quarter of the year, which is three months. In another column, also under expenses, add in estimates of leisure, social, and car expenditures. Add both columns and total them for the three-month period. Then multiply by four to calculate the yearly amount. Divide this figure by fifty weeks. The end weekly figure is the amount you must have set aside for bills, running costs, and leisure. It should be no more than one third of your combined income.

You are a creator and manifester, there is no doubt about that, but your incomings and outgoings must be reassessed and rebalanced.

Where debt is created, more debt is likely to be created. Automatic repayment plans are fabulous because you can focus on creation rather than repayment. Deciding and honouring a repayment system and commitment of any type will correct the balance in favour of prosperity. Make a list of these, including councils and credit card facilities, and instruct a weekly amount to be automatically deducted.

Take the initiative to gain control in a sensible manner and let go of any fear or projection of outcome. The ideal situation is repayment of all debts without thought or emotion, particularly fear, anger, or bitterness.

Make your lists today.

(1) Repayment of existing

(2) Recovery plan to avoid further debt

(List all utilities and insurances, total for the year, then divide into a weekly amount to set aside)

Thank you.

From an elevated viewpoint, many metres into the sky, I am looking down upon the city of New York. Only a few metres from the top of the Empire State Building and only a short distance away (approximately fifteen kilometres), I can see the Statue of Liberty.

The noise at ground level is a hum in the distance. Feelings of detachment and peace are imminent here. This nation, or rather its people, require elevation. Much of their influences and obstacles are external at ground level. Basic survival is being compromised each and every day. Lack of money, food, empowerment, and education, and an over exposure to violence, greed, and power, tip the scales. What needs to happen for these people to reignite faith in themselves? To invoke a higher consciousness means to embrace an elevated attitude of self and a choice to disperse what no longer matches at a soul level. An overextended responsibility as the world's police is a mirror of this nation's exhaustion. They face a greater challenge than most, as they need to heal a great deal.

Ask God to connect some key individuals, those who have some influential power and ability to expose healing and an elevated viewpoint to the masses. *The Healer's Journey* will be a tool of great worth for healing to many. The United States has surpassed much drama, as well as political and military scandals, and the population has created many vortexes of confusion, idealisms, power struggles, and negative influences.

We ask that God continue to inspire and lovingly assist beautiful souls like Oprah Winfrey, Doreen Virtue, and many other healers and teachers of our modern day to continue to spread the wisdom and opportunities to teach and heal all people across the globe.

Thank you. We ask that you keep infusing light and love into our books and our intention to join other great teachers and healers in the quest to heal the world.

Amen

One Step at a Time   7/9/2012

We are climbing steps. They are dug out of the dirt of a steep hillside. Each step has a stone edge to ensure its longevity in the natural process of erosion from wind and rain. That acknowledgement in itself is a message.

The great man walks bedside me on my left as we climb one step at a time together. I can see his robe swirling around his feet as we climb, and I can feel his quiet persistence. He is calm but firmly focused on his goal, which is simply to climb each step. That is all he intends at this moment—the very action of moving upward and onward. This intention and symbology can be a meditative practice when walking in your physical world or do anything at all. See nothing but your intention to walk, and fully embrace each step. This will distract from any perceived dramas that are occurring around you right now and bring you back into the moment at hand. The intention is to invite you into the recovery of peace, of simplicity in your world, and to create a space for mental silence. From here, we listen and we heal.

We can become embroiled in so many dramas and scenarios in daily life, which cause great pain, and all *may* have an element of truth in them. The more you worry and powerfully engage in the unforeseen, and the more emotion you give it, the more you will actually create your greatest fears. So what do we do? Stop. Stop your mind from its engagement in pain and fear. Look down at your feet and focus. Focus on each step. One at a time. In this moment, right here, right now, all you have to do is consider your step. It is movement, it is peaceful, it requires nothing but your attention and intention. It has a goal; it is progressing rhythmically, solidly, calmly, and sacredly one step at a time. Keep going.

The hill we climb and each step leads to a temple at its top. It is the temple that we wish to reside in for prayer and for reconnection to Self and our highest intentions. Feel the air on your skin and sense the movement of life around you with gratitude. You are a part of it, and it is part of you.

New people and new situations are being brought to you as part of your answered prayers and greater direction. Trust in this, each person and each step. It matters not who may want to create obstacles on this path, as you are unaffected by their intentions for themselves. Stay calm and remain focused with each step. The air is still, and the temperature perfect and mild. There is total peace now.

Do not pre-empt battle or difficulties, as they are part of the human world based on past experiences. It may be a prior experience, but it is not real now. It does not serve you to draw on a past negative emotion in fresh circumstances, as this is a new day. Step into this new day, one foot in front of the other, calmly, intentionally. You will be guided, so trust in this.

We stop walking. He turns and overlooks the landscape, assessing the distance travelled thus far. We have come a long way, uninterrupted. The progress has been surprisingly quick. It is humbling to be reminded of this.

The beauty and tranquillity is a scene to behold. There is none other than complete union of peace in body and mind.

With gratitude, we experience the meaning of zen.

We continue our ascent.

Amen

Less Is More 17/9/2012

It is the age-old challenge of man. The fear that paralyses the powerful and the worthy into a pitiful, scratching, injured animal: the energy of deception, which of course is housed within the root of trust.

When one carries past injuries as though they've never healed, it becomes a layering of scar tissues, slowly weakening the body and extinguishing the fire of creation.

This viewpoint implies an attitude of "What's in it for you/me? Why should I trust this idea, or you? I've been burned before!"

Hence the creative fire is extinguished, drowned in the tears of past disappointments. Anything to ensure that we won't be fooled again. Who is fooling who? It is a vicious cycle that ensures nothing but a spiralling downward into bitterness and hatred.

No creative light can enter this vaulted, padded room. It is the worst case of human sabotage and an insanity in one's mind.

To turn around such a concrete belief system, you must surrender entirely. You would need to release any dependence or control. Your only task is the desire to relinquish and release all past disappointments and associated pain. Rebuke all victimhood and begin to self-soothe with appreciation and love of self. The devalued position of scars and trauma become like pain trophies, only reinforcing belief of deservedness of pain. When it is realised that the holding onto pain may temporarily justify further punishment to the world and to Self, eventually this will suffocate all new creative and birthing opportunities. Let go and live.

Until you feel confident, take baby steps. One at a time. Focus on one small step per day, and the rest will be shown to you along the way. If it does not feel comfortable, do not share your personal, creative goals. Skim the surface; it is not required to gain approval from anyone. This is not deception. It is careful planning and creating the mental space you need to keep your goals clear without any unnecessary pressure through another's fears.

Soothe your mind. Doubt is illusionary. Seek calm waters.

Amen

Chapter 6

Ground Zero Healings

A clear, transformative energy streams down over the city of New York. As the energy field hits the ground, it billows up over the people, the buildings, the trees. It instantly clears the heaviness. I walk along the pavement and observe the environment. People hurriedly race towards their focused destinations, whether that be a meeting, a luncheon, or a flight to catch. Their mind chatter is like a machine gun, massive overload of scrambled thoughts. They are all so ungrounded. Their bodies are mostly moving by default, as they have little awareness of each step or how that feels on the body and why. They are responding to a series of demands, no more.

Faster, faster, faster. The entire scene appears to be on fast forward, except for the viewer. Viewing the scene is at normal speed and completely unaffected by the environment. I am walking within it but not a part of it.

I am looking down a major street and passing many buildings. There's bright and dazzling signage on these buildings, traffic lights overhead, power lines, cars, buses, and many people all in silence. There is no audio to match the vision, which is just as well. It's so noisy.

Suddenly, we're led along a street and look up ahead. It's a light as bright as the sun and absolutely huge in size. It would be approximately the size of fifty football fields suspended about fifty metres in the air. The "sunlight" is moving closer, and as it does, it radiates many tubular rays, shining down towards the ground. These rays are multicoloured and have a sound frequency as well. It's like the great light is the mother ship and the light streams (which appear quite solid) are its children. It may sound like a weird analogy, but it's the only way I can explain it.

The rays of light are now transforming into angels of their particular colour ray and frequency. It's beautiful, and my heart wants to explode with joy. It's like I know them all, and I'm so happy to see them again! I suddenly understand why the environment had to be sped up and all was moving so fast! This was to create a frequency that best supports their coming. It's faster, much higher, and lighter than earth.

They all descend and telepathically tell me they are doing much work to assist the nation, its people, and the entire world. America has a significant role for humanity on a variety of levels; however, as we connect to the United States and the world with our mission of global healing, they reveal themselves. Their mighty presence is so whole and miraculous, our true light workers and angel guardians. They are dedicated to our growth and support our quest to heal and reveal our true nature.

"We are God beings, but so many forget. From our dimension, we send much light frequency and vibration or 'healing,' as you call it. We anchor and secure many pillars of light from Ground Zero."

Suddenly, the light beings and light pillars transform into reflecting sparkles of light and disperse, and then rejoin to the huge sunlight.

I am standing near a maple tree. The message is complete.

Thank you. Endless gratitude.

Amen

Ground Zero—Melbourne   1/02/2012

A rumbling, a vibration like that of a great earthquake, can be heard, only it's coming from the sky. An excitability grows, and there is a great feeling of anticipation. It's getting closer and closer! Then a great explosion of energy erupts into our dimension and into the physical plane of the earth, right here. It enters through the rooftop. It begins as a massive stream, very fast and powerful. It comes through the roof and into the building, filling every room and corridor, then streaming and purging out to the streets. From above, the view encompasses the circular radius around the business, then spreads out across Melbourne, Victoria; country Victoria; Sydney, New South Wales; Adelaide, South Australia; Canberra, ACT; Brisbane, Queensland; Cairns and North Queensland, Northern Territory; Darwin and Perth, Western Australia; vibrating across thousands of kilometres clearing, wiping out dense energies. All of nature, the animals, this part of earth that is Australia, are very grateful.

The Ascension Centre stands in all her glory, luminous and energised by the concurrent earth healing for Ground Zero—Melbourne. There are rays of light filtering from and through her. It's sheer perfection. If she could speak, she'd say, "I'm bliss. I'm so happy."

Jesus asks that you don't become too focused on figures. Place your trust and focus on the God energy functioning in and around you always. The building of the Ascension Centre is but a miniscule task for God and her universe, so understand you already have received what you are asking for. Be not within the limited thinking of physical reality, as this is merely the end result of all you put your energy to. Be absolutely clear, act with joy, and see no bills burdening, as this will lower your expectations and plunge you into the illusion of lack. There is no lack. Only if you create lack. Focus on the feeling of having so many clients you are now booking six months in advance! You are so incredibly abundant and prosperous.

You love what you do. Thank God for your blessings, and in return bless all of your clients—new, old, forthcoming—and bless all of your adversaries. Bless your bank account and bless your life. In complete and total joy, bless everything you have experienced and will experience. Bless the phone and her deliverance of all your clients. Bless the web and all who connect who wish to be healed. Your heart has so much love to give to all who know who come and all who will come. Your heart encompasses the love that covers and nurtures the entire earth and all her inhabitants. Nothing is unreachable, nothing is impossible, as you have engaged in the flow of the infinite and its creative force. Ride the frequency like I was riding the back of a dolphin. It is natural, joyful, and effortless. The infinite flow of the universe plays its rhythms within your heart and sings its song.

Reread and reread whenever a thought distracts you. Reread, sing it, and feel it. It's your song.

I love you.

Amen

Ground Zero—Hollywood, California   1/02/2012

The "H" on the Hollywood sign appears luminous. The clearing energy showers down over the mountain and makes its way to the lower valley region, towards the heart of Los Angeles. There is such a polarity of energies here, like an immense light vs. a dark underworld, battling for supremacy. Then the residue disperses into the alleyways until the next time they meet. One can get lost in LA, dreaming of becoming a star, living and riding upon the wings of the angels of this city, or just as easily become one.

There appears a Marilyn Monroe look-alike up on a stage. She is mimicking the famous goddess's persona and style. Her dress is in a fuchsia pink satin, and she wears a stole around her shoulders. The beauty, the glamour, and the fame was an exterior façade. Marilyn's, and likewise this woman's, interior world lay in a devalued, denied, self-sacrificial void. This energy is of pure sadness, and it hovers at street level. There is too much of this on our planet.

Changing course, it is night, and I'm walking up the street. Flashy dressed, flashy mouthed con artists call out to people walking down the street. Scam artists, musicians, and all sorts of weird and wonderful people fill the streets and call out to you. I keep walking. I look up and see a huge Coca-Cola sign in the iconic red and white. I ask to be taken back to the Hollywood sign on the mountain to view the situation from a higher perspective.

Jesus appears: There are enlightened human beings here. They mix in their circles. We need to clear the way. A lot of energy work is being done that allow the awakening. Influences of greed, dominance, and drugs are of high volume, but that is our opportunity to assist and acknowledge and infuse as much light, joy, and hope into their lives as possible.

The wealthier portion of Hollywood has a lot of its roots in creative arts, film making, fashion, and real estate. We allow this healing light to filter to them, perhaps to spark an idea to film or create a documentary based on *The Healer's Journey.*

With love and gratitude.

Amen

I'm hearing a music cart playing festival circus-style music. I can see it; it's colourful and it has white and red stripes along the panels with many ornaments, which appear like carved figures.

You can purchase cold drinks, ice cream, small souvenirs of the Eiffel Tower, and cards of Paris, etc. I turn around and standing before me is a huge structure. It is the Eiffel Tower. The music continues to play softly in the background. You can feel the pride of this nation in its food and wine, its people, the dining, the humming sound of light-hearted chatter.

An energy showers downward from above. A clear, divine energy transmutes the blanket of low vibration at ground level. This city is more in tune with its heart and soul. The heritage and pride of it connects people strongly to tradition and to each other. Whilst work may be necessary to survive, equally important is the enjoyment of life, beauty, the arts, food, culture, tradition, and faith. Fashion, love, romance—all of those elements are firmly conscious and well integrated in the French and certainly Parisians. The energy gently showers down. It's integrating very well. It mainly targets and assists negative ego elements.

Some children run past, cheerful, playing, and joyful. They are advanced evolutionary beings to create a greater spiritual awareness to the people. They are comfortable in their own skin. The young are coming forth with such natural awareness. Education plays a big role here, to be worldly, knowledgeable, and rich in their heritage as well as their spiritual selves.

I cannot see the top of the Eiffel Tower, it's so tall. A red-breasted small bird is sitting in a tree beside me. Distracted by the red breast, so round and beautiful, I am suddenly viewing the entire scene from above, and it's quite high. I am viewing the distance between Paris and Provence, which is a huge area of southern France. The idea of this visual is to see them linked energetically. The actual distance is much more than what I'm seeing but the altering of actual distance is shortened to show me the line of connection. There is the enormous sun shining from above once again. The beams of golden and white light shine towards Paris and then also towards Provence. Then an enormous beam of white energy connects the two on the ground. It looks like an enormous pyramid of light. Little star-like sparks rain off the beams, knowing where they are going. They are in fact assigned angels on their mission: the return of the Magdalene and her beloved daughter.

Learn some French. It will be very beneficial to you when you travel there. Your Mother spoke like she was a native of the region. She was very skilled in languages.

The French will be impacted greatly. They will feel it in their genes.

In unity, with love.

Amen

Jesus appears with tears in his eyes, but they are not his tears. They are the tears of thousands of generations who have cried with grief over his death. Grief that they wish they could have prevented. This pain has an underlying aspect of intense guilt at its core.

Within the heart of every Roman is the subliminal belief, "We killed our Lord Jesus Christ." Some or most will not even be aware of it, and most would passionately and vigorously deny it. But this lies within the core of them, and it is very sad indeed. This is why the great empire outwardly forgave themselves and embarked on a worldwide pledge to turn every man, woman, and child into a Christian and follower of Christ. We know that hundreds and hundreds of years of continued bloodshed of millions of people in the name of Christianity was a bizarre and violent injustice for the great man who lived for love and died for ego.

At that time and thereafter, history saw a manifestation of an extremely low energy upon earth, which grew into mass destruction and death, supposedly to hide a belief that they themselves felt like they were Christ murderers. It was a gross type of overcompensation. But by killing the innocent in Christ's name, they became exactly that—murderers, the most severe form of unlove, of darkness and of evil. The anger and control spread like a cancer.

Today Rome is titled a holy city, one that functions by the very existence, love, and worship of Christ. Still in its mammoth form, it's a force to reckon with and has proven time and time again over the centuries that it will not reveal any of the secret documents or untold secrets that are tightly locked away in the Vatican vaults.

Most traditional worshippers and people of faith practise only by the doctrines of the written, published, and authenticated Bible of the Holy Catholic Church. There have been many books written and theories speculated upon in recent years, providing some thought-provoking evidence and theories, which suggest that the life of Christ as written in the Bible was altered in so many ways.

Hatred was to manipulate certain events. Those in power would focus their attention and blame upon a nation of people, Jesus's own people, the Jews. They were to carry the burden, quite ironically, and would suffer at the hands of hatred, projections, and isolation for thousands of years, lasting to this day. It's humanity's lesson, one that must be righted or, more so, be acknowledged. There have been many lies, and the truth must now be told.

The consciousness sweeping the planet is of the Christ. He showers his love, gratitude, strength, and reform upon us. His physical self could do no more during his life. His enormous task began after his physical death for the human race to awaken from their current existence and ascend into the light.

The perfection is the awakening of the spirit so strong, it reveals the greatest glory of ourselves creating now. We understand the road we've travelled; we need not go back there.

Symbolically, thousands and thousands lay down their swords, revealing many more. Millions and millions follow.

We need not rekindle and support an illusion created in the eyes of man.

The great walls will crumble eventually, one way or another, and the truth will be revealed. The time grows near where humanity will open their hearts and acknowledge their role in these genetic/karmic events, and compassion will rain over all with acceptance.

Amen

A white-turbaned, bearded imam is shown to me. He has a kind face and gentle speaking voice. To fully understand the people of the Muslim faith and all people who come from the Middle East, we need go there.

The entire region has had a tumultuous history, one of changing leadership, family/royalty land entitlements, and sheiks wanting to retain continuing wealth and power. However, in 540 AD when Muhammad was born, the region and its faith would undergo an enormous transition. There were many wars, with the overall outcome in an identical position to the Christian world.

Muhammad, like Jesus, did not come into his knowledge of his great gifts and prophesising until his thirties. His early life was that of a peasant—challenging and not at all glorious. Later he began to hear the words of God, unknowingly channelling his love and guidance. He would also be aware of the messages he received through other people. He respected and loved Jesus the prophet, the man who changed the world. Jesus's teachings were known to Muhammad. He was well aware that Jesus was a child of God and a gift unto the earth.

Muhammad prayed to God a great deal, and once the messages began to come through, he began to speak to those around him and eventually draw forth the assistance from his wife and followers to write the early scriptures. The Koran, as it appears today, has been amended by the religious powers and government to control the masses, just like the Christian Bible. There is not a shred of difference.

We are on the edge of such an evolutionary breakthrough, one that will rock both the Christian and Muslim worlds as we acknowledge Muhammad and Jesus as brothers. Their greatness and their love force connection to God are the same. Man has changed the dynamic and drawn strong boundaries between East and West over a series of events and from a power and supremacy aspect, which we will reveal now.

Christianity implemented their bloody pledge: the Roman Empire wanted complete control over the planet and for every person to be a follower of Christ. In doing so, the Middle East, already suffering under years of bloodshed and dominance from the Romans, had experienced the teachings of Muhammad and had great faith in their beliefs based on his teachings. The battle began, and the Middle East refused to be threatened by the Romans' forceful position: "Take our Bible or die by the sword."

And so the destructiveness of jihad begun. If you die defending Allah, you will be greatly rewarded in the kingdom of heaven. Muslims would furiously protect their choices, and if need be, would die doing so. Surrendering meant that there would be a complete takeover and complete loss of freedom. The Middle East placed many barriers, both social and religious, to enforce opposing rules and practices of a severe nature to keep the West at a great distance.

Turkey was under Greek reign for hundreds of years and therefore had more Christian influence. Later, once they gained their independence and revealed their

Muslim identity, they were seen as the half brother of Islam and weren't to be completely trusted. They were "Europeanised" but had much wealth in gold and riches, similar to that of Egypt. It is the quest of humanity to now recognise that we are all of one Source, that the ways in which history played a part created a mammoth division, an illusion of separation, and an opportunity for peace, forgiveness, and awareness of oneness.

Those dividing walls, Mecca's and Rome's fear, must crumble at this time for liberation, for peace, and for the brotherhood and sisterhood of earth's ascension. It is time.

We are all one.

Amen

The golden shower of God energy rains down upon Westminster Abbey. The love energy blankets, transmutes, and transforms dense energy, which may be associated with ego, shame, scandal, and fear.

The English have a long history with intolerance and indifference, and an egocentric belief of supremacy. Historically, they were a ruthless European empire. The English felt quite threatened by powerful nations around them. So to eliminate the threat of an intruder, they would reveal a merciless force and often savagery.

But the English had a lease of the Magdalene love force, as her feet touched the shores of France with her intent and longing to reach England. But distance would have played a part. Relatives of her late husband Jesus were there; however, it was too unprotected an unfriendly place for her, so she would wait.

England's Stonehenge is its prominent energy vortex; it is the chakra of the United Kingdom and is extremely necessary for balance. Today, many people are low and almost in a mesmerised or hypnotic state. In some ways, they carry the burden of royal scandal, the tragedy of Princess Diana's death (who was an earth angel preparing the royal family's evolvement as a major influence to many millions of people). Now William carries this ongoing task.

Additionally, the history of the Templars, the torching of witches and pagans, the rise, fall, and scandals of various kings and queens, all describe a turbulent, passionate, tumultuous history. Some say this weighs heavily upon the people. England requires some faith and a belief in her strength no longer implemented through brute force. The power and grace of the English rose will deliver her from the low frequency energy of past.

A profound earth angel and Englishman, Mr. Lee Harris, enlightens and assist the masses through his channelling of his guides, "The Z's." He is directly influencing Great Britain, the United States, Australia, and Europe with his gentle but direct counselling of humanity, shifting through dramatic changes on earth as our consciousness expands and sweeps the planet. The heart connectedness of England is blossoming, the sweet-smelling rose is opening the heart even further, and the people are embracing it at a soul level.

There are a few churches, one in particular in England, built in honour of the beloved Mary Magdalene. The priest who built it travelled to France and brought back the knowledge.

Suddenly, the vision now shows an enormous God energy parting some very heavy clouds. The clouds are unable to hold their weight and burst, allowing the rain to fall in buckets of water. A long, solid stream of water begins to take shape like an antenna, as the water falls and then spreads over all of England in a mass flooding of divine rain. It washes away old guilt and releases old patterns, limiting beliefs and structures, pain and savagery.

Love is the only true emotion of God and forgiveness and compassion, its greatest test. In God we trust.

Amen

A bearded man dressed in a caftan and sandals leads a small procession. He wears cloth around his head, which allows for easy coverage of the mouth and nose. The desert winds swoop up heavy blasts of sand. The temperature is very hot. The path is leading towards three large pyramids. We are on sacred land, and the flashbacks of Jesus's footsteps are being viewed, as it was so many years ago. The imagery, a moment in time, his footsteps, mirror ours.

This ancient land comfortably houses many truths, no matter how arrogant the Western or modern world chooses to be. It is an open treasure chest of history and great knowledge; one just has to seek. It is no mystery or surprise that the ancient people were working with energy, manifestation, healing, and miracles way before Jesus walked the earth.

Souls of his own bloodline were his undeniable attraction to the land of the gods, which led him there.

He truly loves the whole world; for this he marks no preference. However, he understands <u>our</u> reflection of his life path and our interest in the energy vortexes and chakras that assist our planet's healing. The earth's vibration and frequency support all inhabitants, including animal and plant life. As the great Mother Earth is shifting, creating, harmonising, rebalancing, and realigning herself to sustain and support growth, it's healing allows all life to proliferate towards perfection.

The kaftan-wearing guide turns to face us. His dark skin and electric blue eyes tell me he is someone more than a human. He is Kathumi. We do not question; we are here to pray and meditate.

We stop thirty metres short of the base of the first pyramid. Jesus stands open-armed a few metres away. He smiles and begins to walk towards us.

Like greeting old friends, he smiles and looks at each one of us with such love. He hugs Kathumi as his brother. The joy he feels is like a reuniting, as he had not seen him for a while. As we seat ourselves on the ground in a circle, the energy begins to circulate clockwise around the circle. Positioned opposite this great being, such love fills the circle—through us, around us.

From behind Jesus's head shines a great sunlight; it encompasses everything and completely envelopes all that could be seen. It is so extraordinarily bright white/golden yellow. The great light and it's very essence is he, and he it.

Communicating telepathically: The light is God, and we are made of light. We are no different from the divinity of the Source and its love. It is unlimited and eternal, and its power exists within us, in and out of physical form. It is the Source that we draw on in all ways and in everything we do, say, love, hate, create, or destroy. It is the universe's mother and father. It is the all. It is God. My mother and father are your mother and father.

We sat in silence with images of the cosmos, the most extraordinarily beautiful Milky Way, endless spheres. Then the imagery changed and became a huge open meadow with long reeds blowing across hilltops, then expanded to enormous snowcapped mountains with valleys below.

Suddenly back within in the circle, Jesus opens his arms and indicates the close of the prayer/healing.

It's sunset. Camels can be seen in the distance. Peace be with you.

Amen

A cross stands solid in the ground with an enormous God light beaming behind it. What a profound symbol to truly remind people to accept responsibility for their actions. Where one places their energies, thoughts, and emotions will create before them. Humanity's journey has been a purposeful series of events, all of which are opportunities for change. Structured religion has been particularly misled because of the avalanche of fear in men, forcing all how to think and what to believe.

But of course, truth has a way of presenting out of the soil like a new sprouting of a tree. Then it grows, matures, and strengthens to eventually bear fruit, as does the olive tree. The knowledge, the life-giving nutrients, can then be passed to so many, yet it is your choice if you dare try its flavour. Chew the fruit and swallow all its juices, all of what it has to offer. If you like it, how lovely. Your experience was fulfilling. You may even share this with your neighbour and offer a piece.

Being part of the energy flow of physical life, the actual practise of it, and all of the experiences you endure sparks the memory of your innate wisdom. You have already done this millions of times before, as one sometimes requires repetition.

The greatest impact on humanity was the crucifixion. This impact has left its mark upon the world on so many levels.

But dear people, it is the message behind the symbol. The cross represents the surrender of man to trust in God to always love and support you. It represents your release of illusionary obstacles of fear, judgement, and non-creation in your life.

My persecutors karmically understood the action they took, that their action caused nothing more than grief within themselves. They hurt none other than themselves. I am not the victim; I am the victor. I embraced the passage to the holy light of love. I surrendered my will and my ego to God and was taken into the arms of great love.

So do not fear your persecutors. Feel compassion, as they are creating for themselves a sad path indeed. The cross reminds us to rejoice, to surrender. The cross reminds us of great love. When you view or feel the sadness of my death (which was only symbolic for humanity to embrace lessons), understand it was my transition to love and freedom in its entirety. It is a cross we all bear at some time. Think about how many you carry on your back right now.

Rejoice! I ascended to exist with love and freedom. Yes, I too was tested in my faith, and I cried out in doubt and fear. But as I walked within the shadow and darkness of death, I reclaimed out of the ashes a great love for thyself. I came forth through my greatest love for you all to help you to truly experience yourselves. Your choices define what sort of life you shall live. Will you choose love, hope, healing, creation? Or will you choose fear, loss, illness, destruction?

The cross represents surrender. I allow my soul to guide me, direct my every choice in faith, in love, light, and awareness of my peace. Viewing the cross from a perspective of courage is also relevant. Sometimes verbalising your truth may lead to disapproval from those around you. Will they crucify me? Liberation is faith. To walk forth with complete peace in knowing your every step is supported is the key to your freedom. We are all connected. The progress and fulfilment of our life missions will be clearer and with less fear if we work together.

Be conscious. Be aware. Live with love and peace, and it will spread across the earth like a soft spring shower. There is much life to live.

Jesus

Ground Zero—Tibet: Shangri-La 9/2/2012

I see the most beautiful valley with a cobalt-coloured river running though; a paradise, no less. The air is clear, cool, crisp, and we are entering this scene airborne, approximately twenty feet from the surface. Jesus is ahead and indicates we should go forth towards a mountainous area ahead. It is a very lush, very green, almost dark-emerald-coloured landscape. The temperature is very moderate.

Shangri-La is the Lotus Kingdom, a place that exists on a higher dimension but accessible via meditation, healing, and stillness. Here it is a kingdom of abundant life, incredible beauty, and very high vibration, and it is open to all who connect to the frequency of it. It is our bliss and certainly a mirror of earth's ascension, and in earth's existence, her desire to become. The lotus is the shape of the kingdom, and within its centre lies the palace of unimaginable beauty. Gold and diamonds and waterfalls abound. The water is almost crystalline in appearance. It is so much lighter than our water on earth. The Shambala (access point) lies in the heart; the encodement is present and activation allows you access to this magnificent region. The kingdom is accessible within self.

The monks of the mountains know, as they have frequently travelled there. Their physical bodies are completely rejuvenated each time they visit, and their energy bodies vibrate very fast (high). They are free of all disease and discomfort, and live to be well over a hundred years old. Jesus travelled a long way to see the monks of the mountain. He spent some time there perfecting the complete disassociation of the body as a meditation practice. (This served him well at the time of his

449

physical crucifixion.) What would normally take people many years, Jesus accomplished in a short time. He would learn to bi-locate to this realm and learn much from the ascended ones, beings of light, and beings from other worlds.

All inhabitants are light and are not of solid body.

There is no falsehood, no obligation, no greed, and no hunger. This dimension lies between heaven and earth and is a foundation of God. Intelligence that surpasses any human brain or intellect exists here. The blueprint or source is only accessible from the heart. True intelligence is the heart.

Here, the beings understand the very nature of disease and discomfort on earth is only an illusion made real by its inhabitants. We have a choice. It is well understood. You will learn though very deep meditation, an understanding of soul. Where God speaks directly to you, you will understand.

Jesus spends much time here.

Through this realm, you will be shown beauty—the beauty with your world and yourself. You have to choose the pathways, the streams, the plant and bird life that bring you joy and coordination. It is about the harmony of the Soul integrating into a harmonious body and a peace-filled mind. When you reach enlightenment, you can reside in Shangri-La. Many great master souls reside or travel here frequently.

Buddha. He was the brother of Jesus and many others of flesh, as love masters with the same father and mother.

Open the door to the lotus within the centre of your heart.

Symbols all in Gold, then imagery of swirling colours that are indescribably beautiful. It is paradise. Turquoise, gold, hot pink, green, orange, purple.

That is all. Thank you.

God

A female voice singing a traditional Indian song can be softly heard. This song is about the Goddess of Birth, incarnation, and fulfilling life contracts. A temple stands against the warm, blue sky. The temple is white and domed. A white-bearded man, a master of ancient teachings, stands outside. His kind eyes are welcoming. His hands hold each other lovingly in front of his chest. I walk towards him.

"You see, my dear, the key to all life is right here." He points to his heart. "Not here (head) or here (stomach). Only here (heart)."

Peace is a result of that. Inner peace provides wisdom beyond the teaching of the classrooms, and it opens an endless stream of solutions to all worldly cares. We are spiritual teacher's insofar as we coordinate the beauty of the body in existence with the mind of greatest landscape with the soul of boundless opportunity.

There you have the holy trinity, the three conceptual aspects of existence in man.

I want you to understand that you were born with all of the knowledge within but have chosen to forget. The Western world has many distractions. Your life, your demands, your cars, your TVs, your lack of daily meditative practice take away attention of true guidance. Right in the centre of your being is your heart. The fire in your passion, for life, for Self, had been almost extinguished as a species. We need to remember. Reconnect to the all, the power of the Source that sustains your every breath. God lovingly provided many teachers and saints upon the earth for your benefit, and we celebrate the joy and gratitude of being blessed with some of the most beautiful souls to accompany us.

Jesus spent much time here, more than you know. He found the balance of earth and heaven. He could practice all he knew, learn perfection, and begin again on another level and continue to experience life without the constant disruption of Roman occupation. Jesus was a scholar. He truly understood all that was unwritten and written. He enjoyed and loved the vessel as much as his conscious connection to God and the messengers of heaven (angels).

He was a prophet and a healer; he was the balance in human form, like many before and after him. He used the power within his body to transcend, bi-locate, perform miracles, and heal, but mistake it not—he still felt. This beautiful man of flesh and blood felt the pain of the body and of the heart, like everyone else does. This is the mark and experience of the teacher. We understand the challenge of the journey when we've travelled there ourselves.

Many earthly practices did not interest Jesus, as he had surpassed the primitiveness of bitterness. Like a well-prepared solider, he was not the enemy, but he understood them well.

Arrogance is the poison and the destruction of man; awareness is her freedom.

Jesus's body functioned in its purest form on earth as he became a master of a study of meditation, which allowed his body to cellularly rejuvenate, even when his heart rate would be slowed. His metabolism to would decrease so that he could survive long periods without food if necessary. He transcended the heaviness of the body but still stayed connected to earth. He understood the power and control he had. He would not need as much food whilst practicing these teachings nor need a tremendous amount of sleep. This couldn't last for long periods, but certainly during long travels, as it was necessary to lighten his body whilst still regenerating cells and infusing light.

Jesus became aware and fully understood the individual system of each chakra and its function. There was a peaceful exchange of the energies when working with him as he was pure love when meeting his brothers. All of his time with us was his peace, as he could live without any dire attention, as previously experienced closer to his birth home.

He had completed his earth contract from a soul perspective.

Jesus spent many years, some in his early life until he was twenty-five years old, and then later returned. He felt a calling to spend his final years on earth living to old age.

That is all.

Ground Zero—As Above So Below   *21/3/2012*

My left ankle pinches in pain. A lower frequency is unravelling from around it like a snake releasing its tightened grip. The cleansing energy, an all-powerful force, flushes anything that is unhealthy. Indeed, you have many angels and light being helpers who are nodding in agreement. You are shown and are seeing clearly. You have the knowledge and the tools. For this, be so very grateful; thank you, God.

Jesus shows his presence, and he beckons me to follow him. It is a tunnel that we must bend slightly to go through. It is off to the side wall of the building, behind your storage cupboard, in your healing room.

We walk quite a long way, and it is dimly lit. Exiting through an opening, we enter a beautiful crystal cave. The interior is of the deepest purple amethyst glistening brilliantly and lining the walls. Inlaid within the amethyst are scattered cut garnets in the most vibrant red and also golden-amber citrines, sea-blue aquamarines, and ocean pearls as well. The cave is so breathtakingly beautiful, and it emanates a very powerful vibration. In the centre of the floor is a small fireplace. We are seated, and a drink is offered from a golden cup. It is spring water, but it is the most pure, sweet water I have ever tasted. It is so light. Oddly, it barely has any volume at all.

I look at Jesus, and he appears to be meditating. I put the cup down and quieten my mind to join in.

A swirl of golden-white energy begins to circulate anticlockwise around our heads. I open my eyes for a moment to see if I can view it with my physical eyes; instead, I see you have appeared,

455

sitting crossed legged in front of me, meditating as well with a slight smile on your face. There is no verbal communication at all. We all sit together in complete silence, and yet we are connected. Aware and at peace. The fire burns quietly, gently popping and crackling, beaming out a comforting warmth. The flames represent our creative fire. Fuel must be present to allow your passion to create, to manifest your goals and desires. The inner landscape of the cave is our interior, our inner beings in a symbolic sense, which is residing in the silence of God. Retreat to inner healing and wisdom.

Here is stillness.

Amen

Chapter 7

Global Shifting:
Ascension to New Earth

The golden God light shines behind many thousands walking the path. There forms silhouette of many, many thousands walking into the realm where we are.

We now invite the awakening. We now welcome the many souls whose divine spark has been lit within them. How blessed are we.

The law of attraction and divine assistants will be led to us, whether it be via the books, through the website, or by contacting you personally. The intent is to heal, learn, and gather together to move onward to the ascension of humanity. This process is inevitable, and our acknowledgement allows us to be directly touched by God in every moment of this awareness.

Archangel Gabriel: "Beloved creators, I thank you for your love-guided service to this planet and her inhabitants. These souls sing a glorious tune of happiness, and they celebrate in true joy fully realized by their immense perfection of creation! For many centuries, the soul, physical, mental, and emotional selves have not been aligned with unity. Many thousands of lifetimes, karmic and genetic releases, and fear-based beliefs have finally been conquered to allow the euphoria of greatness to confirm all that you are. But now, dear beings, you have connected all the elements that make up your true God being. You have awoken to God within you, and as with all souls, you wish to bring this news to the world.

The many who are coming come in search of their answers. Into the highest realms they seek with the true guidance of their hearts. Within their being is a voice, a feeling, an urge to search for clarity within. Question, seek, and thou shall find. They will know they have entered into the house of the Lord and returned home.

Guiding them to their truth is an act of love and is in service to God and God's children, the highest glory in honour. Amen.

The awakening of yourself and others continues and allows the process for humanity to embrace these aspects: "We are humble, we are honourable, we are grateful, dear Lord."

Gabriel

Scene: Cosmos with purple, blue-red hues

As the crowd gathers, there is an air of anticipation, fear, wonder, vulnerability, and need.

Gatherings of the poor, hungry, fearful, and all those who wish to avoid misfortune create a mass of energy that is extremely heavy and draining. On an energy level, a huge spiral or drain can be seen, and many simply collapse into it.

The leaders, the priests, the holy men, the healers, the kings, the emperors, the people's representative: whomever you happen to be, step forth onto the podium, stage, balcony, or to the front of your temple, church, or castle to greet the needy, the frightened, the desperate. The ego inflates as the cries of relief ring out into the air; he then raises his hand in acknowledgement. This one movement of his hand ushers in a silence from the crowd. He looks across the heads and faces, barely glimpsing at them.

Every needy soul expects a blessing, a pardon, hope, faith, freedom, food. Life. There is nothing godly about this historical image; there is nothing holy or miraculous about this primitive scene. This is the very foundation of what has confused people, in the past and in the present. Many church/religious leaders, politicians, occult leaders, royalty, and ego-driven healers served themselves and their egos, not the people, and certainly not God. This root and foundation must be eliminated with a blinding light of God, an explosion of grace and truth.

Tiny particles of light float gently to the earth. They melt like snow on the warm ground. These are days of light; the time of ascension is upon us, and we will choose to experience the arrogance no more. We will no longer connect to the primitive ways of third-dimensional living.

Christ consciousness is a frequency our bodies, our minds, and our souls resonate to. Now we can enjoy this luscious vibration, integrating it through every cell, through a collective existence, rather than a post life reality. We no longer need to pray for salvation; we pray for and expect nirvana.

It lives within us, and it is expanding, surfacing, being.

Thousands of angels, light beings, and masters have travelled into our dimension to support the change in frequency we are experiencing, and all is going well. Those who are unable to continue life in their physical reality will ascend and then incarnate again (if they choose to do so) once their vibration/frequency has undergone an alignment to the new reality and resettled into the new adjustments to best utilize their next descent to earth disease-free, pain-free, illusion-free. This is the new perspective and desire for humanity to experience.

The earth is healing at such a rapid rate, much faster than ever previously recorded. During reports of natural disasters, do not be not afraid. These energetic and subsequent physical shifts must occur for the growth and expansion of new earth.

On earth as it is in heaven.

Such time is coming.

Amen

Jesus sails a small raft, simple in its design. It has a small hand-sewn sail guiding it. The sea is calm. He looks at the horizon and then up at the sky.

Looking up, the grey clouds part. The bluest sky opens up, and a huge beam of glittering-white light shines down. He acknowledges the light is shining over a place on land. The land is Eygpt, and the light is beaming upon Mt. Sinai. He holds a crown of thorns, but it signifies an ending. The crown will be laid on the earth upon arriving at shore. Humanity no longer needs to associate with energy of sacrifice. This is done.

"I am your Lord, God of your conscious and unconscious. I am your guiding light, your angel, your Mother and your Father. I am the one you can rely upon, aspire to, pray with, love, and be loved by. We have journeyed long together side by side. Each and every one of you I know. I know you all so well. Let us walk, my friends."

He lays the crown on the sand, and it sinks as if in quicksand. Upon the shore a short track leads to the base of the mountain. We walk; I am behind him, I am so grateful and feel a love for him I cannot fully explain.

We reach the top, and he stands with his arms extended to the heavens. "How miraculous is this life?" he exclaims. We laugh; the clouds build into a dark purple-blue colour full of water and seemingly stormy. The wind begins to blow, and we observe the miraculous and powerful energy of nature.

"This time is grand and of great importance. The world has run out of time with outdated, disproportionate ways. Fear cannot live within a light body, so it dissipates cellularly. We don't cease to exist, of course; only the illusion, the control, the judgement, the fear, the negative portion of ego dies. The possibilities of your creation are endless. Choose this now. Watch and experience your life unfold.

Now gather ye all around. We join all with my daughters and sons of earth, the high priests and priestesses, the healers and the wise ones, in this gift of love to all living beings upon the earth."

Love is our God
Your grace is upon us
Forever in this moment
We ascend
In unity. Amen.

Global Fear: Opportunity
for Awareness   13/2/2012

The Lord is my shepherd, and I shall not fear the darkness I will walk along my path in full faith and his light will lead before me.

We travel along a road in our car. It is night time, and vision is limited. We can only see a little way in front, as far as the headlights shine. But we trust in full, knowing that the road is prepared before us. We still feel safe to drive for many thousands of miles with very little vision of our full surroundings and no vision at all of our destination until we arrive.

This vibration you feel is on a global level. There are surges of fear. In truth, the planet is changing vibrationally and therefore physically as well. We are embracing and implementing a new consciousness, and regardless of your belief, no one is exempt. All people are feeling some level change. We are experiencing economic shifts and changes in what we truly desire as a global community. Some of the international relationships are strengthening and others are weakening, but all are in truth of the requirements of now and into the future. Technology has simplified the accessibility of needs, and the global community sees money and survival tools as a birthright to all who are living on earth.

Remember, fear is the response to an energy that is not understood but feels uncomfortable. Through this feeling comes a heightened awareness, which gives you the scope to assess and let go of whatever it is you desire that does not resonate as being part of you. It is an opportunity for great learning and enormous growth. Your connection to God who loves you will sustain you now and always throughout any fearful changes and otherwise.

However, it is your choice if you wish to acknowledge him. God, your guardians, and light beings are always there for you. They surround you, particularly during moments of fear or sadness, and they allow you choice and free will so that you may ask for their assistance and guidance. They cannot interfere with your choices, should you choose to act in a particular way, but will always support you with unending love and presence.

Your strength is amicable and is called for in so many occasions. Now is the time for meditation and prayer. There is a balance in all things. You cannot have great speed in nonstop activity without time to reflect upon the next move and your goals. One must integrate the knowledge, lessons, and realizations. This assessment is part of the journey, and it brings forth the next leg of it. There is no journey undertaken without due rest. We require fuel and to look upon the map, to reflect on the journey thus far, and to see where we are heading towards next. You will not miss any signs, as it is always clearly labelled for you.

As connected beings, we do affect each other. We live and associate with all of humanity, our country, our community, our work colleagues and friends, our families. The global energy that is vibrating and changing our way of feeling at this moment is working its way through in a mass consciousness, rippling through all nations and into your community, within you and your family. We are choosing to nurture, love, and acknowledge ourselves. Through the declaration of our value, our worth, and our choices, we are also supporting one another's growth through acknowledging them, their choices, and their individuality. As the frequency adjusts, we send love across our community, friends, and colleagues because it's felt within ourselves.

We are in a great time of change. Those sensitive to the altering frequencies take solace in the ebbs and flows of the vibrational changes as they integrate. Be sure to use the rest periods to reflect and regain perspectives and renewed energy to allow the flow times to bring desire into action and manifestation.

One must be kind and love themselves first to honour the duty of care in allowing through these adjustment phases. Through your example, you teach and guide. The journey is the experience of the soul's evolution and the evolution of the planet. We may desire these changes to be faster, but Mother Earth and all inhabitants are integrating as swiftly and compassionately as they can. As light workers, it would be so beneficial to gather and send healing energy to Mother Earth to help her as she is always loving, clearing, and healing continuously.

Prepare your body, your mind, and your intent for the day at the beginning of each morning.

In love is the freedom to realise all we desire, harmony that we wish to experience with our loved ones. In love is the fulfilment of one's life quest.

Trust the road is illuminated as you travel.

God never leaves your life, nor ever leaves you. Look within, not without.

Healing has taken place.

Amen

Human Life on earth   12/06/2012

Take me to a higher plane so that I may walk with thee. I long
for peace and unconditional love in my life. I see, feel, and hear
segregation, abuse, bullying, and pain. This is not how my life
should be. I'm born too early, and I experience such loneliness.
None of my people are here.

Spirit of light and love animate, you are an earth angel, no
doubt. Your gifts are clear and well refined. The challenge
you experience is not of an earthly manner. One cannot live
fully expressed in etheric form; that's why we take to a body.
The ideals and practices of humanity play a very big point
in your evolvement both in the body and in soul. A monk
who sits on top of the mountain surrounded by the sights
and sounds of nature's beauty, experiencing inner silence and
absolute serenity, has many experiences of expansion and may
reach enlightenment. However, the same monk placed in an
apartment on a low income with a family to raise and many
earthly challenges to meet becomes the master.

Life is precious. The body you were born with is miraculous and
has an interwoven genetic and spiritual coding, which among
many other things inspires the mind. Many pre-contractual and
predetermined dynamics are incomprehensible to most of you.
The energy you contain, use, and expel has a magnetic force as
powerful as the ocean's tide. Your own pull and attraction has a
force that could move oceans. You are a powerful being. Every
single one of you has the ability to create and destroy. The
awareness of your power also calls for spiritual responsibility
to use your energy wisely. Be not aloof about the choices and
directions you seek and the people with whom you choose to
create connection. Whilst your entire experience is unfolding

468

as you continue to choose, be very aware of who you are and whether you are being true to yourself at all times. You are no better and no worse than anyone else. Whether you be rich or poor, able or disabled, black or white, your possessions are not you, nor ever will be. Be it that I look towards myself ten times before I point the finger at another. You are not creating more love in the world by expressing your disapproval of another. You can only choose for you. Make choices wisely.

Choices may be a familiar or unfamiliar dynamic. There is complexity, but there are no rules for God's pleasure. You can well decide that your natural self will only resonate with growth and loved inspired actions. Where a frequency, an energy, or an issue is acknowledged that doesn't feel well within you, look away and look within. If you understand that the issue has no conscious or unconscious connection to you, disassociate from it. Understand that you may have absorbed what you are choosing to experience on some level. Once you have realised this, you may step back and cleanse your energy field to experience perfection again.

If you recognize that it is in fact part of your own thoughts, emotions, or beliefs, then decide whether you wish to hold onto it any longer.

It is only present to show us, and so be kind, be loving, express compassion towards self, and release what no longer serves your truth of who you really are and wish to be. Celebrate your human existence, your human service. Love this entire experience and feel great respect, love, and gratitude to your body, as floating heavenward is not your objective here. You will one day return to the state of your God essence from where you came, and you will long to return.

The key to an expansive, growth-filled, enduring, free, and happy lifetime on earth is to love, learn, give, receive, choose, create, and explore with your magnificent being alongside your soulmates, your fellow travellers. Express love, compassion, and respect to them and yourself concurrently.

No life is ever lost. This is divine truth.

You are all extraordinary beings.

I love you.

God

Chapter 8

Final Story

The Almighty Lion of God

Jesus, Mary Magdalene, and Archangel Michael stand around this precious child of God. Jesus begins, "Oh my loving daughter, we walk with you through these last trails of illusion. This illusion that you will forever release to us is fear. It is actually three kinds of genetic fear: the first being fear of wealth, as you are now ready to allow your inner riches to reflect your material abundance for God's glorious ascension of world healing.

"The second is fear is fear of the unknown. You may not think that we will be there in the hour of your need, but we can never leave you. We create a peaceful and harmonious outcome of abundance for your earthly family.

"The third fear is that of burden, burden experienced by your mother in your earthly family. This old frequency of ignorance, slavery, and conditional love is now replaced with our unending healing and path-making with free-flowing understanding, freedom, and unconditional, loving support.

"Funds within in the vicinity of 7.5 to 8 million dollars will be available for the building of God's Ascension Temple so that all of the men, women, and children of the world may receive the holy gift of perfect health, perfect love, and perfect balance from God through your body to all.

"I love you always, your Father, Jesus."

Archangel Michael then steps forward:

"Oh mighty healer of God, do not underestimate the pure power of God that you are! While I walk with you, I ask only that today you allow my protection, love, and courage to merge with you so that the blocks that reside within your genetic group and their karma do not ever affect the mission of God that you wish to create.

"You should never feel left behind by those around you because of your desire to create a sanctuary of healing. Your family do love you, despite combating unhealthy energies and entities of greed and desperation, challenging you to feel otherwise.

"This is a journey of hope and of love, which begins now. We will gather around you in our ranks to uphold the worldwide goal of salvation, redemption, and uplift towards the truth of life, which is heavenly ascension. The risk you take is not merely a chance to create freedom, but rather healing on a global scale, cleansing the entire planet, just like your Father and Mother did.

"With love, courage, and protection, Archangel Michael."

Mary Magdalene now enters the space:

"My lovely girl, how excited I am to see you thrive as a woman and as the healer you were always meant to be. You are my legacy, and you will teach the world about God and the way of love by shining your light wherever you are.

"We will be present as we have been through the centuries for you. When you are meeting with those who impose their will, we will surround them with loving understanding and the flow of God so that your will and the will of God is done.

"Our Father and Mother God will be watching and guiding all of the events with people in authority so that you can easily receive all the manna from heaven as money on earth to begin this most significant and important mission to ascend and heal the world.

"In this you will be blessed, always with love.

"Your Mother, Mary Magdalene."

The angels of God herald the arrival and beginning of the new apostles and healers who will now flood your new centre in its infancy so that you have all the support you could ever hope for and more.

God, your Mother and Father, bless and gift this life to you to become what your soul already is: a great healer unto earth.

A great healer of God.

Thank you.

Amen

Channeled by guest medium/healer: Ms Clare Murray

In Closing

Now we celebrate the birth, development, and continued practice and education of this revolutionary form of healing. Over thousands of clients, many of whom have enjoyed the life-changing experience of divine healings directly, we have scripted our way to a fascinating text for you all to read and contemplate.

No doubt many of you will find similarities within your own lives reflected within these pages. This amazing and instant form of healing is available to you all. It is empowering and unique, as it allows for one to take responsibility for one's own well being. Through this healing modality, you are able to acknowledge and sever the past and look forward to creating healthy and confident choices for the future.

Be inspired by the blank canvas that lies before you. Having cleared and severed negativity and attachments, and having retrieved any soul fragment from the past, you are able to move forward with excitement and clarity. Paint with as many colours and in whatever style you wish, as there is no limit to your desires and the fruition of your dreams.

God provides unlimited resources and only wishes to see you fulfil your journey with faith, clarity, love, and commitment.

From here, we move forward as a business and as healers to provide a service and education centre for a larger clientele.

We are to open the largest healing and learning centre in the Southern Hemisphere, called the Ascension Centre, in Melbourne, Australia.

With great joy and humility, we look forward to connecting with every one of you in the future to assist you on your tremendous journey. We thank you for being part of ours.

We complete this divine text with one last script and healing, which provided a clear and concise message from Spirit to me directly. I follow this guidance with full faith and love.

See you soon.

Love, Trish

The Ascension Centre

Bringing heaven to earth is no easy task, but at the Ascension Centre you experience just that. With a team of heavenly angel helpers to facilitate your healing, enlightenment, self-reflection, self-development, and divine connection, we aim to bring the body, mind, and soul of all towards a higher state of being wherein all etheric and physical parts of the self can be made whole and unified with their souls' purposes.

As we are a universal group, we wish to extend our energies throughout the nation, world, and all planes of existence so that those who walk the path, those who are beginning their journey, and those in need of divine nurture and love can feel welcomed to the realisation of the infinite union of all energy bodies as one in the self, because we aim to be at one with you.

The master, saint, and angel energies each member of our team embodies and channels allows for the reunion of all who come for healing, readings, clearings, mediation, and inspiration to elevate their lives to an ascended state in holy alignment with their master, saint, angel, God, and soul selves to walk in grace and bliss on a lifetime basis.

We are at this time embracing a never-before-seen centre for enlightenment and universal ascension because the earth herself is an ascension state. We wish to enable all to rise to their souls' advancement with her.

We invite all peoples from all corners of God's universe to take part in this learning, healing, sharing, nurturing, and loving venue for the growth, inspiration, and ascension for all who come to us.

We the four archangels of heaven extend our hearts, souls, love, and devotion to all beings that exist in the universe. We act as anchors to the north, south, east, and west of the heavenly portal of light that is the Ascension Centre.

In God's grace and with God's blissful blessings. Thank you.

Archangel Gabriel

Channeled by guest medium/healer: Ms Clare Murray

CPSIA information can be obtained at www.ICGtesting.com
Printed in the USA
LVOW06s0255250913

353908LV00003B/4/P